A Dictionary of

English and Italian

Equivalent Proverbs

Teodor Flonta

A Dictionary of
English and Italian
Equivalent Proverbs

DeProverbio.com

2001

DeProverbio.com

DeProverbio.com is an imprint of *De Proverbio* (www.deproverbio.com)

© Teodor Flonta 2001

All rights reserved. No part of this publication may be reproduced, stored in a retrieval system, or transmitted, in any form or by any means, electronic, mechanical, photocopying, recording, or otherwise, without the prior permission of DeProverbio.com

ISBN 1-875943-18-8

CONTENTS

INTRODUCTION vii

BIBLIOGRAPHY xi

DICTIONARY 1

INDEX 236

INTRODUCTION

From time immemorial proverbs have fascinated people of all ages and from all walks of life. As it happened throughout centuries, common people today still avail themselves of the proverb's rich oral tradition to convey their culture and values, while scholars collect and study them from a wide range of angles: linguistic, social, psychological, political... Although the problem of proverb definition is still open, it is broadly accepted that proverbs were born from experience and that they generally express, in a very succinct way, common-sense truths, give sound advice and reflect the human condition. But, as we know and as this dictionary proves, human nature is both good and bad and the latter is often mirrored by discriminatory proverbs, be they against women, different nationalities or particular social groups. For a thorough discussion of proverb definition, see *Popular Views of the Proverb* (www.deproverbio.com) by Prof. Wolfgang Mieder.

As to the origin of proverbs we tend to assume that they were born in times when human society began to self-impose rules and embrace principles necessary for communal living. Research can trace them back only to the time when language was recorded by means of some type of writing. The Sumerian civilisation of more than five thousand years ago is the oldest known civilisation to have made use of proverbs, some of which have been passed on through its cuneiform inscriptions. One such proverb, in its Latin version, is "Canis festinans caecos parit catulos" which spread to other languages such as English, in the form "The hasty bitch brings forth blind whelps," French, "La chienne dans sa hâte a mis bas des chiots aveugles," Italian, "La gatta frettolosa fece i gattini ciechi" (here the 'bitch' has been replaced by 'cat'), Portuguese, "Cadelas apressadas parem cães tortos," and Romanian, "Cățeaua de pripă își naște cățeii fără ochi."

Given their widespread use over the millennia, it is no wonder that scholars of the past started assembling proverbs in collections. Aristotle is believed to be among the first paremiographers (collectors of proverbs), but, unfortunately, his collection was lost. In more recent times a great impetus to the collection of proverbs was given by Erasmus, whose fame spread from Venice throughout Europe after the publication in 1508 of his *Adagiorum Chiliades* which contained 3,260 proverbs drawn from classical authors. The success of the book led to several augmented editions culminating with that of 1536, revised by Erasmus himself, which contains 4,151 proverbs. Erasmus' work was translated into several European languages and became the model for future proverb collections in those languages. The latter were, in turn, widely copied and translated. One good example of such a practice is the 1591 Italian collection *Giardino di Ricreatione, nel quale crescono fronde, fiori e frutti, vaghe, leggiadri e soavi, sotto nome di sei miglia proverbii, e piacevoli riboboli Italiani, colti e scelti da Giovanni Florio,* which appeared in French two decades later as *Le Jardin de Récréation, au quel croissent rameaux, fleurs et fruits très-beaux, gentils et souefs, soubz le nom de Six mille proverbes et plaisantes rencontres françoises, recueillis et triéez par GOMÈS DE TRIER, non seulement utiles mais délectables pour tous espritz désireux de la très-noble et copieuse langue françoise, nouvellement mis en lumière, à Amsterdam, par PAUL DE RAVESTEYN.*

Apart from use on a wide scale in day-to-day speech, there is ample evidence that proverbs were essential tools in teaching and learning. The pedagogical use of proverbs was encountered first in Sumerian society and subsequently this use became widespread throughout Medieval Europe. In the preface to the first edition of the *Oxford Dictionary of English Proverbs,* J. Heseltine states that proverbs and proverbial expressions are found in religious manuscripts of the first half of the eighth century. The aim of introducing proverbs into religious texts was to help novices to learn Latin, and this practice became widespread by the tenth century. The use of proverbs in teaching and learning was not circumscribed to England. Relatively new research attests to the use of proverbs in teaching in the eleventh century in Liège, France. In Italy the famous medical School of Salerno of the eleventh century formulated medical precepts which later became proverbs adopted by different cultures, such as "Post prandium stabis, post coenam ambulabis" translated "After dinner sit awhile, after supper walk a mile" in English, "Après dîner repose un peu, après souper promène une mille" in French, "Dopo pranzo riposar un poco, dopo cena passeggiar un miglio" in Italian, "Después de yantar reposad un poco, después de cenar pasead una milla" in Spanish and "Depois de jantar, dormir; depois de cear, passos mil" in Portuguese.

Joanna Wilson, in her *Introduction* to the third edition of *The Oxford Dictionary of English Proverbs,* said, regarding the foreign proverbs' contribution to the English proverbial stock, that "these enriched our language, for many proverbs of foreign origin were quickly absorbed into English life and these have a rightful place in an English dictionary." And, indeed, a close scrutiny of that dictionary reveals that more than two hundred and fifty proverbs are listed as first existing in Italian. This is also true for other modern languages, particularly French and Spanish. The translation is not always literal; at times it is adapted to the new language and the resulting proverb is often enriched in its expression, for instance the Latin "Homo sine pecunia est imago mortis" (A man without money is the image of death) is rather closely translated in Italian as "Uomo senza quattrini è un morto che cammina" (A man without money is a dead man walking), but in English the metaphor changes and the proverb becomes "A man without money is a bow without an arrow," in French "Un homme sans argent / Est un loup sans dents" (A man without money is a wolf without teeth) where an element of rhyme is introduced, while the Rumanian adaptation is a real poetic gem "Omul fără bani e ca pasărea fără aripi; Când dă să zboare / Cade jos și moare" (A man without money is like a bird without wings; When he tries to fly / He falls down and dies). The concept is essentially the same: the man without money lacks something important...

But from use comes abuse, as a Spanish proverb says, and there is no doubt that the capacity of the proverb to convey universal truths concisely led to their abuse and manipulation. Hitler and his Nazi regime employed proverbs as emotional slogans for propaganda purposes and encouraged the publication of anti-semitic collections of proverbs. For a thorough analysis of this phenomenon, please read the fascinating article " ... *as if I were the master of situation.*" *Proverbial Manipulation in Adolf Hitler* (www.deproverbio.com) by Prof. Wolfgang Mieder. At the opposite end of the political spectrum, communist regimes of the past have not only manipulated proverbs, but also 'purged' popular collections of features which did not reflect their political ends. The former Soviet regime is at the forefront of such actions. One type of manipulation described by Jean Breuillard in *Proverbes et pouvoir politique: Le cas de l'U.R.S.S.* (published in "Richesse du proverbe", Eds. François Suard and Claude Buridant. Lille: Université de Lille, 1984. II, 155-166) consisted in modifying ancient proverbs like "La vérité parcourt le monde" (Truth spreads all over the world) into "La vérité de Lénine parcourt le monde" (Lenin's truth spreads all over the world) where the new 'creation' is unequivocably charged with a specific ideological message. Manipulation did not stop at individual proverbs, it extended to entire collections. The first Soviet edition (1957) of Vladimir Dal's mid-nineteen century collection of Russian proverbs reduces the proverbs containing the word *God* from 283 to 7 only, while proverbs which express compassion for human weaknesses, such as alcoholism, disappear altogether. In more recent years, in Ceausescu's Romania, the 1985 edition of *Proverbele românilor* (published in 1877 by I.C. Hințescu) suffered the same treatment: more than 150 proverbs were eliminated or changed in order to respond rigidly to the communist ideology.

In spite of their ups and downs, proverbs and their study are alive and well today as illustrated by the hundreds of studies and collections published every year all over the world. For a bibliography of the most recent publications see the invaluable *international bibliographies* (www.deproverbio.com) published each year by Prof. Wolfgang Mieder.

While proverbs are still used today in a traditional way, that is in speech, literature and teaching, they have found a new ever expanding use in the advertising industry and in the mass media. Proverbs like "Here today, gone tomorrow" become "Hair today, gone tomorrow" in the hair-removal industry, while the mass media has a variety of paraphrases such as "Hear today, gone tomorrow," "Heir today, gone tomorrow." Before the Barcelona Olympic Games the old proverb "All roads lead to Rome" became "All roads lead to... Barcelona" in many English language newspapers and magazines. This is a phenomenon encountered in many languages nowadays and is undoubtedly a sign of the proverb's resilience and vitality.

* * *

This dictionary assembles 2,513 English proverbs and their Italian equivalents. Equivalent proverbs are those which express the same concept, be it literally, such as "Love is blind" = "L'amore è cieco," or with completely different words, such as "Every cloud has a silver lining" = "Non tutto il male viene per nuocere."

The *Dictionary* is a very useful reference tool for scholars of the two languages, for researchers working in various associated fields such as linguistics, literature, folklore, anthropology, psychology, sociology, history, and for workers in newer areas such as advertising and contemporary media. The *Dictionary* is also of interest to diplomats and politicians who try to improve their communication by sharing ideas formulated in some common meaningful expressions; it will assist interpreters and translators, and teachers and students for whom it is important to understand not only what the target culture expresses in the same way as their own, but also what is formulated in a different way. The *Dictionary* is also of benefit to non-professionals who, for the sheer enjoyment of it, wish to savour the wisdom, wit, poetry and the colourful language of proverbs.

BIBLIOGRAPHY

Arthaber, A. *Dizionario comparato di proverbi e modi proverbiali,* Ulrico Hoepli, Milano, 1981

Battaglia, S. *Grande Dizionario della Lingua Italiana,* voll. I-XII, UTET, Torino, 1961-1984

Bellonzi, F. *Proverbi toscani,* Aldo Martello - Giunti Editore, Firenze, 1975

Bohn, Henry G. *A Polyglot of Foreign Proverbs,* London, 1857

Browning, D. C. *Everyman's Dictionary of Quotations and Proverbs,* Octopus Books Limited, London, 1982

Devoto, G. - Oli G. C. *Dizionario della lingua italiana,* Le Monnier, Firenze, 1980

Diccionario de Aforismos, Proverbios y Refranes, Editorial Sintes, Barcelona, 1967

Dispenza, Gioacchino *Dice il proverbio...,* Edizioni Paoline, Milano, 1988

Dizionario Garzanti della lingua italiana, Garzanti, Milano, XVII edizione, 1979

Dizionario Sandron della lingua italiana, Istituto Geografico De Agostini, Novara, 1980

Düringsfeld (von), Ida und Otto Freiherrn *Sprichwörter der germanischen und romanischen Sprachen vergleichend zusammengestellt,* Verlag von Hermann Fries, Leipzig, vol. 1 - 1872, vol. 2 - 1875

Falassi, Alessandro *Proverbi toscani commentati,* Il Vespro, Palermo, 1979

Flonta, Teodor *Dicţionar englez-italian-român de proverbe echivalente / English-Italian-Romanian Dictionary of Equivalent Proverbs,* Editura Teopa, Bucureşti, 1993

Florio, Giovanni *Florio's Second Frutes,* Thomas Woodcock, London, 1591, reprint Da Capo Press and Theatrum Orbis Terrarum Ltd., New York and Amsterdam, 1969

Franceschi, G. *Proverbi e modi proverbiali italiani,* reprint Hoepli edition of 1908, Istituto Editoriale Cisalpino-Goliardica, Milano, 1982

Gheorghe, G. *Proverbele româneşti şi proverbele lumii romanice,* Editura Albatros, Bucureşti, 1986

Giusti, G. *Raccolta di Proverbi Toscani,* reprint of 1911 edition, Edikronos, Palermo, 1981

Gluski, Jerzy *Proverbs - A Comparative Book of English, French, German, Italian, Spanish and Russian Proverbs with a Latin Appendix,* Elsevier Publishing Company, Amsterdam-London-New York, 1971

Hazlitt, W. C. *English Proverbs and Proverbial Phrases,* London, 1882

Hazon, Mario *Grande Dizionario inglese-italiano, italiano-inglese,* Garzanti, Milano, 1975

Lapucci, Carlo *Dizionario dei modi di dire della lingua italiana,* Garzanti-Vallardi, Milano, 1979

Macchi, Vladimiro (a cura di) *Dizionario inglese-italiano, italiano-inglese,* Sansoni Editore, Firenze, 1981

Mieder, Wolfgang - Kingsbury, Sewart A. - Harder, Kelsie B. *A Dictionary of American Proverbs,* Oxford University Press, New York, 1992

Mieder, Wolfgang *The Prentice-Hall Encyclopedia of World Proverbs,* Prentice-Hall Inc., Englewood Cliffs, N.J., 1986

Passarini, Ludovico *Modi di dire proverbiali e motti popolari italiani,* ristampa anastatica dell'edizione di Roma, 1875, Forni, Bologna, 1970

Pauli, Sebastiano *Modi di dire toscani ricercati nella loro origine,* ristampa anastatica dell'edizione di Venezia, 1740, Insubria, Milano, 1979

Pescetti, Orlando *Proverbi italiani,* Venezia, 1629

Ragazzini, Giuseppe *Dizionario inglese italiano, italiano inglese,* Zanichelli Editore, 1984

Ridout, Ronald & Witting Clifford *English Proverbs Explained,* Pan Books, London, 10th printing, 1983

Schwamenthal R. - Straniero M. L. *Dizionario dei proverbi italiani,* BUR, Milano, 1991

Simpson, J. A. *The Concise Oxford Dictionary of Proverbs,* Oxford University Press, Oxford, 1982 & 1992

Skey, Malcom (a cura di) *Dizionario inglese italiano, italiano inglese,* S.E.I., Torino, 1979

The Random House Dictionary of English Language, Random House, New York, 1973

The Shorter Oxford English Dictionary, voll. 1-2, Oxford University Press, Oxford, 1980

Torriano, Giovanni *Piazza universale di proverbi italiani,* London, 1666

Wilson, F. P. *The Oxford Dictionary of English Proverbs,* 3rd edition, Oxford University Press, Oxford, 1982

A

1 **ABSENCE makes the heart grow fonder.**
Se vuoi che ti ami, fa che ti brami.

    Sim. *Absence sharpens love, presence strengthens it.*

2 **The ABSENT are always in the wrong.**
Chi è assente ha sempre torto.
Gli assenti hanno sempre torto.

    Var. *He is neither absent without fault, nor present without excuse.*

3 **ABUNDANCE of things engenders disdainfulness.**
L'abbondanza genera fastidio.

    Cf. *TOO MUCH breaks the bag / You can have TOO MUCH of a good thing.*

4 **Out of the ABUNDANCE of the heart the mouth speaketh.**
Per l'abbondanza del cuor la bocca parla.

    Var. *Out of the fullness of the heart the mouth speaks.*
    Cf. *What the HEART thinks, the tongue speaks.*

        o Matthew 12, 34 / Matteo 12, 34; Luke 6, 45 / Luca 6, 45

5 **There is no ACCOUNTING for tastes.**
Dei gusti non se ne disputa.

    Sim. *Everyone as they like best.*
    Cf. *Every man to his TASTE / TASTES differ.*

6 **ACQUAINTANCE of the great will I naught, for first or last, dear it will be bought.**
Amor di signore e vin di fiasco, se la mattina è buono, la sera è guasto.

    Sim. *Great men's favours are uncertain.*
    Cf. *A king's FAVOUR is no inheritance.*

7 **ACTIONS speak louder than words.**
I fatti contano più delle parole.
Contano più i fatti che le parole.
Val più un fatto che cento parole.

    Cf. *DEEDS, not words.*

8   **When ADAM delved and Eve span, who was then the gentleman?**
    Quando Adamo zappava ed Eva filava, dov'era il primo nobile?

9   **We are all ADAM's children.**
    Tutti siamo figli di Adamo ed Eva.
    Veniamo tutti da Adamo ed Eva.

    Var. *We are all Adam's children but silk makes the difference.*

10 **Much ADO about nothing.**
    Molto rumore per nulla.

    Cf. *Much CRY and little wool.*

11 **ADVERSITY makes a man wise, not rich.**
    Danno fa far senno.

    Cf. *EXPERIENCE is the mother of knowledge.*

12 **Good ADVICE is beyond all price.**
    A buon consiglio non si trova prezzo.
    Dono di consiglio più vale che d'oro.

    Sim. *Good counsel has no price.*

13 **If you wish good ADVICE, consult an old man.**
    Chiedi consiglio a chi è vecchio.
    Consiglio di vecchio non rompe mai la testa.
    Fatti di giovani e consigli di vecchi.

    Sim. *If the old dog barks, he gives counsel.*

14 **Take the first ADVICE of a woman and not the second.**
    Il primo consiglio della donna prendi.
    La donna decide all'improvviso, e l'uomo a caso pensato.

15 **When a thing is done, ADVICE comes too late.**
    Dopo il fatto il consiglio non vale.

    Cf. *When the HOUSE is burned down, you bring water / It is too late to shut the STABLE -DOOR after the horse has bolted / It is easy to be WISE after the event.*

16 **Write down the ADVICE of him who loves you, though you like it not at present.**
    Consiglio di chi ti vuol bene, scrivilo ancor che ti paia male.

17 **AFFECTION blinds reason.**
    Affezione accieca ragione.

    Cf. *LOVE is blind.*

18 **He that is AFRAID of wounds must not come nigh a battle.**
Chi ha paura, non vada alla guerra.

> Sim. *He that is afraid of the wagging of feathers must keep from among wild fowl / He that fears every grass must not walk in a meadow.*
> Cf. *He that fears LEAVES, let him not go into the wood / He that forecasts all PERILS will never sail the sea.*

19 **AGE is a heavy burden.**
La vecchiaia è una grave soma.

20 **For AGE and want save while you may: no morning sun lasts a whole day.**
Chi fatica in gioventù gode in vecchiaia.
È gran saviezza di risparmiar per la vecchiezza.

> Sim. *Keep something for him that rides on the white horse / Spare when you're young and spend when you're old.*
> Cf. *Make ample PROVISION for old age / Keep SOMETHING for a rainy day.*

21 **Old AGE is sickness of itself.**
La vecchiaia è in se stessa una infermità.
Chi ha degli anni, ha dei malanni.

> Sim. *An old man is a bed full of bones.*

22 **A lean AGREEMENT is better than a fat judgement.**
Meglio un magro accordo che una grassa sentenza.

> Var. *A bad peace is better than a good quarrel / A lean compromise is better than a fat lawsuit.*

23 **Autumnal AGUES are long or mortal.**
Febbre autunnale, o è lunga o è mortale.

24 **Quartan AGUES kill old men, and cure young.**
Febbre quartana, il vecchio uccide e il giovane risana.

25 **A man cannot live by AIR.**
Non si campa d'aria.

26 **The AIR of a window is as the stroke of a cross-bow.**
Aria di finestra, colpo di balestra.

27 **ALMS never make poor.**
L'elemosina non fa impoverire.

> Var. *No one becomes poor through giving alms / You shall not lose by giving alms.*
> o Proverbs 28, 28 / Proverbi 28, 27

28 **When thou doest ALMS, let not thy left hand know what thy right hand doeth.**
Quando fai elemosina, non sappia la tua mano sinistra quello che fa la destra.

    o Matthew 6, 3 / Matteo 6, 3

29 **It is not good that the man should be ALONE.**
Non è bene che l'uomo sia solo.

   Cf. *A MAN without a wife is but half a man.*

    o Genesis 2, 18 / Genesi 2, 18

30 **He that serves at the ALTAR ought to live by the altar.**
Chi serve all'altare vive d'altare.
Il prete dove canta vi mangia.

31 **He that doth AMISS may do well.**
Chi ha fatto il male faccia la penitenza.

32 **Like the ANCHOR of a ship that is always at sea and never learns to swim.**
È come l'ancora, che sta sempre nel mare e non impara mai a nuotare.
L'ancora sta sempre nell'acqua, pur non nuota mai.

33 **Good riding at two ANCHORS, men have told, for if one break the other may hold.**
La nave è più sicura con due ancore che con una sola.

34 **ANGER and haste hinder good counsel.**
L'ira è cattiva consigliera.
A sangue caldo, nessun giudizio è saldo.
Chi s'adira non è consigliato.

35 **ANGER cannot stand without a strong hand.**
Corruccio è vano senza forte mano.
L'ira senza forza non vale una scorza.
Ira senza forza nulla vale.

36 **ANGER is a short madness.**
L'ira accieca la ragione.
L'ira turba la mente ed accieca la ragione.

37 **A soft ANSWER turneth away wrath.**
Una risposta gentile calma la collera.

   Cf. *Good WORDS cool more than cold water.*

    o Proverbs 15, 1 / Proverbi 15, 1

38 **The ANT had wings to her hurt.**
    Quando la formica vuol morire, mette le ali.

39 **An iron ANVIL should have a hammer of feathers.**
    A dura incudine, martello di piuma.

40 **The ANVIL fears no blows.**
    Buona incudine non teme martello.
    Dura più l'incudine che il martello.

41 **When you are an ANVIL, hold you still; when you are a hammer, strike your fill.**
    Quando s'è incudine convien soffrire; quando s'è martello convien percuotere.
    A questo mondo bisogna essere incudine o martello.

42 **The higher the APE goes, the more he shows his tail.**
    Quanto più la scimmia va in alto, più mostra il deretano.
    Come la scimmia, chi più va in alto, più mostra il culo.

    Var. *The higher the monkey climbs, the more he shows his tail.*

43 **An APE's an ape, a varlet's a varlet, though they be clad in silk or scarlet.**
    La scimmia è sempre scimmia, anche vestita di seta.

    Sim. *An ape is never so like an ape as when he wears a doctor's cape / An ass is but an ass, though laden with gold.*

44 **APPEARANCES are deceptive.**
    L'apparenza inganna.

    Var. *Appearances are deceiving.*
    Sim. *Things are not always what they seem.*

45 **Never judge from APPEARANCES.**
    Non bisogna fidarsi delle apparenze.
    L'uomo si giudica male alla cera.
    Non giudicate secondo le apparenze.

    Cf. *Under a ragged COAT lies wisdom.*

    o John 7, 24 / Giovanni 7, 24

46 **APPETITE comes with eating.**
    L'appetito vien mangiando.
    Mangiando viene l'appetito.

    Cf. *EATING and scratching wants but a beginning.*

47 **For a good APPETITE there is no hard bread.**
A chi ha fame è buono ogni pane.
Quando si ha fame, il pane sa di carne.

48 **An APPLE a day keeps the doctor away.**
Una mela al giorno toglie il medico di torno.

49 **An APPLE never falls far from the tree.**
La mela non cade lontano dall'albero.

   Cf. *A CHIP off the old block / Like FATHER, like son / Like MOTHER, like daughter.*

50 **The rotten APPLE injures its neighbours.**
Una mela marcia ne guasta cento.
Una pera fradicia ne guasta un monte.
Una pera fradicia ne infradicia cento.

   Var. *It takes only one bad apple to spoil the lot / One bad apple spoils the lot / One rotten apple can spoil the whole bunch / One rotten apple destroys the barrel / One rotten apple will spoil a bushel / The rotten apple injures its companion.*

51 **A cold APRIL the barn will fill.**
Aprile freddo, molto pane e poco vino.

52 **APRIL and May are the keys of the year.**
Aprile e maggio son la chiave di tutto l'anno.

53 **APRIL rains for men; May, for beasts.**
D'aprile piove per gli uomini e di maggio per le bestie.

   Var. *April rains for corn; May, for grass.*
   Cf. *A dry MARCH, wet April and cool May, fill barn and cellar and bring much hay.*

54 **APRIL showers bring forth May flowers.**
Aprile fa il fiore, e maggio ne ha l'onore.
Aprile fa il fiore e maggio si ha il colore.

   Var. *March winds and April showers always bring May flowers.*

55 **APRIL weather, rain and shower both together.**
La pioggia d'aprile dura quaranta giorni.

56 **Till APRIL's dead, change not a thread.**
Per tutto aprile, non ti scoprire.
D'April non ti scoprire.
April, Aprilone, non mi farai metter giù il pelliccione.

   Cf. *Cast ne'er a clout till MAY be out.*

57 **Every man is the ARCHITECT of his own fortune.**
Ciascuno è fabbro della sua fortuna.
Ognuno è artefice del proprio destino.

58 **An ARMY of stags led by a lion would be more formidable than one of lions led by a stag.**
È meglio un esercito di cervi sotto il comando di un leone, che un esercito di leoni sotto il comando di un cervo.

59 **An ARROW shot upright falls on the shooter's head.**
La saetta gira, gira, torna addosso a chi la tira.

Sim. *Evil that comes out of thy mouth flieth into thy bosom.*
Cf. *Who SPITS against the wind, it falls in his face / Piss not against the WIND.*

o Ecclesiasticus 27, 25 / Siràcide 27, 25

60 **ART consists in concealing art.**
L'arte che tutto fa, nulla si scopre.

Var. *The best art conceals art.*

61 **ART has no enemy but ignorance.**
L'arte non ha maggior nemico dell'ignorante.

Var. *Science has no enemy but the ignorant.*

62 **ART improves nature.**
Dove manca natura, arte procura.

Cf. *NURTURE passes nature.*

63 **ART is long and life is short.**
La vita è breve e l'arte è lunga.
Arte lunga, vita breve.

64 **He who has an ART has everywhere a part.**
Chi ha arte, ha parte.

Cf. *Who has a TRADE, has a share everywhere.*

65 **In every ART it is good to have a master.**
In ogni arte convien aver maestro.

66 **Divine ASHES are better than earthly meal.**
Più val la cenere divina che la mondana farina.

67 **ASK, and it shall be given you.**
Chiedete e vi sarà dato.

o Matthew 7, 7 / Matteo 7, 7

68 **An ASS endures his burden, but not more than his burden.**
L'asino, per tristo che sia, se tu lo batti più del dovere tira calci.

Sim. *It is not the burden, but the overburden that kills the beast.*

69 **An ASS in a lion's skin.**
Al ragliar si vedrà che non è leone.

70 **An ASS is known by his ears.**
L'asino si conosce all'orecchie.

71 **An ASS must be tied where the master will have him.**
Lega l'asino dove vuole il padrone.

72 **An ASS pricked must needs trot.**
Asino punto convien che trotti.

73 **Better ride on an ASS that carries me than a horse that throws me.**
Piuttosto un asino che porti che un cavallo che butti a terra.

74 **Did you ever hear an ASS play on a harp?**
Essere come l'asino al suono della lira.

Sim. *A sow to a fiddle.*

75 **He that cannot beat the ASS, beats the saddle.**
Chi non può dare all'asino, dà al basto.

Cf. *He that cannot beat the HORSE, beats the saddle.*

76 **If an ASS goes a-travelling, he'll not come home a horse.**
Chi bestia va a Roma, bestia ritorna.
Molti vanno a studio vitelli e tornano a casa buoi.

Var. *Never went out ass and came home horse.*
Sim. *Send a fool to the market (far, to France) and a fool he will return again / How much the fool who goes to Rome excels the fool who stays at home.*
Cf. *He that sends a FOOL expects one.*

77 **Jest with an ASS, and he will slap you in the face with his tail.**
Chi accarezza la mula, buscherà dei calci.

78 **One ASS scrubs another.**
Un asino gratta l'altro.

79 **The ASS loaded with gold still eats thistles.**
Asino carico d'oro mangia cardoni e ortiche.
Fare come l'asino, che porta il vino e beve l'acqua.

80 The ASS that brays most eats least.
    Asino che raglia mangia poco fieno.

    Cf. *A bleating SHEEP loses her bit.*

81 When all men say you are an ASS, it is time to bray.
    Quando tutti ti diranno che sei asino, e tu raglia.
    Quando tutti ti dicono ubriaco, va a dormire.

    Sim. *If one, or three tell you, you are an ass, put on a bridle (tail).*
    Cf. *What everybody says must be TRUE.*

82 Wherever an ASS falls, there will he never fall again.
    L'asino, dove è cascato una volta, non ci casca più.

    Var. *Even an ass will not fall twice in the same quicksand.*

83 Who drives an ASS and leads a whore, has toil and sorrow evermore.
    Chi asino caccia e puttana mena, non esce mai di pena.

84 You go to an ASS for wool.
    Dall'asino non cercar lana.

    Sim. *Look not for musk in a dog's kennel.*

85 He that washes an ASS's head loses both his lye and his labour.
    Chi lava la testa all'asino perde il ranno e il sapone.
    Chi lava la testa all'asino perde la spugna e il sapone.
    A lavar la testa all'asino si perde il ranno e il sapone.

    Var. *He that washes an ass's head loses both his soap and his labour.*

86 ATTACK is the best form of defence.
    La miglior difesa è l'attacco.

87 Like AUTHOR, like book.
    Tal autor, tal opera.

88 The AVARICIOUS man is always in want.
    L'uomo avaro e l'occhio sono insaziabili.

    Var. *The miser is always in want.*
    Sim. *Avarice is never satisfied.*

B

89 **Don't throw the BABY out with the bathwater.**
Gettare il manico dietro la scure.
Gettare la fune dietro la secchia.

    Sim. *To throw the helve after the hatchet.*

90 **He would fall on his BACK and break his nose.**
Chi nasce sfortunato, s'ei va indietro a cader si rompe il naso.

    Sim. *An unfortunate man would be drowned in a tea-cup.*

91 **Scratch my BACK and I'll scratch yours.**
Grattami e ti gratterò.

    Var. *Scratch me and I'll scratch you.*
    Sim. *Claw me, and I'll claw thee.*
    Cf. *Roll my LOG, and I'll roll yours.*

92 **Nothing so BAD in which there is not something of good.**
Non c'è cosa così cattiva, che non sia buona a qualche cosa.

    Var. *Nothing but is good for something.*
    Sim. *No great loss but some small profit .*
    Cf. *ILL LUCK is good for something.*

93 **There is no great BANQUET, but some fare ill.**
Non fu mai sì gran banchetto, che qualcun non desinasse male.

94 **A BARBER learns to shave by shaving fools.**
Alla barba dei pazzi il barbiere impara a radere.

95 **A young BARBER and an old physician.**
Medico vecchio e barbiere giovane.

    Var. *The barber must be young, and the physician old.*

96 **One BARBER shaves another gratis.**
Un barbiere tosa l'altro.

97 **A good BARGAIN is a pick-purse.**
Buon mercato sfonda la borsa.
Sotto il buon prezzo ci cova la frode.
Le buone derrate vuotano la borsa.

    Cf. *GOOD cheap is dear.*

98 **BASHFULNESS is a great hindrance to a man.**
Fra Modesto non fu mai priore.
Chi vuole impetrare, la vergogna ha da levare.
Sim. *A modest dog seldom grows fat.*

99 **He that makes a BASKET can make one hundred.**
Chi fa una trappola ne sa fare cento.
Chi fa trenta può fare trentuno.

100 **A BEAN in liberty is better than a comfit in prison.**
Meglio è una fava in libertà che un confetto in carcere.
Cf. *LIBERTY is more worth than gold.*

101 **BEAR and forbear.**
Sostienti e astienti.
Soffri e taci, ogni cosa ha fine.

102 **Don't sell the BEAR's skin before you have caught him.**
Non si vende la pelle prima che s'ammazzi l'orso.
Non vendere la pelle dell'orso prima di averlo preso.
Non vendere la pelle dell'orso prima di averlo ucciso.

Sim. *Don't cross the bridge till you come to it / Do not count your chickens before they are hatched / It is not good praising a ford till a man be over / Do not halloo till you are out of the wood / Never fry fish till it's caught.*
Cf. *Count not FOUR, except you have them in the wallet.*

103 **A BEARD well lathered is half shaved.**
Barba bagnata è mezza fatta.

Var. *A good lather is half a shave.*

104 **A red BEARD and a black head, catch him with a good trick and take him dead.**
Barba rossa e mal colore, sotto il cielo non è peggiore.

Cf. *Red HAIR; devil's hair.*

105 **He that hath a BEARD is more than youth; and he that hath no beard is less than a man.**
Gallo senza cresta è un cappone, uomo senza barba è un minchione.

106 **It is not the BEARD that makes the philosopher.**
La barba non fa il filosofo.

Var. *The beard does not make the doctor or philosopher.*

107 **The BEARD will not pay for the shaving.**
Il barbiere non si contenta del pelo.

108 **A poor BEAUTY finds more lovers than husbands.**
Le belle senza dote trovano più amanti che mariti.

109 **BEAUTY and chastity seldom agree.**
Di rado s'accoppiano bellezza e castità.

110 **BEAUTY and folly are often companions.**
Beltà e follia vanno spesso in compagnia.

111 **BEAUTY carries its dower in its face.**
Bellezza è mezza dote.
Chi nasce bella non nasce povera.

Sim. *A fair face is half a portion.*

112 **BEAUTY draws more than oxen.**
Tira più un pel di donna che cento paia di buoi.

Cf. *NATURE draws more than ten teams.*

113 **BEAUTY fades like a flower.**
Bellezza è come un fiore che nasce e presto muore.

Sim. *Beauty is but a blossom.*

114 **BEAUTY is but skin-deep.**
La bellezza è effimera.

115 **BEAUTY is no inheritance.**
Bellezza di corpo non è eredità.

116 **BEAUTY may have fair leaves, yet bitter fruit.**
La bellezza ha belle foglie, ma il frutto amaro.

117 **As you make your BED, so you must lie on it.**
Come uno si fa il letto, così dorme.

Sim. *As you bake, so shall you eat / As they brew, so let them bake.*
Cf. *As they BREW, so let them drink.*

118 **Better go to BED supperless than to rise in debt.**
Meglio andare a letto senza cena, che alzarsi con debiti.

119 **Early to BED and early to rise, makes a man healthy, wealthy, and wise.**
Presto a letto e presto alzato fa l'uomo sano, ricco e fortunato.

120 **He that goes to BED thirsty rises healthy.**
Chi a letto con la sete se ne va, si leva la mattina con sanità.

121 **Who goes to BED supperless, all night tumbles and tosses.**
Chi va a letto senza cena tutta la notte si dimena.

122 **A dead BEE makes no honey.**
Ape morta non fa miele.

123 **The BEE sucks honey out of the bitterest flowers.**
I fiori amari, giunti alla bocca delle pecchie, diventano miele.

124 **Better BEG than steal.**
È meglio mendicare che sulla forca sgambettare.

125 **It is better to be a BEGGAR than a fool.**
È meglio esser mendicante che ignorante.

126 **Set a BEGGAR on horseback, and he'll ride to the Devil.**
Quando il villano è a cavallo, non vorrebbe mai che si facesse sera.
Quando la merda monta in scanno, o che la puzza, o che fa danno.

Sim. *Beggars mounted run their horse to death.*
Cf. *When a KNAVE is in a plum-tree, he has neither friend nor kin / No PRIDE like that of an enriched beggar.*

127 **The BEGGAR is never out of his way.**
Gli accattoni non sono mai fuori di strada.

128 **The BEGGAR may sing before the thief.**
Il mendicante può cantare dinanzi al ladro.
Cento ladri non possono spogliare un uomo nudo.

Sim. *A beggar can never be bankrupt.*
Cf. *No NAKED man is sought after to be rifled.*

129 **BEGGARS can't be choosers.**
Chi mendica non può scegliere.

130 **What is got by BEGGING is dear bought.**
Niuna cosa costa più cara di quella che comprano le preghiere.

131 **Better never to BEGIN than never to make an end.**
Meglio è non dire che cominciar e non finire.

Sim. *Let him that beginneth the song make an end.*

132 **A bad BEGINNING, a bad ending.**
Chi comincia male, finisce peggio.
Quando si comincia male, si finisce peggio.

133 **A good BEGINNING makes a good ending.**
Buon principio fa buon fine.

134 **Every BEGINNING is hard.**
Ogni principio è difficile.
Il difficile sta nel cominciare.

BEGINNING

Var. *All beginnings are hard (difficult).*
Cf. *It is the first STEP that is difficult.*

135 **Everything must have a BEGINNING.**
Ogni cosa vuol principio.

136 **Such BEGINNING, such end.**
Qual principio, tal fine.

137 **Well BEGUN is half done.**
Chi ben comincia è a metà dell'opera.
Chi ben comincia è a metà dell'opra.

Sim. *The first blow is half the battle.*

138 **BELIEVE nothing of what you hear, and only half of what you see.**
Quel che vedi, poco credi; quel che senti non creder niente.

139 **We soon BELIEVE what we desire.**
Quel che si vuol, presto si crede.

140 **He that BELIEVES all, misses; he that believes nothing, misses.**
Tristi guai, chi crede troppo e chi non crede mai.

141 **BELLS call others, but themselves enter not into the church.**
Non entra a messa la campana e ognun ci chiama.
Le campane chiamano gli altri e non entrano in chiesa.

142 **A BELLY full of gluttony will never study willingly.**
A buzzo pieno mal si lavora.

Sim. *Fat paunches have lean pates.*

143 **A fat BELLY, a lean brain.**
Il ventre pieno fa la testa vuota.

144 **A full BELLY neither fights nor flies well.**
Pancia piena, piede addormentato.

145 **Better BELLY burst than good meat lost.**
Piuttosto crepa panza che roba avanza.

146 **He whose BELLY is full believes not him who is fasting.**
Chi ha pien il ventre non crede a chi ha fame.
Corpo satollo non crede al digiuno.

Cf. *Little knows the FAT man what the lean does mean.*

147 **The BELLY carries the legs.**
La bocca porta le gambe.

148 The BELLY hates a long sermon.
Messa corta e lunga tavola.

149 The BELLY robs the back.
Meglio buon desinare che una bella giubba.

Sim. *Back may trust, but belly won't.*

150 The BELLY teaches all arts.
Il ventre è maestro delle arti.
Il ventre insegna il tutto.

Cf. *HUNGER is the teacher of the arts / NECESSITY is the mother of invention / POVERTY is the mother of all arts.*

151 The BELLY wants ears.
Ventre digiuno non ode nessuno.

Var. *Hungry bellies have no ears.*

152 To a full BELLY all meat is bad.
A ventre pieno ogni cibo è amaro.
Colombo pasciuto, ciliegia amara.
Allo svogliato il miele pare amaro.

Sim. *When the mouse has had enough, the meal is bitter.*

o Proverbs 27, 7 / Proverbi 27, 7

153 A BELLYFUL is a bellyful, whether it be meat or drink.
O di paglia o di fieno, il corpo ha da esser pieno.

154 Better BEND than break.
È meglio piegare che rompere.
Meglio è piegarsi che scavezzarsi.

Cf. *All that SHAKES falls not.*

155 BEST is best cheap.
La buona roba non fu mai cara.

156 The BEST is behind.
Il meglio va serbato all'ultimo.

157 The BEST is the enemy of the good.
Il meglio è nemico del bene.
L'ottimo è nemico del bene.

158 The BETTER-natured, the sooner undone.
Troppo buono, troppo minchione.

159 **A BIRD in the hand is worth two in the bush.**
Un uccello in mano ne val due nel bosco.
Meglio fringuello in man che tordo in frasca.
Val più fringuello in man che tordo in frasca.
È meglio un uccello in gabbia che cento per aria.
È meglio un uccello in gabbia che cento al bosco.

Sim. *Better a fowl in hand nor two flying.*
Cf. *A FEATHER in hand is better than a bird in the air.*

160 **A little BIRD is content with a little nest.**
A picciol uccello, picciol nido.

161 **Each BIRD loves to hear himself sing.**
Ogni uccello canta il suo verso.

162 **Far shooting never killed BIRD.**
Bel colpo non ammazzò mai uccello.

163 **It is an ill BIRD that fouls its own nest.**
Cattivo quell'uccello che sporca il suo nido.

164 **Such BIRD, such egg.**
Qual uccello, tal uovo.

Sim. *Like crow, like egg.*
Cf. *An evil CROW, an evil egg.*

165 **Such BIRD, such nest.**
Qual uccello, tal nido.

166 **The BIRD is known by his note.**
Dal canto si conosce l'uccello.

Cf. *The BIRD is known by his note, the man by his words.*

167 **The BIRD is known by his note, the man by his words.**
Al canto l'uccello, al parlare il cervello.
Gli uomini si conoscono al parlare e le campane al sonare.

Cf. *The BIRD is known by his note.*

168 **The BIRD loves her nest.**
Ad ogni uccello il suo nido è bello.
Ogni uccello fa festa al suo nido.

Var. *Every bird likes his own nest best.*

169 **The early BIRD catches the worm.**
L'uccello mattiniero si becca il verme.

170 **The more the BIRD caught in lime strives, the faster he sticks.**
    Chi nel fango è cascato, più si dimena, più vien imbrattato.
    Chi nel fango casca, quanto più si dimena, più s'imbratta.

171 **Thou art a bitter BIRD, said the raven to the starling.**
    Il ciuco dà del bue all'asino.

   Sim. *The kettle calls the pot black-brows (burnt-arse) / The pot calls the kettle black.*
   Cf. *The FRYING-PAN said to the kettle, "Avaunt, black brows!"*

172 **To fright a BIRD is not the way to catch her.**
    Chi vuol pigliare uccelli non dee trar loro dietro randelli.

   Cf. *To hunt for a HARE with a tabor.*

173 **BIRDS of a feather flock together.**
    Gli uccelli si appaiono coi loro pari.
    Pari con pari ben sta e dura.
    Dio li fa e poi li accoppia.

   Sim. *Likeness causes liking.*
   Cf. *LIKE will to like.*

   o Ecclesiasticus 27, 9 / Siràcide 27, 9

174 **Small BIRDS must have meat.**
    Uccellin che mette coda vuol mangiare in ogni ora.

   Cf. *Growing YOUTH has a wolf in his belly.*

175 **You cannot catch old BIRDS with chaff.**
    Nuova rete non piglia uccello vecchio.
    Passero vecchio non entra in gabbia.

   Cf. *An old FOX is not easily snared.*

176 **The BIT that one eats no friends makes.**
    Boccon inghiottito, amici non catta.

177 **The hasty BITCH brings forth blind whelps.**
    La gatta frettolosa fece i gattini ciechi.

   Cf. *HASTE makes waste / Too HASTY burned his lips.*

178 **That which was BITTER to endure may be sweet to remember.**
    Quel che fu duro a patire è dolce da ricordare.

   Sim. *The remembrance of past sorrow is joyful.*
   Cf. *SORROWS remembered sweeten present joy.*

179 **Who has BITTER in his mouth spits not all sweet.**
Chi ha dentro amaro non può sputare dolce.
Chi ha in bocca il fiele non può sputar miele.
Chi ha agro in bocca non può sputar dolce.

180 **Above BLACK there is no colour, and above salt no savour.**
Sopra il sal non è sapore, sopra Dio non è signore.
Sopra il nero non v'è colore.

181 **BLACK will take no other hue.**
Il nero non piglia altro colore.

182 **He that BLAMES would buy.**
Chi biasima vuol comprare.
Chi disprezza compra.

Cf. *He that speaks ill of the MARE would buy her.*

183 **A BLIND man may sometimes hit the mark.**
Talvolta anche una gallina cieca trova un granello.

Sim. *A blind man may perchance catch the hare (crow).*

184 **A BLIND man will not thank you for a looking-glass.**
Al cieco non giova pittura, color, specchio o figura.

Var. *A blind man has no need of a looking-glass.*

185 **A man were better to be half BLIND than have both his eyes out.**
Meglio losco che cieco in tutto.

Sim. *Better to have one eye than be blind altogether.*

186 **Better to be BLIND than to see ill.**
È meglio esser cieco che veder male.

187 **BLIND men should judge no colours.**
Il cieco non giudichi dei colori.

188 **If the BLIND lead the blind, both shall fall into the ditch.**
Se un cieco guida l'altro, tutti e due cascano nella fossa.

o Matthew 15, 14 / Matteo 15, 14

189 **There's none so BLIND as those who will not see.**
Non c'è peggior cieco di chi non vuol vedere.
Non c'è maggior cieco di quello che non vuol vedere.

Var. *None so blind as those who won't see.*

190 **Every BLOCK will not make a Mercury.**
Non d'ogni legno si può fare un Santo.

Sim. *Every reed will not make a pipe.*

191 **BLOOD is thicker than water.**
Il sangue non è acqua.
È la voce del sangue.

Var. *Blood is not water.*

192 **BLOOD will tell.**
Buon sangue non mente.

193 **Like BLOOD, like good, and like age, make the happiest marriage.**
Moglie e buoi dei paesi tuoi.
Moglie e ronzino, pigliali dal vicino.

Cf. *MARRY your equal.*

194 **You cannot get BLOOD from a stone.**
Dalla rapa non si cava il sangue.

Var. *You cannot get milk (water) from a stone.*

195 **The first BLOW is as much as two.**
Il primo colpo val per due.
Chi mena per primo mena due volte.

196 **Great BOAST and small roast.**
Molto fumo e poco arrosto.

Cf. *Great BRAGGERS, little doers / Much CRY and little wool / The greatest TALKERS are the least doers / A longue TONGUE is a sign of a short hand.*

197 **Ill goes the BOAT without the oar.**
Ben faremo, ben diremo, mal va la barca senza remo.
Mal va la barca senza remo.

198 **A little BODY often harbours a great soul.**
Poca mole, gran valore.

199 **He that gives thee a BONE would not have thee die.**
Chi ti dà un osso non ti vorrebbe morto.

Sim. *He that gives me small gifts would have me live.*

200 **The nearer the BONE, the sweeter the flesh.**
La carne più vicina all'osso è più saporita.

201 **What is bred in the BONE will not out of the flesh.**
Vizio per natura, fino alla fossa dura.

Sim. *Though you cast out nature with a fork, it will still return.*

202 **A closed BOOK does not produce a learned man.**
Libro serrato non fa l'uomo letterato.
La libreria non fa l'uomo dotto.

   Sim. *A book that remains shut is but a block.*

203 **A wicked BOOK is the wickeder because it cannot repent.**
Un cattivo libro è anche più cattivo perché non si può pentire.

204 **Beware of the man of one BOOK.**
Dio ti guardi da chi legge un libro solo.
Dio mi guardi da chi studia un libro solo.

   Cf. *GOD keep me from the man that has but one thing to mind.*

205 **There is no BOOK so bad, but something good may be found in it.**
Non vi è libro così cattivo che non abbia qualcosa di buono.

206 **As soon as a man is BORN he begins to die.**
Dalle fasce, si comincia a morir quando si nasce.
Quando si nasce s'incomincia a morire.
Il primo passo che ci conduce alla vita, ci conduce alla morte.

   Sim. *It is as natural to die as to be born / Our lives are but our marches to the grave.*
   Cf. *He that is once BORN, once must die / All that LIVES must die / All MEN are mortal.*

207 **He that is once BORN, once must die.**
Chi nasce convien che muoia.

   Sim. *It is as natural to die as to be born / Our lives are but our marches to the grave.*
   Cf. *As soon as a man is BORN he begins to die / All that LIVES must die / All MEN are mortal.*

208 **Men know where they were BORN, not where they shall die.**
Si sa dove si nasce, ma non si sa dove si muore.

209 **Who would BORROW when he has not, let him borrow when he has.**
Chi vuol pigliar in prestito quando non ha, ne pigli quando ne ha.

210 **A good BORROWER is a lazy payer.**
Buon esattore, cattivo pagatore.

211 **The BORROWER is servant to the lender.**
Chi prende in prestanza è servo del prestatore.

   o Proverbs 22, 7 / Proverbi 22, 7

212 **He that goes a-BORROWING, goes a-sorrowing.**
Finché si è debitori, si è nei dolori.
Chi è debitore non riposa come vuole.
Dorme chi ha dolore, e non dorme chi è debitore.

213 **Cut not the BOUGH that thou standest upon.**
Tagliare il ramo su cui si è seduti.
Var. *Don't cut the bough you are standing on.*

214 **Short BOUGHS, long vintage.**
Ramo corto, vendemmia lunga.

215 **A BOW too much bent will break.**
Il troppo tirar, l'arco fa spezzar.
La corda troppo tesa si rompe.
La corda, a forza di tirarla, si rompe.
Corda che troppo è tesa, spezza se stessa e l'arco.
Var. *A bow long bent at last waxes weak / When the bow is too much bent, it breaks.*

216 **BOYS will be boys.**
Gioventù non ha virtù.

217 **BOYS will be men.**
Anche i fanciulli diventano uomini.

218 **Great BRAGGERS, little doers.**
Gran vantatore, piccol facitore.
Var. *They brag most that can do least.*
Sim. *Much bruit and little fruit.*
Cf. *Great BOAST and little roast / Much CRY and little wool / The greatest TALKERS are the least doers / A long TONGUE is a sign of a short hand.*

219 **The BRAINS don't lie in the beard.**
La sapienza non sta nella barba.
I peli non pensano.

220 **Much BRAN and little meal.**
Molta paglia, poco grano.

221 **The BRAYING of an ass does not reach heaven.**
Raglio d'asino non arrivò mai in cielo.
Sim. *The prayers of the wicked won't prevail.*

222 **Another's BREAD costs dear.**
Il pane degli altri è troppo salato.
Il pane degli altri ha sette croste.

223 **BREAD and circuses.**
Pane e feste tengon il popolo quieto.

224 **BREAD with eyes, cheese without eyes, and wine that leaps up to the eyes.**
Pane cogli occhi, e cacio senz'occhi.
Pan leggero e grave formaggio, piglia sempre, se sei saggio.

225 **Dry BREAD at home is better than roast meat abroad.**
Pan asciutto in casa propria, anzi che l'arrosto nell'altrui.

226 **Dry BREAD is better with love than a fat capon with fear.**
Più vale un pan con amore che un cappone con dolore.

Cf. *Better an EGG in peace than an ox in war.*

227 **Eaten BREAD is soon forgotten.**
Il pan mangiato, presto è dimenticato.

Cf. *Fair-weather FRIENDS are not worth having.*

228 **He would have better BREAD than is made of wheat.**
Non cercar miglior pane che di grano.

229 **Man cannot live by BREAD alone.**
L'uomo non vive di solo pane.

> o Matthew 4, 4 / Matteo 4, 4; Luke 4, 4 / Luca 4, 4; Deuteronomy 8, 3 / Deuteronomio 8, 3

230 **Who fasts and does no other good spares his BREAD and goes to hell.**
Chi digiuna e altro ben non fa, avanza il pane, e a casa il diavol va.

231 **Who has no more BREAD than need must not keep a dog.**
A chi ha pane, non gli manca il cane.

232 **BREAK it, you pay for it.**
Chi rompe paga, e i cocci sono suoi.
Chi rompe paga, e porta via i ciottoli.

Var. *He pays for the glasses who breaks them.*

233 **One man's BREATH another's death.**
Morte tua, vita mia.

Cf. *One man's LOSS is another man's gain.*

234 **The first BREATH is the beginning of death.**
Il primo passo che ci conduce alla vita, ci conduce alla morte.

235 **Not where one is BRED, but where he is fed.**
Non d'onde sei, ma d'onde pasci.

236 **As they BREW, so let them drink.**
Chi l'ha fatta, la beva.

Sim. *As you bake, so shall you eat / As they brew, so let them bake.*
Cf. *As you make your BED, so you must lie on it.*

237 **It is meet that a man be at his own BRIDAL.**
Tristo a colui che non si trova alle sue nozze.
Chi non è alle sue nozze, o che son crude o che son troppo cotte.

238 **It is the BRIDLE and spur that makes a good horse.**
Briglia e speron fanno il cavallo buon.

239 **A new BROOM sweeps clean.**
Granata nuova spazza ben tre giorni.
Granata nuova, tre dì buona.

Var. *New brooms sweep clean.*

240 **Between two BROTHERS two witnesses and a notary.**
Corruccio di fratelli fa più che due flagelli.
Ira di fratelli, ira di diavoli.
Fratelli, flagelli.

241 **Three BROTHERS, three castles.**
Tre fratelli, tre castelli.

Sim. *Three helping one another bear the burden of six.*

242 **BUILDING and marrying of children are great wasters.**
Chi edifica, la borsa purifica.

Cf. *BUILDING is a sweet impoverishing.*

243 **BUILDING is a sweet impoverishing.**
Il fabbricare è un dolce impoverire.

Cf. *BUILDING and marrying of children are great wasters.*

244 **He may bear a BULL that has borne a calf.**
Ben può sostenere il toro chi ha già portato il vitello.

245 **A BURDEN of one's own choice is not felt.**
Il proprio fardello pesa poco.

246 **Every man shall bear his own BURDEN.**
Ciascuno porterà il suo proprio peso.

o Galatians 6, 5 / Galati 6, 5

247 **He that BURNS shines most.**
Chi più arde più splende.

248 **One beats the BUSH and another catches the birds.**
Uno scuote il cespuglio, l'altro acchiappa l'uccello.

Sim. *The poor man turns his cake and another comes and takes it away.*
Cf. *Little DOGS start the hare, the great get her / One SOWS and another reaps.*

249 **BUSINESS before pleasure.**
Prima il dovere, poi il piacere.

250 **BUSINESS is business.**
Gli affari sono affari.

251 **Every man knows his own BUSINESS best.**
Ognuno è maestro nell'arte sua.

252 **No man fouls his hands in his own BUSINESS.**
Nessuno s'ha da vergognare della sua arte.

253 **The BUTCHER looked for his knife and it was in his mouth.**
Fare come quello che cercava la pipa e l'aveva in bocca.

Cf. *You look for the HORSE you ride on.*

254 **It is not all BUTTER that the cow yields.**
Non è tutto burro ciò che fa la vacca.

255 **It rains BUTTER and cheese.**
Quando piove d'agosto, piove miele e piove mosto.

256 **The BUYER needs a hundred eyes, the seller but one.**
A chi compra non bastano cent'occhi; a chi vende ne basta uno solo.
Due occhi per chi vende, ma cento per chi prende.

Var. *The seller needs but one eye; the buyer one hundred.*
Sim. *Let the buyer beware.*

257 **He that BUYS what he does not want, must often sell what he does want.**
Chi compra il superfluo, venderà il necessario.

Var. *Buy what you do not want and you will sell what you cannot spare.*

C

258 CABBAGE twice cooked is death.
Cavolo riscaldato non fu mai buono.

    Sim. *Take heed of reconciled enemies and of meat twice boiled.*
    Cf. *A broken FRIENDSHIP may be soldered, but will never be sound.*

259 Either CAESAR or nobody.
O Cesare o niente.

260 Render unto CAESAR the things which are Caesar's.
Rendete a Cesare quello che è di Cesare, e a Dio quello che è di Dio.
A Cesare quel che è di Cesare, a Dio quel che è di Dio.
Quel che è di Cesare è di Cesare.

    Var. *Give back to Caesar what is Caesar's, and to God what is God's.*
    Cf. *Every MAN should take his own.*

        o Matthew 22, 21 / Matteo 22, 21; Mark 12, 17 / Marco 12, 17; Luke 20, 25 / Luca 20, 25

261 CAESAR's wife must be above suspicion.
Esser come la moglie di Cesare.

262 A fine CAGE won't feed a hungry bird.
La bella gabbia non nutrisce l'uccello.
La bella gabbia non nutre l'uccello.

263 You can't eat your CAKE and have it too.
Non si può avere la botte piena e la moglie ubriaca.

    Var. *You can't have your cake and eat it too.*

264 If thou suffer a CALF to be laid on thee, within a little they'll clap on the cow.
Se ti lasci metter in spalla il vitello, quindi a poco ti metteran la vacca.

265 It is easier for a CAMEL to go through the eye of a needle than it is for a rich man to enter the kingdom of heaven.
È più facile per un cammello passare per la cruna di un ago che per un ricco entrare nel regno di Dio.

        o Matthew 19, 24 / Matteo 19, 24; Luke 18, 25 / Luca 18, 25

266 **He who CAN, does; he who cannot, teaches.**
Chi sa fa e chi non sa insegna.

267 **A CANDLE lights others and consumes itself.**
La candela alluma, e se stessa consuma.

268 **It is sometimes good to hold a CANDLE to the devil.**
È bene accendere una candela a Dio e due al diavolo.

> Sim. *Like the old woman who burned one candle to St. Michael and another to the Dragon.*
> Cf. *Give the DEVIL his due.*

269 **If CANDLEMAS day be fair and bright, winter will have another flight: if on Candlemas day it be shower and rain, winter is gone, and will come not again.**
Per la santa Candelora, se nevica o se plora, dall'inverno siamo fora; ma s'è sole e solicello noi siam sempre a mezzo il verno.

> Var. *If Candlemas day be sunny and bright, winter will have another flight; if Candlemas day be cloudy with rain, winter is gone, and won't come again.*

270 **When the CANDLES are out, all women are fair.**
A lume spento è pari ogni bellezza.
Al buio la villana è bella quanto la dama.
Al lume di lucerna ogni rustica è bella.

271 **If thou hast not a CAPON, feed on an onion.**
Sono meglio le fave che durano, che i capponi che vengon meno.

> Sim. *Acorns were good till bread was found / Better a louse (mouse) in the pot than no flesh at all.*
> Cf. *They that have no other MEAT, bread and butter are glad to eat.*

272 **Where the CARCASE is, there shall the eagles be gathered together.**
Dove son carogne, son corvi.

> Var. *Wheresoever the carcase is, there will the ravens be gathered together.*
>
> o Matthew 24, 28 / Matteo 24, 28; Luke 17, 37 / Luca 17, 37

273 **Lucky at CARDS, unlucky in love.**
Chi ha fortuna in amore, non giochi a carte.
Fortuna al gioco, sfortuna in amore.

> Var. *Lucky at play, unlucky in love / Unlucky in love, lucky in play.*
> Cf. *Unlucky at CARDS, lucky in love.*

274 **Unlucky at CARDS, lucky in love.**
Sfortuna al gioco, fortuna in amore.

Cf. *Lucky at CARDS, unlucky in love.*

275 **CARE brings grey hair.**
Le preoccupazioni fanno venire i capelli bianchi.
I pensieri fanno mettere i peli canuti.

276 **He CARRIES well to whom it weighs not.**
A chi non pesa, ben porta.

277 **A creaking CART goes long on the wheels.**
Dura più un carro rotto che uno nuovo.
Dura più una pentola fessa che una nuova.
Basta più una conca fessa che una sana.
Tutto il giorno ahi! non muor mai.

Sim. *A creaking door hangs long on its hinges.*

278 **Don't put the CART before the horse.**
Non mettere il carro davanti ai buoi.
Non bisogna mettere il carro davanti ai buoi.

Var. *Don't get the carriage before the horse / To put the cart before the horse.*

279 **Every CASK smells of the wine it contains.**
La botte dà del vino che ha.

Var. *The cask savours of the first fill.*
Cf. *There comes nought out of the SACK, but what was there.*

280 **A CAT always falls on its legs.**
Cascare in piè come le gatte.

281 **A CAT has nine lives.**
Gatti hanno nove vite.
La gatta ha sette vite, e la donna sette più.

Var. *A cat has nine lives; a woman has nine cat's lives.*

282 **A CAT in gloves catches no mice.**
Gatta inguantata non prese mai topi.
Gatta guantata non piglia sorci.

283 **A CAT may look at a king.**
Un gatto può ben guardare un re.
Anche un gatto può guardare un re.

284 **A scalded CAT fears cold water.**
Gatto scottato dall'acqua calda ha paura della fredda.

Var. *A scalded dog fears cold water.*
Sim. *Once bitten twice shy / He that has been bitten by a serpent is afraid of a rope.*
Cf. *A burnt CHILD dreads the fire / Whom a SERPENT has bitten, a lizard alarms.*

285 **How can the CAT help it if the maid be a fool?**
Che colpa ne ha la gatta, se la massaia è matta?

286 **Never was CAT or dog drowned that could but see the shore.**
Né can né gatta mai s'affogan pur che vedan la ripa.

287 **That that comes of a CAT will catch mice.**
Chi di gatta nasce, sorci piglia.
Chi di gatta nasce, sorci piglia; se non li piglia non è sua figlia.
I figliuoli dei gatti pigliano i topi.

Sim. *Cat after kind, good mouse-hunt.*
Cf. *Who is born of a CAT will run after mice / He that comes of a HEN must scrape.*

288 **The CAT would eat fish and would not wet her feet.**
La gatta vorrebbe mangiar pesci, ma non pescare.

Var. *The cat loves fish, but dares not wet his feet.*
Cf. *He who would catch FISH must not mind getting wet.*

289 **Who is born of a CAT will run after mice.**
Non fu mai gatta che non corresse ai topi.

Sim. *The son of a cat pursues the rat / Cat after kind, good mouse-hunt.*
Cf. *That that comes of a CAT will catch mice / He that comes of a HEN must scrape.*

290 **When the CAT's away, the mice will play.**
Quando il gatto non c'è, i topi ballano.
Quando la gatta non c'è, i sorci ballano.
Quando la gatta non è in paese, i topi ballano.

291 **All CATS are grey in the dark.**
Di notte tutti i gatti sono grigi.

Var. *All cats are alike grey in the night.*

292 **CATS eat what hussies spare.**
Chi serba, serba al gatto.
Chi sparagna, vien la gatta e glielo magna.

293 Two CATS and a mouse, two wives in one house, two dogs and a bone, never agree in one.
Due gatti e un topo, due mogli in una casa, due cani e un osso non vanno mai d'accordo.

294 Take away the CAUSE and the effect must cease.
Tolta la causa, cessato l'effetto.

295 Without CERES and Bacchus, Venus grows cold.
Senza Cerere e Bacco, è amor debole e fiacco.

296 Never quit CERTAINTY for hope.
Non lasciare il certo per l'incerto.
Mal si lascia il certo per prendere il forse.

297 He is not free that draws his CHAIN.
Non è scappato chi si strascina dietro la catena.

Cf. *The HORSE that draws after him his halter is not altogether escaped.*

298 The CHARITABLE give out at the door, and God puts in at the window.
Il caritatevole dà dalla porta, e Iddio mette dentro dalle finestre.

299 CHARITY begins at home.
La prima carità comincia da sé.

Sim. *Love your friend, but look to yourself.*
Cf. *Every MAN is nearest himself.*

300 CHARITY covers a multitude of sins.
La carità dona il paradiso.
La carità ricopre ogni misfatto.

o I Peter 4, 8 / I Pietro 4, 8

301 He that CHASTENS one, chastens twenty.
Chi ne castiga uno, cento ne minaccia.

302 CHASTISE the good and he will mend; chastise the bad and he will grow worse.
Batti il buono, egli migliora; batti il cattivo, egli peggiora.

Cf. *Show a good man his ERROR and he turns it to virtue; but an ill, it doubles his fault / PRAISE makes good men better, and bad men worse.*

303 In the Kingdom of a CHEATER, the wallet is carried before.
In terra di ladri, la valigia dinanzi.

304 **Those that eat CHERRIES with great persons shall have their eyes squirted out with the stones.**
Non è buono mangiar ciliege coi signori.

> Var. *Eat peas with the king, and cherries with the beggar.*
> Cf. *Share not PEARS with your master, either in jest or in earnest.*

305 **Take the CHESTNUTS out of the fire with the cat's paw.**
La scimmia leva le castagne dal fuoco colla zampa della gatta.

> Sim. *To take the nuts from the fire with the dog's foot / It is good to strike the serpent's head with your enemy's hand.*

306 **A burnt CHILD dreads the fire.**
L'uomo scottato ha paura del fuoco.
Chi è scottato una volta, l'altra vi soffia su.

> Sim. *Once bitten twice shy / A scalded dog fears cold water / He that has been bitten by a serpent is afraid of a rope.*
> Cf. *A scalded CAT fears cold water / Whom a SERPENT has bitten, a lizard alarms.*

307 **A CHILD may have too much of his mother's blessing.**
Figlio troppo accarezzato non fu mai ben allevato.

> Sim. *Give a child till he craves, and a dog while his tail doth wave, and you'll have a fair dog, but a foul knave.*

308 **Happy is the CHILD whose father goes to the devil.**
Per essere ricco bisogna avere un parente a casa del diavolo.

309 **It is a wise CHILD that knows its own father.**
Quello è un fanciullo accorto che conosce il padre suo.

310 **Praise the CHILD, and you make love to the mother.**
Si bacia il fanciullo a cagion della madre, e la madre a cagion del fanciullo.

> Var. *Many kiss the child for the nurse's sake.*
> Cf. *He that would the DAUGHTER win must with the mother first begin.*

311 **The CHILD says nothing, but what it heard by the fire.**
Quando il piccolo parla, il grande ha parlato.

> Sim. *What children hear at home, soon flies abroad.*

312 **Better CHILDREN weep than old men.**
È meglio pianga il figliuolo che il padre.

> Sim. *The man who has not been flogged is not educated.*
> Cf. *Spare the ROD and spoil the child.*

313 **CHILDREN and chicken must be always picking.**
Ragazzi e polli non si trovan mai satolli.

314 **CHILDREN and fools tell the truth.**
I fanciulli e i pazzi dicono la verità.
I fanciulli e i pazzi profetizzano.
Chi vuol sapere la verità, lo domandi alla purità.

Var. *Children and fools cannot lie.*
Cf. *DRUNKARDS and fools cannot lie.*

315 **CHILDREN are poor men's riches.**
I figli sono la ricchezza dei poveri.

316 **CHILDREN suck the mother when they are young, and the father when they are old.**
I figliuoli succhiano la madre quando son piccoli, e il padre quando son grandi.

317 **CHILDREN when they are little make parents fools, when they are great they make them mad.**
Figli piccoli, guai piccoli; figli grandi, guai grandi.

Var. *Children when little make parents fool, when great, mad.*

318 **He that has CHILDREN all morsels are not his own.**
Chi ha figliuoli, tutti i bocconi non son suoi.

319 **He that has no CHILDREN knows not what is love.**
Chi non ha figliuoli non sa che sia amore.

Sim. *It takes children to make a happy home.*

320 **Late CHILDREN, early orphans.**
Chi tardi mette i denti, vede morire tutti i suoi parenti.

321 **She spins well that breeds her CHILDREN.**
Fila buona tela chi allatta il suo figliuolo.

322 **When CHILDREN stand quiet they have done some ill.**
Quando i ragazzi stan cheti, han fatto qualche malestro.
Quando i ragazzi stanno fermi, cattivo segno.

323 **A CHIP off the old block.**
La scheggia ritrae dal ceppo.

Var. *A chip of the old block.*
Cf. *An APPLE never falls far from the tree / Like FATHER, like son / Like MOTHER, like daughter.*

324 **From CHIPPING come chips.**
Dove piove ci sono gocciole.

325 **CHRISTMAS comes but once a year.**
Natale viene una sola volta l'anno.

    Cf. *Every DAY is not Sunday.*

326 **CHRISTMAS in mud, Easter in snow.**
Chi fa il Natale al sole, fa la Pasqua al fuoco.

    Cf. *Green CHRISTMAS brings white Easter.*

327 **Green CHRISTMAS brings white Easter.**
Verde Natale, bianca Pasqua.

    Cf. *CHRISTMAS in mud, Easter in snow.*

328 **They talk of CHRISTMAS so long that it comes.**
Tanto si chiama Natale ch'ei viene poi.

329 **The nearer the CHURCH, the farther from God.**
Vicino alla chiesa, lontano da Dio.

    Var. *He who is near the church is often far from God.*
    Sim. *He has one face to God and another to the devil.*

330 **Hasty CLIMBERS have sudden falls.**
Chi troppo in alto sal, cade repente, precipitevolissimevolmente.

    Sim. *The bigger they are, the harder they fall.*
    Cf. *The higher the MOUNTAIN, the greater descent / The higher STANDING, the lower fall.*

331 **It is a bad CLOTH that will take no colour.**
Cattiva è quella lana che non si può tingere.

332 **The best CLOTH may have a moth in it.**
In panno fino sta la tarma.

333 **CLOTHE thee warm, eat little, drink enough, and thou shalt live.**
Vesti caldo, mangia poco e bevi assai che vivrai.

334 **Every CLOUD has a silver lining.**
Non tutto il male vien per nuocere.

335 **All CLOUDS bring not rain.**
Non tutte le nuvole fanno pioggia.

336 **Cut your COAT according to your cloth.**
Bisogna fare la veste secondo il panno.

    Sim. *Stretch your arm no further than your sleeve will reach.*
    Cf. *Everyone stretches his LEGS according to the length of his coverlet.*

337 **Near is my COAT, but nearer is my shirt.**
Stringe più la camicia che il giubbone.
Tocca più la camicia che il giubbone.
Stringe più la camicia che la gonnella.

Sim. *Near is my doublet (kirtle, petticoat), but nearer is my smock.*
Cf. *Near is my SHIRT, but nearer is my skin.*

338 **The COAT makes the man.**
L'abito fa l'uomo.
L'abito fa il monaco.

Var. *Apparel makes the man / The garment makes the man.*
Cf. *Fine FEATHERS make fine birds / Dress up a STICK and it does not appear to be a stick.*

339 **Under a ragged COAT lies wisdom.**
Spesso sotto abito vile s'asconde uom gentile.
Spesso sotto abito vile s'asconde tesor gentile.

Cf. *Never judge from APPEARANCES.*

340 **Let the COBBLER stick to his last.**
Ciabattino, parla sol del tuo mestiere.

Var. *Let not the cobbler (shoemaker) go beyond his last.*

341 **A COCK is bold on his own dunghill.**
È ardito il gallo sopra il suo letame.

Var. *Every cock crows on his own dunghill.*
Sim. *Every dog is valiant at his own door.*
Cf. *Every DOG is a lion at home / Every man is a KING in his own house.*

342 **As the old COCK crows, so crows the young.**
Come canta il gallo, canterà il galletto.
Risponde il frate come canta l'abate.

Sim. *The young pig grunts like the old sow.*
Cf. *Where the DAM leaps over, the kid follows.*

343 **Who eats his COCK alone, must saddle his horse alone.**
Chi mangia solo, crepa solo.

Var. *He that eats his fowl alone, must saddle his horse alone / Who eats his dinner alone, must saddle his horse alone.*

344 **Many a shabby COLT makes a good horse.**
Di puledro scabbioso, talvolta hai cavallo prezioso.

Var. *A ragged colt may make a good horse / The wilder the colt, the better the horse.*
Cf. *Wanton KITTENS make sober cats.*

345 **Young COLTS will canter.**
Ogni puledro vuol romper la sua cavezza.

346 **If thou wilt COME with me, bring with thee.**
In casa mia non entrerai, se tu non porterai.

Cf. *They are WELCOME that bring.*

347 **The COMFORTER's head never aches.**
A buon confortatore il capo non duole.

348 **COMMAND your man, and do it yourself.**
Comanda e fai da te.

349 **He is not fit to COMMAND others that cannot command himself.**
Chi vuol regnare, convien se stesso dominare.

350 **He who COMMENCES many things finishes but few.**
Chi troppo comincia, poco finisce.
Chi troppo intraprende, poco finisce.

Var. *He who begins many things finishes but few.*
Sim. *Overdoing is doing nothing to purpose.*

351 **Evil COMMUNICATIONS corrupt good manners.**
Le cattive compagnie guastano i buoni costumi.
Cattive conversazioni corrompono buoni costumi.

o I Corinthians 15, 33 / I Corinzi 15, 33

352 **A merry COMPANION is a waggon in the way.**
Compagno allegro per cammino ti serve per ronzino.

353 **A man is known by the COMPANY he keeps.**
Dimmi con chi vai, e ti dirò chi sei.

Sim. *Show me your company, and I'll tell you who you are / Tell me with whom thou goest, and I'll tell thee what thou doest.*

354 **Better be alone than in bad COMPANY.**
Meglio soli che male accompagnati.

Sim. *Better to be beaten than be in bad company.*

355 **Ill COMPANY brings many a man to the gallows.**
Le cattive compagnie conducono l'uomo alla forca.

356 **It is good to have COMPANY in trouble.**
Mal comune, mezzo gaudio.

Sim. *Company in distress makes trouble less / Company in misery makes it light / Two in distress makes sorrow less / A trouble shared is a trouble halved.*

357 **Keep good men COMPANY, and you shall be of the number.**
Accostati ai buoni e sarai uno di essi.
Accompagnati con chi è meglio di te, e fagli le spese.

Sim. *Associate with the good and you will be one of them.*

358 **COMPARISONS are odious.**
I paragoni sono tutti odiosi.
I confronti sono odiosi.

359 **A clear CONSCIENCE fears not false accusations.**
Buona coscienza non ha paura.

360 **A good CONSCIENCE is a soft pillow.**
Una buona coscienza è un buon guanciale.

Sim. *A good conscience is a continual feast.*

361 **CONSCIENCE is a thousand witnesses.**
La coscienza vale per mille testimoni.
La coscienza vale per mille accusatori e per mille testimoni.
La coscienza vale per mille prove.

362 **Some make a CONSCIENCE of spitting in the church, yet rob the altar.**
Molti si fanno coscienza di sputare in chiesa, che poi cacano sull'altare.

363 **CONTENT is happiness.**
Chi si contenta gode.

Cf. *A contented MIND is a continual feast.*

364 **CONTENT is more than a kingdom.**
Contentezza passa ricchezza.

365 **He who is CONTENT in his poverty is wonderfully rich.**
Cuor contento non sente stento.

366 **No man is CONTENT with his lot.**
E non è un per cento di sua sorte contento.

Sim. *None is satisfied with his fortune.*

367 **They need much whom nothing will CONTENT.**
Sempre stenta chi mai si contenta.

368 **Better wait on the COOK than on the doctor.**
Meglio il cuoco che il medico.
È meglio che ci venga il fornaio che il medico.

369 **He is an ill COOK that cannot lick his own fingers.**
Tristo quel cuoco che non si sa leccar le dita.

370 **Too many COOKS spoil the broth.**
Troppi cuochi rovinano la minestra.
Troppi cuochi rovinano il brodo.
I troppi cuochi guastano la cucina.
Dove son molti cuochi, la minestra sarà troppo salata.

371 **A threefold CORD is not quickly broken.**
Il cordone a tre fili non si rompe prestamente.

    o Ecclesiastes 4, 12 / Qoèlet 4, 12

372 **Three things COST dear: the caresses of a dog, the love of a whore, and the invitation of a host.**
Carezze di cani, cortesia di puttane, e inviti d'osti, non puoi far che non ti costi.

Cf. *An HOST's invitation is expensive.*

373 **A dry COUGH is the trumpeter of death.**
La tosse è il tamburo della morte.

374 **COUNSEL must be followed, not praised.**
Il consiglio non va lodato, ma seguito.

375 **Give neither COUNSEL nor salt till you are asked for it.**
Non dare consigli a chi non li chiede.

Sim. *Come not to counsel uncalled.*

376 **It is an ill COUNSEL that has no escape.**
Tristo quel consiglio che non ha sconsiglio.

377 **The COUNSEL thou wouldst have another keep, first keep it thyself.**
Male altrui consiglia, chi per sé non lo piglia.

378 **There is none so simple but can give COUNSEL.**
È più facile consigliare che fare.

Sim. *We may give advice, but we cannot give conduct.*

379 **To the COUNSEL of fools, a wooden bell.**
A consiglio di pazzo, campana di legno.

380 **He that will not be COUNSELLED cannot be helped.**
Chi non vuol esser consigliato, non può esser aiutato.
A chi non si lascia consigliare, non si può aiutare.

Sim. *In vain he craves advice that will not follow it.*

381 **He that is his own COUNSELLOR knows nothing sure but what he has laid out.**
Chi si consiglia da sé, da sé si ritrova.

382 **COUNSELS in wine seldom prosper.**
Consiglio in vino non ha mai buon fine.

383 **So many COUNTRIES, so many customs.**
Tanti paesi, tanti costumi.

Cf. *Every LAND has its own law.*

384 **For our COUNTRY it is bliss to die.**
Chi per la patria muor, vissuto è assai, la fronde dell'allor non muore mai.

Sim. *He lives in fame that died in virtue's cause.*

385 **In every COUNTRY dogs bite.**
In ogni paese mozzicano i cani.

386 **In every COUNTRY the sun rises in the morning.**
In ogni paese si leva il sole la mattina.

387 **In the COUNTRY of the blind the one-eyed man is king.**
In terra di ciechi chi ha un occhio è signore.

Var. *In the Kingdom of blind men, the one-eyed is king.*

388 **Where is well with me, there is my COUNTRY.**
La patria è dove s'ha del bene.

Sim. *A wise (valiant) man esteems every place to be his own country.*

389 **At COURT every one for himself.**
Alla corte del re ognun faccia per sé.

390 **He that lives in COURT dies upon straw.**
Chi vive in corte muore in paglia.

391 **Full of COURTESY, full of craft.**
La molta cortesia fa temere che inganno vi sia.
Chi t'accarezza più di quel che suole, o t'ha ingannato, o ingannar ti vuole.

Sim. *Credulous men are prey of crafty ones / He that is kinder than he was wont, has a design upon you.*

392 **All COVET, all lose.**
Chi tutto vuole, tutto perde.

Sim. *Grasp all, lose all.*
Cf. *He that too much EMBRACETH holds little.*

393 **A COVETOUS man does nothing that he should till he dies.**
L'avaro è come il porco, che è buono dopo morto.
L'avaro non fa mai bene, se non quando tira le calze.

  Sim. *He is like a swine, he'll never do good while he lives.*

394 **A COVETOUS man serves his riches, not they him.**
L'avaro non possiede l'oro, ma è posseduto dall'oro.

  Sim. *The rich are rather possessed by their money than possessors.*

395 **The COVETOUS spends more than the liberal.**
L'avaro spende più che il liberale.

396 **COVETOUSNESS breaks the bag.**
La cupidigia rompe il sacco.

  Var. *Covetousness bursts the sack.*
  Sim. *Over covetous was never good.*
  Cf. TOO MUCH breaks the bag / You can have TOO MUCH of a good thing.

397 **COVETOUSNESS is the root of all evil.**
La radice di tutti i mali è l'avarizia.
L'avarizia è scuola d'ogni vizio.

  o I Timothy 6, 10 / I Timoteo 6, 10

398 **COVETOUSNESS often starves other vices.**
L'avarizia fa stentare gli altri vizi.

399 **A curst COW has short horns.**
A cattiva vacca Dio dà corte corna.

  Cf. *A curst DOG must be tied short.*

400 **Let him that owns the COW, take her by the tail.**
Di chi è l'asino, lo pigli per la coda.

401 **Set a COW to catch a hare.**
Bisogna saper prendere la lepre col carro.

402 **The COW knows not what her tail is worth till she has lost it.**
L'asino non conosce la coda, se non quando non l'ha più.

  Cf. *A GOOD thing lost is a good thing valued / We never know the worth of WATER till the well is dry.*

403 **The COWL does not make the monk.**
L'abito non fa il monaco.

  Var. *The hood (habit) does not make the monk.*
  Sim. *It is not the gay coat that makes the gentleman.*

404 Plant the CRAB-TREE where you will, it will never bear pippins.
Il pruno non fa melaranci.
La quercia non fa limoni.
Il leccio non fa olive.
I castagni non fecero mai aranci.

405 He that has not the CRAFT, let him shut up shop.
Chi non sa l'arte, non apra bottega.

406 To a CRAFTY man, a crafty and a half.
Per conoscere un furbo ci vuole un furbo e mezzo.

407 Who buys dear and takes up on CREDIT, shall ever sell to his loss.
Chi compra caro e toglie a credenza, consuma il tempo e perde la semenza.

408 CREDITORS have better memories than debtors.
I creditori hanno miglior memoria dei debitori.

409 He that dwells next door to a CRIPPLE will learn to halt.
Chi pratica lo zoppo, impara a zoppicare.

410 He that mocks a CRIPPLE, ought to be whole.
Chi burla lo zoppo, badi di essere diritto.

Sim. *If you mock the lame, you will go so yourself in time.*
Cf. *It is hard to halt before a CRIPPLE.*

411 It is hard to halt before a CRIPPLE.
Davanti gli zoppi non bisogna zoppicare.

Cf. *He that mocks a CRIPPLE, ought to be whole.*

412 That which is CROOKED cannot be made straight.
Le cose torte non si possono dirizzare.

o Ecclesiastes 1, 15 / Qoèlet 1, 15

413 Every man has his CROSS to bear.
Ognuno porta la sua croce.

Cf. *Every HEART has its own ache.*

o Matthew 10, 38; 16, 24 / Matteo 10, 38; 16, 24; Mark 8, 34; 10, 21 / Marco 8, 34; 10, 21; Luke 9, 23; 14, 27 / Luca 9, 23; 14, 27.

414 The CROSS on his breast and the devil in his heart.
Parole d'angioletto, unghie di diavoletto.
Parole di santo e unghie di gatto.

Sim. *Beads about the neck and the devil in the heart / The beads in the hand and the devil in capuch.*

415 **An evil CROW, an evil egg.**
Dal mal corvo, mal uovo.

Sim. *Like crow, like egg.*
Cf. *Such BIRD, such egg.*

416 **Breed up a CROW and he will tear out your eyes.**
Nutri il corvo e ti caverà gli occhi.

Var. *He has brought up a bird to pick out his own eyes.*
Cf. *To nourish a SNAKE in one's bosom.*

417 **The CROW thinks her own bird fairest.**
Ogni cornacchia ama i suoi cornacchiotti.
Il corvo pensa che i suoi pulcini siano i più belli.

Cf. *FAIR is not fair, but that which pleases / The OWL thinks her own young fairest.*

418 **The CROWN is no cure for the headache.**
Dolor di capo non toglie la corona reale.

419 **Carrion CROWS bewail the dead sheep, and then eat them.**
Il corvo piange la pecora, e poi la mangia.

420 **CROWS will not pick out crows' eyes.**
Corvi con corvi non si cavano gli occhi.

Var. *Hawks will not pick out hawks' eyes.*

421 **Put not an embroidered CRUPPER on an ass.**
Chi mette all'asino la sella, la cigna va per terra.

Sim. *My old mare would have a new crupper.*

422 **Much CRY and little wool.**
Assai rumore e poca lana.

Sim. *Much bruit and little fruit.*
Cf. *Much ADO about nothing / Great BOAST and little roast / Great BRAGGERS, little doers / The greatest TALKERS are the least doers / A long TONGUE is a sign of a short hand.*

423 **It is no use CRYING over spilt milk.**
È inutile piangere sul latte versato.

Var. *Don't cry over spilt milk.*

424 **What can't be CURED must be endured.**
Sopporta e non biasimare quel che non puoi cambiare.

425 **CURSES, like chickens, come home to roost.**
Le maledizioni fanno come le processioni che tornano donde partono.
La bestemmia gira gira, e ricade su chi la tira.
Le imprecazioni sono foglie, chi le semina le raccoglie.

426 **CUSTOM is a second nature.**
L'abitudine è una seconda natura.

427 **CUSTOM rules the law.**
L'uso fa legge.

428 **Once is no CUSTOM.**
Una volta non fa usanza.

Var. *Once, and use it not.*

429 **The command of CUSTOM is great.**
Grande è la forza dell'abitudine.

D

430 **Where the DAM leaps over, the kid follows.**
Le capre, dove ne salta una, saltan tutte.

> Sim. *The young pig grunts like the old sow.*
> Cf. *As the old COCK crows, so crows the young.*

431 **He that will not be ruled by his own DAME shall be ruled by his stepdame.**
Chi non crede alla buona madre, crede poi alla matrigna.

> Sim. *He that will not hear motherhead, shall hear step-motherhead.*

432 **Better pass a DANGER once than be always in fear.**
Meglio è pericolar un tratto che star sempre in pericolo.

433 **DANGER itself the best remedy for danger.**
Il pericolo s'ha a vincer col pericolo.

> Sim. *Without danger we cannot get beyond danger.*

434 **He that runs into DANGER must expect to perish therein.**
Chi ama il pericolo perirà in esso.

> Sim. *He that brings himself into needless dangers, dies the devil's martyr.*
>
> o Ecclesiasticus 3, 26 / Siràcide 3, 26

435 **The DANGER past and God forgotten.**
Passato il pericolo, gabbato il santo.
Passata la festa, gabbato lo Santo.

> Sim. *Call the bear 'uncle' till you are safe across the bridge / Once on shore, we pray no more.*
> Cf. *The RIVER past and God forgotten.*

436 **He that would the DAUGHTER win must with the mother first begin.**
Chi vuol la figlia, carezzi la madre.

> Cf. *Praise the CHILD, and you make love to the mother.*

437 **DAUGHTERS and dead fish are no keeping wares.**
Le ragazze sono come i cavalli: se non si danno via da giovani, perdono la loro ventura.

Sim. *Marry your daughter and eat fresh fish betimes / Marry your daughters betimes, lest they marry themselves.*

438 DAUGHTERS are brittle ware.
Figlie da maritare, fastidiose da guardare.
Dove ci son ragazze innamorate è inutile tener porte serrate.

439 All's alike at the latter DAY: a bag of gold and wisp of hay.
Al giorno del giudizio, tanto vale il marchetto quanto il ducato.

Cf. *DEATH is the great leveller / DEATH makes equal the high and low / At the END of the game the King and the pawn go into the same bag / Six FEET of earth make all men equal.*

440 At Twelfth DAY the days are lengthened a cock-stride.
San Tommè, cresce il dì quanto il gallo alza un piè.

441 Every DAY brings its bread with it.
Ogni dimane porta il suo pane.

442 Every DAY comes night.
Non vien dì che non venga sera.
Ogni dì vien sera.

Sim. *Be the day never so long, at length cometh evensong.*
Cf. *The longest DAY must have an end.*

443 Every DAY is not Sunday.
Ogni dì non è festa.
Ogni giorno non si fanno nozze.

Var. *Every day is no Yule-day.*
Cf. *CHRISTMAS comes but once a year.*

444 No DAY passes without some grief.
A ogni giorno basta il suo affanno.
Ogni giorno ha il suo amore e dolore.

Cf. *Sufficient unto the DAY is the evil thereof.*

445 No DAY without a line.
Ogni giorno deve avere il suo compito.
Ogni dì è nostro.

Sim. *No day should pass without something being done.*

446 One DAY of pleasure is worth two of sorrow.
Un'ora di contento sconta cent'anni di tormento.

447 Praise a fair DAY at night.
Non lodar il bel giorno innanzi sera.

Sim. *Praise day at night, and life at the end / The evening crowns the day.*
Cf. *Say no ill of the YEAR till it be past.*

448 Sufficient unto the DAY is the evil thereof.
A ciascun giorno basta la sua pena.

Cf. *No DAY passes without some grief.*

o Matthew 6, 34 / Matteo 6, 34

449 Take each DAY as it comes.
Bisogna prendere il tempo come viene.

Sim. *Take things as they are, not as you'd have them.*

450 The longest DAY must have an end.
Non vi è giorno sì lungo che non lo segua la notte.

Sim. *Be the day never so long, at length cometh evensong.*
Cf. *Every DAY comes night.*

451 Two good DAYS for a man in his life: when he weds and when he buries his wife.
Due dì gode il marito la sua metà: il dì che la porta a casa, e quello che la se ne va.

452 DEAD men don't bite.
Uomo morto non fa guerra.

453 It is only the DEAD who do not return.
I morti non tornano.

454 Let the DEAD bury the dead and let the living lead a gay life.
Lascia i morti seppellire i loro morti.

Var. *Let the dead bury their dead.*
Cf. *We must LIVE by the quick, not by the dead.*

o Matthew 8, 22 / Matteo 8, 22

455 Never speak ill of the DEAD.
All'assente e al morto non si deve far torto.
Al morto non si deve far torto.

Sim. *Speak well of the dead.*
Cf. *Say nothing of the DEAD but what is good.*

456 Say nothing of the DEAD but what is good.
Dei morti non si deve dire che bene.

Cf. *Never speak ill of the DEAD.*

457 Speak not of a DEAD man at the table.
Non ricordare i morti a tavola.

458 To lament the DEAD avails not and revenge vents hatred.
Il pianger i morti non rileva e la vendetta sfoga l'odio assai.

459 There's none so DEAF as those who will not hear.
Non c'è peggior sordo di chi non vuol sentire.
Gran sordo è quello che non vuol udire.

Var. *None so deaf as those who won't hear.*

460 The DEARER it is the cheaper.
Chi più spende, meno spende.

461 A fair DEATH honours the whole life.
Un bel morir tutta la vita onora.

Cf. *Better DIE with honour than live with shame.*

462 After DEATH the doctor.
Dopo la morte non val medicina.

Cf. *After MEAT, mustard.*

463 DEATH is common to all.
La morte è un debito comune.

464 DEATH is deaf and will hear no denial.
La morte non riceve alcuna scusa.

465 DEATH is the end of all.
La morte è la fine delle miserie umane.

466 DEATH is the great leveller.
La morte pareggia tutti.

Cf. *All's alike at the latter DAY: a bag of gold and wisp of hay / DEATH makes equal the high and low / At the END of the game the king and the pawn go into the same bag / Six FEET of earth make all men equal.*

467 DEATH keeps no calendar.
La morte non guarda calendario.

468 DEATH makes equal the high and low.
L'eccelse ed umil porte batte egualmente morte.

Cf. *All's alike at the latter DAY: a bag of gold and wisp of hay / DEATH is the great leveller / At the END of the game the king and the pawn go into the same bag / Six FEET of earth make all men equal.*

469 **DEATH pays all debts.**
   La morte paga i debiti, e l'anima li purga.

470 **Fear of DEATH is worse than death itself.**
   La paura del morire è peggio della morte.

471 **He has not lived that lives not after DEATH.**
   Chi non può viver dopo morte non è vissuto.

472 **Nothing so certain as DEATH.**
   Di sicuro non c'è che la morte.

   Var. *Nothing is certain but death and taxes (quarter day).*

473 **Old men go to DEATH, death comes to young men.**
   I vecchi vanno verso la morte e ai giovani la gli va incontro.

474 **The DEATH of the wolves is the safety of the sheep.**
   La morte dei lupi è la salute delle pecore.

475 **DEATHS foreseen come not.**
   La morte viene quando meno s'aspetta.

476 **Let him that sleeps too sound, buy the DEBTOR's bed.**
   Compra il letto d'un gran debitore.

477 **Of ill DEBTORS men take oats.**
   Da cattivo debitor togli paglia per lavor.

   Sim. *From a bad paymaster get what you can.*

478 **He who pays his DEBTS begins to make a stock.**
   Chi paga debito fa capitale.

   Sim. *Out of debt, out of danger.*

479 **To deceive a DECEIVER is no deceit.**
   Merita onore chi inganna l'ingannatore.

480 **A good DEED is never lost.**
   Piacer fatto non va perduto.

   Sim. *One good turn deserves another / One never loses by doing a good turn.*
   Cf. *DO well and have well / GOOD finds good.*

481 **DEEDS are males, and words are females.**
   I fatti sono maschi e le parole sono femmine.

   Var. *Deeds are masculine; words are feminine.*

482 **DEEDS, not words.**
   Fatti, non parole.

   Cf. *ACTIONS speak louder than words.*

483 Ill DEEMED, half hanged.
Chi è diffamato, è mezzo impiccato.

Sim. *An ill wound is cured, not an ill name.*
Cf. *He that has an ill NAME is half hanged.*

484 He that soon DEEMETH, shall soon repent.
Chi presto giudica, presto si pente.

485 All is not lost that is DELAYED.
Quello che è differito non è perduto.

Sim. *Delays are not denials.*

486 DELAYS are dangerous.
L'indugiare è pericoloso.
Come la cosa indugia, piglia vizio.

487 After us the DELUGE.
Dopo di noi il diluvio.

Cf. *When I die, the WORLD dies with me.*

488 He that asks faintly begs a DENIAL.
Non c'è intoppo per avere, più che chiedere e temere.

489 He who DENIES all, confesses all.
Chi tutto nega, tutto confessa.

490 Better the DEVIL you know than the devil you don't know.
Chi lascia la via vecchia per la nuova, sa quel che lascia, ma non quel che trova.

491 Give the DEVIL his due.
Dare al diavolo ciò che gli spetta.

Sim. *Give credit where credit is due.*
Cf. *It is sometimes good to hold a CANDLE to the devil.*

492 He that has shipped the DEVIL must make the best of him.
Chi ha imbarcato il diavolo, ha a passare in sua compagnia.

Sim. *He that takes the devil into his boat must carry him over the sound.*

493 It is easier to raise the DEVIL than to lay him.
Il diavolo è facile a chiamare, difficile a mandarlo via.

494 One DEVIL drives out another.
Un diavolo scaccia l'altro.

Cf. *LIKE cures like / One NAIL drives out another / One POISON drives out another.*

o Matthew 9, 34 / Matteo 9, 34

495 Seldom lies the DEVIL dead in a ditch.
Rare volte il diavolo giace morto nella fossa.

496 Talk of the DEVIL, and he is bound to appear.
Quando si nomina il diavolo se ne vede spuntar la coda.

Sim. *The devil is never nearer than when we are talking of him / The devil is never far off.*
Cf. *Talk of the WOLF, and his tail appears.*

497 The DEVIL finds work for idle hands to do.
Le mani oziose sono il regno del diavolo.

498 The DEVIL is not always at one door.
Il diavolo non sta sempre in un luogo.

499 The DEVIL is not so black as he is painted.
Il diavolo non è brutto quanto si dipinge.
Il diavolo non è così nero come lo si dipinge.

Sim. *The lion is not so fierce as he is painted.*

500 The DEVIL is subtle, yet weaves a coarse web.
Il diavolo è sottile, e fila grosso.

501 The DEVIL is the father of lies.
Il diavolo è padre di menzogna.

502 The DEVIL knows many things because he is old.
Il diavolo è cattivo perché è vecchio.

503 The DEVIL lurks behind the cross.
Il diavolo si nasconde dietro la croce.

504 The DEVIL makes his Christmas-pies of lawyers' tongues and clerks' fingers.
Di tre cose il diavolo si fa l'insalata, di lingua d'avvocati, di dita di notai, e la terza è riservata.

505 The DEVIL sometimes speaks the truth.
La verità qualche volta può uscire dalla bocca del diavolo.

506 The DEVIL take the hindmost.
All'ultimo tocca il peggio.

507 The DEVIL tempts all, but the idle man tempts the devil.
Il diavolo tenta tutti, ma l'ozioso tenta il diavolo.
Quando facciam del male, il diavolo ci tenta, quando non facciamo niente, noi tentiamo lui.

508 The DEVIL turns away from a closed door.
Alla porta chiusa il diavolo volta le spalle.

Var. *The devil turns his back when he finds the door shut against him.*

509 **The DEVIL was sick, the devil a monk would be; the devil was well, the devil a monk was he.**
Il diavolo, quando è vecchio, si fa romito.
Il diavolo, quando è vecchio, si fa cappuccino.

    Var. *The devil was sick, the devil a monk would be / When the devil was sick he thought to become a monk.*

510 **The DEVIL wipes his tail with the poor man's pride.**
Della superbia dei poveri il diavolo se ne netta il sedere.

511 **When the DEVIL prays, he has a booty in his eye.**
Quando il diavolo prega, tien d'occhio a una preda.

    Cf. *When the DEVIL says his Pater Noster he means to cheat you.*

512 **When the DEVIL says his Pater Noster he means to cheat you.**
Quando il diavolo fa orazione, ti vuole ingannare.

    Cf. *When the DEVIL prays, he has a booty in his eye.*

513 **Where the DEVIL can't go, he sends his grandmother.**
Dove il diavolo non può entrare, manda una vecchia.
Il diavolo dove non può mettere il capo vi mette la coda.

    Var. *Where the devil cannot come, he will send.*

514 **Give a thing, and take a thing, to wear the DEVIL's gold ring.**
Chi dà e ritoglie, il diavolo lo raccoglie.

    Sim. *Give a thing and take again, and you shall ride in hell's wain.*

515 **The DEVIL's meal is all bran.**
La farina del diavolo va tutta in crusca.
La farina del diavolo se ne va tutta in semola.

516 **What is got over the DEVIL's back is spent under his belly.**
Diavol reca, diavol porta.

    Cf. *Ill-gotten GOODS never prosper.*

517 **A man can DIE but once.**
La morte è una cosa che non si può fare due volte.
Si muore una volta sola.

518 **Better DIE with honour than live with shame.**
Meglio è assai morte onorata, che una vita svergognata.
È meglio morir con onore che vivere con vergogna.

    Var. *Better a glorious death than a shameful life.*
    Cf. *A fair DEATH honours the whole life.*

519 **The DIE is cast.**
Il dado è tratto.

520 **They DIE well that live well.**
Chi ben vive, ben muore.

Sim. *A good life makes a good death.*

521 **He that DIED half a year ago is as dead as Adam.**
I morti e gli andati presto son dimenticati.

522 **He that DIES this year is excused for the next.**
Morto che s'è una volta, non vi s'ha più a pensare.

523 **DILIGENCE is the mother of good luck.**
Diligenza passa scienza.

524 **After DINNER rest a while, after supper walk a mile.**
Dopo desinare, non camminare; dopo cena, con dolce lena.

Var. *After dinner sit a while, after supper walk a mile.*

525 **Sweet DISCOURSE makes short days and nights.**
Bel discorso accorcia giornata.

526 **A deadly DISEASE neither physician nor physic can ease.**
A mal mortale né medico né medicina vale.

Sim. *Death defies the doctor.*
Cf. *There is a REMEDY for everything but death.*

527 **A DISEASE known is half cured.**
Il male previsto è mezza sanità.

Sim. *A danger foreseen is half avoided.*

528 **Desperate DISEASES must have desperate remedies.**
A mali estremi, estremi rimedi.

Var. *Desperate cuts must have desperate remedies.*

529 **DISEASES come on horseback, but go away on foot.**
Il male viene a cavallo e se ne va a piedi.

Cf. *MISCHIEF comes by the pound and goes away by the ounce.*

530 **DISGRACES are like cherries, one draws another.**
Le disgrazie sono come le ciliege, una tira l'altra.

Cf. *Of one ILL come many / MISFORTUNES never come singly.*

531 **Of two DISPUTANTS, the warmer is generally in the wrong.**
Chi ha torto, grida più forte.
Chi ha meno ragione, grida più forte.
Chi ha più torto, strilla, più forte.

532 **In too much DISPUTE truth is lost.**
Per troppo battere la verità si perde.

533 **Who knows not how to DISSEMBLE, knows not how to live.**
Chi non sa dissimulare, non sa regnare.
Chi non sa fingere, non sa regnare.

534 **DISTRUST is the mother of safety.**
La diffidenza è la madre della sicurtà.

Cf. *In TRUST is treason.*

535 **Remember to DISTRUST.**
Fidarsi è bene, non fidarsi è meglio.

536 **DIVIDE and rule.**
Dividi e impera.

Cf. *KINGDOMS divided soon fall.*

537 **Make me a DIVINER and I will make thee rich.**
Fammi indovino, e ti farò ricco.

538 **Anyone who can DO more can do less.**
Chi ha fatto il più, può fare il meno.

539 **DO as I say, not as I do.**
Fate quel che dico e non quel che faccio.

Cf. *DO as the friar says, not as he does.*

540 **DO as the friar says, not as he does.**
Fa' quel che il prete dice, non quel che il prete fa.

Cf. *DO as I say, not as I do.*

541 **DO as you may if you can't do as you would.**
Chi non può fare come vuole, faccia come può.

Var. *He who can't do what he wants, must want what he can do / They who cannot as they would, must do as they can.*

542 **DO as you would be done by.**
Come volete che gli uomini facciano a voi, così fate voi a loro.

Sim. *Do unto others as you would they should do unto you.*

o Matthew 7, 12 / Matteo 7, 12; Luke 6, 31 / Luca 6, 31

543 **DO not all you can; spend not all you have; believe not all you hear; and tell not all you know.**
Non far tutto ciò che tu puoi, non spender tutto ciò che tu hai; non creder tutto ciò che tu odi, e non dire tutto ciò che tu sai.

544 DO right and fear no man.
Fa' il dovere e non temere.
Mal non fare, paura non avere.

Sim. *Do well and dread no shame.*

545 DO well and have well.
Chi fa bene, ha bene.

Sim. *Do good: thou doest it for thyself / One good turn deserves another / One never loses by doing a good turn.*
Cf. *A good DEED is never lost / GOOD finds good.*

546 DO what you ought, come what may.
Fa' che devi e sia che può.
Fa' quel che devi, avvenga quel che può.

547 Don't DO to others what you would not have done to you.
Non fare agli altri quello che non vorresti che fosse fatto a te.
Non fare ad altri quel che non vuoi sia fatto a te.

Var. *What you do not like done to yourself, do not do to others.*

548 If thou thyself canst DO it, attend no other's help or hand.
Quel che tu stesso puoi dire e fare, che altri il faccia mai non aspettare.

549 If you want a thing well done, DO it yourself.
Chi vuol presto e bene, faccia da sé.
Chi fa da sé, fa per tre.
Non v'è più bel messo che se stesso.

Sim. *If you would be well served, serve yourself.*

550 It is better to DO well than to say well.
È meglio ben fare che ben dire.

551 Self DO, self have.
Chi fa, fa a sé.

552 Who would DO ill ne'er wants occasion.
A chi vuol far del male, non gli manca mai occasione.
A chi fa male, mai mancano scuse.

553 DOCTORS' faults are covered with earth, and rich men's with money.
Gli errori dei medici sono ricoperti dalla terra, quelli dei ricchi dai denari.

Sim. *Doctors bury their mistakes / If the doctor cures, the sun sees it; but if he kills, the earth hides it.*
Cf. *PHYSICIANS' faults are covered with earth.*

554 **Ill DOERS, ill deemers.**
Chi mal fa, mal pensa.

555 **He that DOES what he will, does not what he ought.**
Chi fa quel che vuole, non fa quel che deve.

556 **A barking DOG never bites.**
Can che abbaia non morde.

> Var. *Barking dogs seldom bite.*
> Sim. *His bark is worse than his bite / Great barkers are no biters / Brag's a good dog, but dares not bite.*

557 **A curst DOG must be tied short.**
A cattivo cane, corto legame.

> Cf. *A curst COW has short horns.*

558 **A dead DOG never bites.**
Cane morto non morde.
Morta la bestia, morto il veleno.

> Var. *Dead dogs bite not.*

559 **A DOG will bark ere he bite.**
Ogni cane abbaia prima che mordere.

560 **A DOG will not howl if you beat him with a bone.**
Cane affamato non teme bastone.

561 **A living DOG is better than a dead lion.**
Piuttosto can vivo che leone morto.
Meglio un asino vivo che un dottore morto.

> Var. *Better live dog than dead lion.*
>
> o Ecclesiastes 9, 4 / Qoèlet 9, 4

562 **An old DOG barks not in vain.**
Cane vecchio non abbaia indarno.

> Sim. *If the old dog barks, he gives counsel.*

563 **Beat the DOG before the lion.**
Se vuoi che il leone ti tema, batti il cane.

564 **DOG does not eat dog.**
Cane non mangia cane.

565 **Every DOG is a lion at home.**
Ogni cane è leone a casa sua.
Ogni tristo cane abbaia da casa sua.

Sim. *Every dog is valiant at his own door.*
Cf. *A COCK is bold on his dunghill / Every man is a KING in his own house.*

566 **Give a DOG a bad name and hang him.**
Chi vuol ammazzare il suo cane, basta che dica che è arrabbiato.
Chi il suo cane vuole ammazzare, qualche scusa sa pigliare.

Sim. *He that would hang his dog gives out first that he is mad.*
Cf. *It is easy to find a STICK to beat a dog.*

567 **He that keeps another man's DOG shall have nothing left him but the line.**
Chi dà del pane ai cani altrui, spesso viene abbaiato dai suoi.

568 **Into the mouth of a bad DOG often falls a good bone.**
Ogni tristo cane talvolta trova buon osso.

Cf. *The worst HOG often gets the best pear.*

569 **Like the gardener's DOG, that neither eats cabbages himself, nor lets anybody else.**
Can dell'ortolano non mangia la lattuga e non la lascia mangiar agli altri.

Sim. *The dog in the manger won't eat the oats nor let anyone eat them.*

570 **Like the smith's DOG that sleeps at the noise of the hammer, and wakes at the crashing of teeth.**
Il cane del fabbro dorme al rumor del martello e si desta a quello delle ganasce.

571 **Love me, love my DOG.**
Chi ama me, ama il mio cane.

572 **The DOG bites the stone, not him that throws it.**
Il can dà alla pietra, non alla mano che la scagliò.

573 **The DOG returns to his vomit.**
Il cane torna al suo vomito.

o Proverbs 26, 11 / Proverbi 26, 11

574 **The DOG that licks ashes trust not with meal.**
A can che lecca cenere, non gli fidar farina.

575 **The hindmost DOG may catch the hare.**
L'ultimo cane talvolta prende la lepre.

576 **You cannot teach an old DOG new tricks.**
Can vecchio mal s'avvezza a portar collare.
Malamente can vecchio s'avvezza a portar cavezza.

Var. *It is hard to teach an old dog tricks.*

577 Cut off a DOG's tail and he will be a dog still.
Taglia la coda al cane, e riman cane.

578 DOGS gnaw bones because they cannot swallow them.
Il cane rode l'osso perché non può inghiottirlo.

579 DOGS wag their tails not so much in love to you as to your bread.
Muove la coda il cane, non per te, ma per il pane.

Sim. *If you would wish the dog to follow you, feed him.*

580 If you lie down with DOGS, you will get up with fleas.
Chi va a letto con i cani si sveglierà con le pulci.
Chi dorme con cani, si leva con pulci.

Var. *He that sleeps with dogs must rise up with fleas / Lay down with dogs, get up with fleas.*

581 Let sleeping DOGS lie.
Non svegliare il can che dorme.
Non destare il can che dorme.
Chi tocca il can che giace, ha qualcosa che non gli piace.

Var. *Don't wake a sleeping dog.*
Sim. *Wake not a sleeping lion.*
Cf. *When SORROW is asleep, wake it not.*

582 Little DOGS start the hare, the great get her.
I picciol cani trovan, ma i grandi han la lepre.

Cf. *One beats the BUSH and another catches the birds / One SOWS and another reaps.*

583 Many DOGS may easily worry* one hare.
Molti cani son la morte della lepre.
* *kill*

584 Quarrelling DOGS come halting home.
Can ringhioso e non forzoso, guai alla sua pelle!

Sim. *Brabbling curs never want sore ears.*

585 Two DOGS strive for a bone, and a third runs away with it.
Tra due litiganti il terzo gode.

586 Two DOGS to one bone, may never accord in one.
Due cani che un sol osso hanno, difficilmente in pace stanno.

Var. *Two dogs over one bone seldom agree.*

587 While the DOGS yelp, the hare runs to the wood.
Mentre il cane piscia, la lepre se ne va.

Sim. *While the dogs snarl among themselves, the wolf devours the sheep.*

588 **By DOING nothing we learn to do ill.**
Niente facendo, s'impara a far male.

  Cf. *Of IDLENESS comes no goodness.*

589 **In DOING we learn.**
Facendo s'impara.
Il fare insegna fare.

590 **If you want a thing DONE, go; if not, send.**
Chi vuole vada e chi non vuole mandi.

591 **What's DONE cannot be undone.**
Quel ch'è fatto, è fatto.
Il fatto non si può disfare.

  Sim. *Things done cannot be undone.*
  Cf. *The THING that's done has an end.*

592 **An open DOOR may tempt a saint.**
Porta aperta i Santi tenta.
A porta aperta anche il giusto vi pecca.

  Cf. *The back DOOR robs the house / EASE makes thief / OPPORTUNITY makes the thief.*

593 **The back DOOR robs the house.**
La porta di dietro è quella che ruba la casa.

  Sim. *A postern door makes a thief.*
  Cf. *An open DOOR may tempt a saint / EASE makes thief / OPPORTU-NITY makes the thief.*

594 **When one DOOR closes, another one opens.**
Mai si serra una porta che non se n'apra un'altra.
Non si serra mai una porta che non se ne apra un'altra.

  Var. *Where one door shuts, another opens.*

595 **When in DOUBT, do without.**
Nel dubbio, astienti.

  Var. *When in doubt what to do, do nothing.*

596 **He that is DOWN, down with him.**
Quand'un'è per terra, ognun grida: dagli, dagli!
A can che fugge, dagli, dagli.

  Cf. *HARES may pull dead lions by the beard.*

597 **A great DOWRY is a bed full of brambles.**
Gran dote, gran baldezza.

598 DREAMS are lies.
I sogni non son veri, e i disegni non riescono.

599 Who likes not the DRINK, God deprives him of bread.
A chi non piace vino, Dio gli tolga l'acqua.

600 The more one DRINKS, the more one may.
Più si beve, più si vorrebbe bere.

601 The last DROP makes the cup run over.
È l'ultima goccia che fa traboccare il vaso.

Sim. *The last straw breaks the camel's back.*

602 Constant DROPPING wears away the stone.
A goccia a goccia si scava la pietra.
A goccia a goccia si fora la pietra.
La goccia scava la pietra.

Var. *Constant dripping wears away a stone / The constant drip of water will wear away the hardest stone.*

o Job 14, 19 / Giobbe 14, 19

603 Many DROPS make a shower.
I piccoli ruscelli fanno i grandi fiumi.

Sim. *Large streams from little fountains flow.*
Cf. *MANY small make a great / PENNY and penny laid up will be many.*

604 A DROWNING man will clutch at a straw.
Chi sta per affogar s'attacca a ogni spina.
Chi è portato giù dall'acqua s'attacca a ogni spino.
Chi si affoga s'attaccherebbe ai rasoi.
Chi affoga s'appiccherebbe alle funi del cielo.

Var. *A drowning man catches at a thread.*

605 When DRUMS beat, laws are silent.
Dove parlano i tamburi, taccion le leggi.
Dove parlano i cannoni, taccion le leggi.

606 DRUNKARDS and fools cannot lie.
Dagli ubriachi e dai bambini si sa la verità.

Var. *Drunkards and fools speak truth.*
Cf. *CHILDREN and fools tell the truth.*

607 If you would know the value of a DUCAT, try to borrow one.
Vuoi saper quanto val un ducato, domandalo in prestito.

608 **All are of the DUST, and all turn to dust again.**
Tutti sono stati fatti di polvere, e tutti ritornano in polvere.

    o Ecclesiastes 3, 20; 12, 7 / Qoèlet 3, 20; 12, 7; Genesis 3, 19 / Genesi 3, 19; Psalms 145, 4 / Salmi 145, 4

609 **He that blows in the DUST fills his eyes with it.**
Chi soffia nella polvere, se n'empie gli occhi.

E

610 **EAGLES do not breed doves.**
D'aquila non nasce colomba.

611 **EAGLES don't catch flies.**
L'aquila non piglia mosche.

612 **In at one EAR and out at the other.**
Per un orecchio entra e per l'altro esce.
Gli entra da un orecchio e gli esce dall'altro.

> Var. *Go in one ear and out the other.*

613 **He who has EARS to hear, let him hear.**
Chi ha orecchie per intendere, intenda.

> o Mark 4, 9; 4, 23 / Marco 4, 9; 4, 23

614 **One pair of EARS draws dry a hundred tongues.**
Un buon paio d'orecchi stancano cento male lingue.

615 **EASE makes thief.**
La comodità fa l'uomo ladro.

> Sim. *The hole calls the thief.*
> Cf. *An open DOOR may tempt a saint / The back DOOR robs the house / OPPORTUNITY makes the thief.*

616 **EASTER so longed for is gone in a day.**
Pasqua tanto desiata, in un giorno è passata.

617 **EASY come, easy go.**
Quel che vien di salti, va via di balzi.
Quel che vien di ruffa raffa, se ne va di buffa in baffa.

> Sim. *Quickly come, quickly go / Lightly gained, quickly lost.*
> Cf. *So GOT, so gone / Come with the WIND, go with the water.*

618 **EAT at pleasure, drink by measure.**
Mangia da sano e bevi da malato.
Pane fin che dura, vino con misura.

619 **EAT to live, not live to eat.**
Si deve mangiar per vivere, non vivere per mangiare.

> o Ecclesiasticus 37, 31 / Siràcide 37, 31

620 **Never be ashamed to EAT your meat.**
Dove si mangia e si beve non ci vuol vergogna.

621 **EATING and scratching wants but a beginning.**
Mangiare e grattare, tutto sta nel cominciare.

Cf. *APPETITE comes with eating.*

622 **Often and little EATING makes a man fat.**
Col poco e collo spesso mangiare s'ingrassa.

623 **He that EATS till he is sick must fast till he is well.**
Chi mangia finché s'ammala, digiuna finché risana.

624 **Better an EGG in peace than an ox in war.**
Val più un buon giorno con un uovo che un mal'anno con un bue.

Cf. *Dry BREAD is better with love than a fat capon with fear.*

625 **Better an EGG today than a hen tomorrow.**
Meglio un uovo oggi che una gallina domani.
È meglio aver oggi un uovo che domani una gallina.

Var. *An egg today is worth a hen tomorrow.*

626 **He that will steal an EGG will steal an ox.**
Il ladro dall'ago va all'uovo, dall'uovo al bue, dal bue alla forca.

Var. *He that steals an egg will steal a chicken.*
Cf. *He that will steal a PIN will steal a better thing.*

627 **One should drink as much after an EGG as after an ox.**
Bevi sopra l'uovo, quanto sopra a un bue.

628 **You cackle often, but never lay an EGG.**
Gallina che schiamazza non fa uova.

629 **Don't put all your EGGS in one basket.**
Chi ha tutto il suo in un loco, l'ha nel fuoco.

Var. *Don't carry all your eggs in one basket.*

630 **He that would have EGGS must endure the cackling of hens.**
Chi vuol l'uovo, deve soffrire lo schiamazzo della gallina.

631 **He that too much EMBRACETH holds little.**
Chi troppo abbraccia, nulla stringe.

Sim. *Grasp all, lose all.*
Cf. *All COVET, all lose.*

632 **At the END of the game the King and the pawn go into the same bag.**
Alla fin del gioco, tanto va nel sacco il re quanto la pedina.

Cf. *All's alike at the latter DAY: a bag of gold and wisp of hay / DEATH is the great leveller / DEATH makes equal the high and low / Six FEET of earth make all men equal.*

633 Better is the END of a thing than the beginning thereof.
Meglio vale il fin della cosa che il principio di essa.

o Ecclesiastes 7, 8 / Qoèlet 7, 8

634 Everything has an END.
Tutto ha una fine.
Tutto finisce.

o I Peter 4, 7 / I Pietro 4, 7; II Esdras 9, 5 / II Esdra 9, 5

635 The END crowns the work.
La fine corona l'opera.
Il fine dimostra la cosa.

Sim. *The end tries all / The evening crowns the day.*

636 The END justifies the means.
Il fine giustifica i mezzi.

637 Think on the END before you begin.
Chi da savio operar vuole, pensi al fine.

Cf. *LOOK before you leap / First THINK, and then speak.*

o Ecclesiasticus 7, 40 / Siràcide 7, 40

638 He that ENDURES is not overcome.
Chi la dura, la vince.

Sim. *He conquers who endures / He that can stay obtains / Perseverance overcomes all things.*

639 He that ENDURETH to the end shall be saved.
Chi avrà sostenuto fino alla fine, sarà salvato.

o Matthew 10, 22; 24, 13 / Matteo 10, 22; 24, 13; Mark 13, 13 / Marco 13, 13

640 If you have no ENEMIES it's a sign fortune has forgot you.
Chi non ha nemici non ha vanto.

641 A wise ENEMY is better than a foolish friend.
Meglio un nemico saggio di un amico sciocco.

642 For a flying ENEMY make a golden bridge.
A nemico che fugge, ponti d'oro.
Al nemico che fugge, il ponte d'oro.

Var. *For a flying enemy make a silver bridge / It is good to make a bridge of gold to a flying enemy.*

643 **He is no man's ENEMY but his own.**
Non ha maggior nemico l'uomo di se stesso.

644 **His own ENEMY is no one's friend.**
È male amico chi a sé è nemico.

645 **If you would make an ENEMY, lend a man money, and ask it of him again.**
Chi dà a credenza spaccia assai, perde l'amico e denar non ha mai.
Chi presta denaro perde un amico e si fa un nemico.

Sim. *When I lent, I had a friend; but when I asked, he was unkind.*
Cf. *Lend your MONEY and lose your friend.*

646 **Nothing worse than a familiar ENEMY.**
Peggio l'invidia dell'amico, che l'insidia del nemico.

o Matthew 10, 36 / Matteo 10, 36

647 **One ENEMY is too many; and a hundred friends too few.**
Un nemico è troppo e cento amici non bastano.

Sim. *One enemy can do more hurt than ten friends can do good.*

648 **There is no little ENEMY.**
Nessun disprezzerai; che il più piccolo nemico può darti briga assai.

Sim. *Though thy enemy seem a mouse, yet watch him like a lion.*

649 **ENGLAND is the paradise of women, the hell of horses, and the purgatory of servants.**
L'Inghilterra è il paradiso delle donne, il purgatorio degli uomini, e l'inferno dei cavalli.

650 **He that will ENGLAND win, must with Ireland first begin.**
Chi vuol vincer l'Inghilterra, cominci dall'Irlanda.

651 **The ENGLISHMAN Italianate is a devil incarnate.**
Inglese italianato è un diavolo incarnato.

652 **An ENGLISHMAN's home is his castle.**
Casa mia, casa mia, per piccina che tu sia, tu mi sembri una badia.

Var. *A man's house is his castle.*
Sim. *East, west, home's best / Home is home, though it be never so homely / There is no place like home.*
Cf. *One's own HEARTH is gowd's worth.*

653 **There was never ENOUGH where nothing was left.**
Non si può dire abbondanza se non n'avanza.

654 An old ENSIGN is a captain's honour.
Bandiera vecchia, onor di capitano.
Bandiera vecchia fa onore al capitano.

655 Better be ENVIED than pitied.
È meglio essere invidiati che compianti.

656 ENVY always shoots at a high mark.
Non fu mai gloria senza invidia.

657 ENVY never dies.
L'invidia non morì mai.
L'invidia nacque e morirà con gli uomini.
Var. *The envious die, but envy never.*
Sim. *Envy never has a holiday.*

658 ENVY shoots at others, and wounds herself.
L'invidia fa agli altri la fossa, e poi vi casca dentro.
L'invidia rode se stessa.

o Proverbs 14, 30 / Proverbi 14, 30

659 If ENVY were a fever, all mankind would be ill.
Se l'invidia fosse febbre, tutto il mondo n'avrebbe.

660 To ERR is human.
Errare è umano.
Umana cosa è errare.
Cf. *To ERR is human; to forgive, divine / To fall into SIN is human, to remain in sin is devilish.*

661 To ERR is human; to forgive, divine.
L'errore è umano, il perdono divino.
Cf. *To ERR is human / To fall into SIN is human, to remain in sin is devilish.*

662 Show a good man his ERROR and he turns it to virtue; but an ill, it doubles his fault.
Mostrando al buon, l'error torna virtute.
Cf. *CHASTISE the good and he will mend; chastise the bad and he will grow worse / PRAISE makes good men better, and bad men worse.*

663 EVENING red and morning grey help the traveller on his way: evening grey and morning red bring down rain upon his head.
Sera rossa e nero mattino, rallegra il pellegrino.

664 Bear with EVIL and expect good.
Soffri il male e aspetta il bene.

665 **Welcome EVIL if thou comest alone.**
Benedetto è quel male che vien solo.

666 **EVILS come without calling for.**
I guai vengono senza chiamarli.

667 **Of two EVILS choose the lesser.**
Di due mali, scegli il minore.

Var. *Choose the lesser of two evils.*

668 **The EVILS we bring on ourselves are the hardest to bear.**
Chi è causa del suo mal pianga se stesso.

669 **EXAMPLE is better than precept.**
Val più un esempio che mille parole.
Contan più gli esempi che le parole.

Sim. *A good example is the best sermon.*

670 **He is an ill case that gives EXAMPLE to another.**
Tristo colui che dà esempio altrui.

671 **The EXCEPTION proves the rule.**
L'eccezione conferma la regola.

Cf. *There is an EXCEPTION to every rule.*

672 **There is an EXCEPTION to every rule.**
Ogni regola ha la sua eccezione.

Var. *There is no general rule without some exception.*
Cf. *The EXCEPTION proves the rule.*

673 **EXCHANGE is no robbery.**
Cambio non è furto.

Var. *Change is no robbery / A fair exchange is no robbery.*

674 **He who EXCUSES himself, accuses himself.**
Chi si scusa, si accusa.
Chi si scusa senz'esser accusato, fa chiaro il suo peccato.

675 **EXPERIENCE is the best teacher.**
Esperienza è una maestra muta.

Cf. *EXPERIENCE is the mother of knowledge.*

676 **EXPERIENCE is the mother of knowledge.**
Esperienza, madre di scienza.

Var. *Experience is the mother of wisdom.*
Cf. *ADVERSITY makes a man wise, not rich / EXPERIENCE is the best teacher / An ounce of PRACTICE is worth a pound of precept.*

677 **EXTREMES meet.**
Gli estremi si toccano.

678 **Every EXTREMITY is a fault.**
Ogni eccesso è vizioso.

679 **An EYE for an eye, and a tooth for a tooth.**
Occhio per occhio, dente per dente.

    o Matthew 5, 38 / Matteo 5, 38

680 **He that has but one EYE must be afraid to lose it.**
Chi ha un occhio solo ben lo guarda.

681 **Jest not with the EYE, or with religion.**
Tre cose lascia da per sé: l'occhio, la donna e la fè.

    Cf. *You should never touch your EYE but with your elbow.*

682 **Look not too high, lest something fall into thine EYE.**
Non mirar troppo alto, per paura che qualche cosa non ti caschi nell'occhio.

    Var. *Hew not to high lest the chips fall in thine eye.*

683 **The EYE is bigger than the belly.**
Piuttosto si satolla il ventre che l'occhio.
Lo stomaco non abbraccia quanto l'occhio.

684 **The EYE is the mirror of the soul.**
Gli occhi sono lo specchio dell'anima.

    Sim. *The eyes are the window of the soul.*

685 **The EYE lets in love.**
L'occhio attira l'amore.
Dove è l'amore, l'occhio corre.

    Sim. *Looks breed love / Loving comes by looking.*
    Cf. *The HEART's letter is read in the eye.*

686 **The EYE of the master does more work than both his hands.**
La presenza del signore è aumento del lavor.

687 **The EYE will have his part.**
Anche l'occhio vuol la sua parte.

688 **The master's EYE makes the horse fat.**
L'occhio del padrone ingrassa il cavallo.

    Var. *The eye of the master fattens his herd.*

689 **What the EYE doesn't see, the heart doesn't grieve over.**
Occhio non vede, cuore non duole.
Occhio che non vede, cuore che non sente.
Se occhio non mira, cuor non sospira.

> Var. *What the eye sees not, the heart craves (rues) not.*
> Cf. *Out of SIGHT, out of mind.*

690 **What the EYE sees, the heart believes.**
Quel che l'occhio vede, il cuor crede.

691 **You can see a mote in another's EYE, but cannot see a beam in your own.**
Vedere la pagliuzza che è nell'occhio altrui, e non vedere la trave che è nel proprio.
Si vede la scheggia nell'occhio altrui e non si vede la trave nel proprio.

> Var. *You see the splinter in your brother's eye; but not the beam in your own.*
> Cf. *The HUNCHBACK does not see his own hump, but sees his companion's.*

o Matthew 7, 3-5 / Matteo 7, 3-5; Luke 6, 41-42 / Luca 6, 41-42

692 **You should never touch your EYE but with your elbow.**
Gli occhi s'hanno a toccare con le gomita.

> Cf. *Jest not with the EYE, or with religion.*

693 **Four EYES see more than two.**
Vedono meglio quattro occhi che due.
Quattro occhi vedono più di due.

Sim. *Two eyes can see more than one.*

694 **Neither EYES on letters nor hands in coffers.**
Né occhi in lettera, né man in tasca.

695 **One EYEWITNESS is better than ten hear-so's.**
Val più un testimonio di vista che dieci d'udita.
Gli occhi hanno più credenza che le orecchie.

> Cf. *SEEING is believing.*

F

696 **A fair FACE, foul heart.**
Bella in vista, dentro è trista.

Sim. *Fair without, foul within.*

697 **The FACE is the index of the mind.**
Il viso è lo specchio dell'anima.
Immagine dell'animo è il volto.

698 **We carry our neighbours' FAILINGS in sight; we throw our own crimes over our shoulders.**
Contro i difetti del vicin t'adiri, e gli stessi difetti in te non miri.

699 **Buy at a FAIR, but sell at home.**
Vendi in casa e compra in fiera.

700 **FAIR in the cradle, and foul in the saddle.**
Bello in fascia, brutto in piazza.
Bello in fasce, brutto in piazza.

Cf. *FOUL in the cradle and fair in the saddle.*

701 **FAIR is not fair, but that which pleases.**
Non è bello quel ch'è bello, ma è bello quel che piace.

Sim. *Beauty is in the eye of the beholder.*
Cf. *The CROW thinks her own birds fairest / The OWL thinks her own young fairest.*

702 **Who is born FAIR is born married.**
Chi nasce bella nasce maritata.

703 **FAITH will move mountains.**
La fede può smuovere le montagne.

o Matthew 17, 20 / Matteo 17, 20

704 **He that is FALLEN cannot help him that is down.**
Chi è cascato non può rilevar il cascato.

705 **Common FAME is a liar.**
La fama e il suono, fan le cose maggior di quel che sono.

Var. *Common fame is seldom to blame.*

706 **FAME is a magnifying glass.**
La fama è un microscopio.

707 **FAMILIARITY breeds contempt.**
Troppa famigliarità genera disprezzo.
Confidenza toglie riverenza.

708 **FAMINE in England begins at the horse-manger.**
La fame in Inghilterra comincia dalla mangiatoia del cavallo.

709 **He FASTS enough that has had a bad meal.**
Digiuna assai chi mal mangia.

710 **Little knows the FAT man what the lean does mean.**
Il grasso non sa ciò che pensa il magro.

   Var. *Little knows the fat sow what the lean does mean.*
   Sim. *It is ill speaking between a full man and a fasting.*
   Cf. *He whose BELLY is full believes not him who is fasting.*

711 **There is no flying from FATE.**
Nessuno può sfuggire al suo destino.

   Sim. *The fated will happen / Whatever happens, all happens as it should.*
   Cf. *He that is born to be HANGED shall never be drowned / What MUST be, must be.*

712 **After a thrifty FATHER, a prodigal son.**
A padre avaro, figliuol prodigo.

   Cf. *After a great GETTER comes a great spender.*

713 **Like FATHER, like son.**
Quale il padre, tale il figlio.
Come il padre, tale è il figlio.

   Cf. *An APPLE never falls far from the tree / A CHIP off the old block / Like MOTHER, like daughter.*

714 **Like FATHER, like son; like mother like daughter.**
Il figlio al padre s'assomiglia, alla madre la figlia.

   Cf. *An APPLE never falls far from the tree / A CHIP off the old block / Like MOTHER, like daughter.*

715 **One FATHER can support ten children; ten children cannot support one father.**
Un padre mantiene sette figli, ma sette figli non mantengono un padre.

   Cf. *One FATHER is enough to govern one hundred sons, but not a hundred sons one father.*

716 **One FATHER is enough to govern one hundred sons, but not a hundred sons one father.**
Basta un padre a governare cento figliuoli e cento figliuoli non bastano a governare un padre.
Un padre campa cento figli e cento figli non campano un padre.
Cf. *One FATHER can support ten children; ten children cannot support one father.*

717 **One FATHER is more than a hundred schoolmasters.**
Più vale un padre che cento pedagoghi.

718 **The FATHER a saint, the son a devil.**
Di padre santolotto, figlio diavolotto.

719 **The FATHERS have eaten sour grapes, and the children's teeth are set on edge.**
Tal susina mangia il padre che allega i denti al figliuolo.

o Ezekiel 18, 2 / Ezekiele 18, 2

720 **A FAULT confessed is half redressed.**
Peccato confessato è mezzo perdonato.
Var. *A fault confessed is half forgiven.*

721 **Every one can find FAULT; few can do better.**
È più facile criticare che fare meglio.
Sim. *Don't find fault with what you don't understand.*

722 **He that commits a FAULT thinks everyone speaks of it.**
Chi è in peccato crede che tutti dicano male di lui.
Cf. *The FAULTY stands on his guard.*

723 **He that is foolish in FAULT, let him be wise in punishment.**
Chi è stolto nella colpa sia saggio nella pena.

724 **The FAULT is as great as he that is faulty.**
Tanto è grande l'errore come quel che erra.

725 **Where no FAULT is, there needs no pardon.**
Dove non v'è mancamento, è superfluo il perdonare.

726 **Who is in FAULT suspects everybody.**
Chi ha colpa sospetta ognuno.
Pensa il ladrone che tutti sian di sua condizione.

727 **He is lifeless that is FAULTLESS.**
Nessuno è perfetto.
Nessun uomo senza difetti.

728 **He that corrects not small FAULTS will not control great ones.**
Chi non gastiga culino non gastiga culaccio.

729 **The first FAULTS are theirs that commit them, the second theirs that permit them.**
I primi falli sono di quelli che li commettono, i secondi di chi non li castiga.

730 **The FAULTY stands on his guard.**
Chi è in difetto è in sospetto.

Cf. *He that commits a FAULT thinks everyone speaks of it.*

731 **A king's FAVOUR is no inheritance.**
Amicizia di signore non è retaggio.

Sim. *Great men's favours are uncertain.*
Cf. *ACQUAINTANCE of the great will I naught, for first or last, dear it will be bought.*

o Proverbs 16, 15 / Proverbi 16, 15

732 **FAVOUR is deceitful, and beauty is vain.**
La grazia è cosa fallace, e la bellezza è cosa vana.

o Proverbs 31, 30 / Proverbi 31, 30

733 **FEAR gives wings.**
La paura mette le ali.
La paura fa i passi lunghi.
La paura fa novanta.

734 **FEAR keeps and looks to the vineyard, and not the owner.**
La paura guarda la vigna.

Var. *Fear keeps the garden better than the gardener.*

735 **Foolish FEAR doubleth danger.**
La paura ingrossa il pericolo.
La paura ha cent'occhi.

Sim. *Fear takes molehills for mountains.*

736 **He that lives ill, FEAR follows him.**
Chi mal vive, lo segue la paura.

737 **Whom many FEAR must needs fear many.**
Chi a molti dà terrore, di molti abbia timore.
Chi fa temere ogni uomo, teme ogni cosa.

Var. *The prince that is feared of many, must fear many.*

738 **He that FEARS you present will hate you absent.**
Chi in presenza ti teme, in assenza ti nuoce.

739 **A FEATHER in hand is better than a bird in the air.**
È meglio una penna in mano che un uccello in aria.

Cf. *A BIRD in hand is worth two in the bush.*

740 **FEATHER by feather, the goose is plucked.**
Piuma a piuma si pela l'oca.
A penna a penna si pela l'oca.

Cf. *By one and one the SPINDLES are made.*

741 **Fine FEATHERS make fine birds.**
Le belle penne fanno il bel uccello.

Cf. *The COAT makes the man / Dress up a STICK and it does not appear to be a stick.*

742 **All FEET tread not in one shoe.**
Non tutti i piedi stanno bene in una scarpa.

Cf. *One SHOE will not fit all feet.*

743 **Keep your FEET dry, and your head hot; and for the rest live like a beast.**
Asciutto il piede e calda la testa, e nel resto vivi da bestia.

744 **Six FEET of earth make all men equal.**
Sei piè di terra ne uguaglia tutti.

Cf. *DEATH is the great leveller / DEATH makes equal the high and low / At the END of the game the king and the pawn go into the same bag.*

745 **He that has a FELLOW-RULER has an over-ruler.**
Chi ha compagno, ha padrone.

746 **No FENCE against ill fortune.**
Non val sapere, a chi ha fortuna contro.

747 **No man loveth his FETTERS, be they made of gold.**
Nessuno ama ceppi ancor che siano d'oro.

748 **A FIELD requires three things; fair weather, sound seed, and a good husbandman.**
Tre cose vuole il campo: buon lavoratore, buon seme e buon tempo.

749 **FIELDS have eyes, and woods have ears.**
Il piano ha occhi, e il bosco orecchi.
Anche i boschi hanno l'orecchie.

Sim. *Hedges have eyes, and walls have ears / The day has eyes, the night has ears.*
Cf. *WALLS have ears.*

750 Peel a FIG for your friend and a peach for your enemy.
Sbuccia il fico all'amico e la pesca al nemico.
All'amico, monda il fico; al nemico, la pesca.

751 He that FIGHTS and runs away, may live to fight another day.
Gambe mie, non è vergogna di fuggir quando bisogna.
È meglio che si dica: qui il tale fuggì, che qui il tale morì.
Un bel morir tutta la vita onora, un bel fuggir salva la vita ancora.
Soldato che fugge, buon per un'altra volta.

752 The FILTH under the white snow the sun discovers.
La neve si strugge e le immondezze si scoprono.
Quando la neve si scioglie si scopre la mondezza.

753 Take heed you FIND not that you do not seek.
Chi cerca trova, e talor quel che non vorrebbe.

Cf. *SEEK and you shall find.*

754 Give a clown your FINGER, and he will take your hand.
Al villano, se gli porgi il dito, ei prende la mano.

Sim. *Give a fool an inch and he will take a mile / Give him an inch and he'll take an ell.*

755 A little FIRE burns up a great deal of corn.
Piccola scintilla può bruciare una villa.

Cf. *Of a small SPARK a great fire.*

756 Covered FIRE is always the strongest.
Sotto la bianca cenere, sta la brace ardente.

757 FIRE and water are good servants, but bad masters.
L'acqua e il fuoco son buoni servitori, ma cattivi padroni.

758 FIRE cannot be hidden in flax.
Stoppa e fuoco non stan bene in un loco.
Non mettere la stoppa vicino al fuoco.

Cf. *Keep FLAX from fire and youth from gaming / A WOMAN is flax, man is fire, the devil comes and blows the bellows.*

759 FIRE is the test of gold; adversity of friendship.
L'oro s'affina al fuoco e l'amico nelle sventure.

Var. *Fire is the test of gold.*
Cf. *GOLD is tried in the fire.*

760 **If you play with FIRE you get burnt.**
Col fuoco non si scherza.
Scherzando col fuoco ci si bruciano le ali.

Sim. *He warms too near that burns.*

761 **No FIRE, no smoke.**
Dove si fa fuoco, nasce del fumo.

Var. *Make no fire, raise no smoke.*
Cf. *No SMOKE without fire.*

762 **Better be FIRST in a village than second at Rome.**
È meglio essere il primo a casa sua che il secondo a casa d'altri.

763 **FIRST born, first fed.**
Chi prima nasce, prima pasce.

764 **FIRST come, first served.**
Chi prima arriva, prima alloggia.

Cf. *He who comes FIRST grinds first.*

765 **He that rises FIRST is first dressed.**
Chi primo si alza, si calza.

766 **He who comes FIRST grinds first.**
Chi primo arriva, primo macina.
Chi è primo al mulino, primo macini.
Chi prima arriva, meglio macina.

Cf. *FIRST come, first served.*

767 **Big FISH eat little fish.**
Il pesce grosso mangia il pesce piccolo.
I pesci grossi mangiano i piccoli.

Var. *The great fish eat up the small.*
Cf. *The great THIEVES hang the little ones.*

768 **FISH and guests stink after three days.**
L'ospite è come il pesce: dopo tre giorni puzza.
L'ospite e il pesce, dopo tre dì rincresce.

Var. *Fresh fish and new-come guests smell in three days.*
Sim. *A constant GUEST is never welcome.*

769 **FISH mars water, and flesh mends it.**
Il pesce guasta l'acqua, la carne la concia.
Carne fa carne, pesce fa vesce.

770 **FISH must swim thrice.**
Il pesce vuol nuotar tre volte, nell'acqua, nell'olio, e nel vino.
Sui pesci mesci.

771 **He who would catch FISH must not mind getting wet.**
Chi vuol pescare, si bagni il sedere.
Chi vuole pesce, bisogna che s'ammolli.

Cf. *The CAT would eat fish and would not wet her feet.*

772 **Neither FISH nor flesh.**
Non essere né carne né pesce.

773 **Old FISH and young flesh do feed men best.**
Carne giovane e pesce vecchio.

774 **Old FISH, old oil, and an old friend are the best.**
Pesce, olio e amico vecchio.

775 **The best FISH swim near the bottom.**
I pesci grossi stanno in fondo.

776 **The FISH always stinks from the head downwards.**
Il pesce comincia a putire dal capo.
Dal capo vien la tigna.

Var. *Fish begins to stink at the head.*

777 **The FISH will soon be caught that nibbles at every bait.**
Il pesce che va cercando l'amo, va cercando il suo gramo.

778 **You must not teach FISH to swim.**
Insegnare a nuotare ai pesci.

Sim. *An old fox needs learn no craft.*

779 **The FISHERMAN with a rod eats more than he earns.**
Chi pesca a canna, perde più che non guadagna.

Sim. *An angler eats more than he gets.*

780 **It is good FISHING in troubled waters.**
A fiume torbido, guadagno di pescatore.

Var. *It is good fishing in muddled waters / There's always good fish in muddled waters.*

781 **It is ill FISHING before the net.**
Non fa buon pescar innanzi la rete.

782 **No FISHING to fishing in the sea.**
Vai al mare, se ben vuoi pescare.
Nel mar grosso si pigliano i pesci grossi.

783 **A FLATTERER's throat is an open sepulchre.**
Gola degli adulatori, sepolcro aperto.

o Psalms 5, 9 / Salmi 5, 9

784 **Keep FLAX from fire and youth from gaming.**
La stoppa lontan dal fuoco e la gioventù dal gioco.

Cf. *FIRE cannot be hidden in flax / A WOMAN is flax, man is fire, the devil comes and blows the bellows.*

785 **FLIES haunt lean horses.**
Ai cani e cavalli magri vanno addosso le mosche.
A cani magri, mosche ingorde.

786 **Hungry FLIES bite sore.**
Mosche e pulci magre son le più affamate.

787 **You will catch more FLIES with a spoonful of honey than with a gallon of vinegar.**
Si pigliano più mosche in una goccia di miele che in un barile d'aceto.

Var. *Honey catches more flies than vinegar.*

788 **It is not FLOUR from thy mill.**
Questa non è farina del tuo sacco.

789 **From the same FLOWER the bee extracts honey and the wasp gall.**
Dallo stesso fiore, l'ape cava il miele e la vespa il fiele.

Sim. *Where the bee sucks honey, the spider sucks poison.*

790 **One FLOWER makes no garland.**
Un fior non fa ghirlanda.

Cf. *One SWALLOW does not make a summer.*

791 **A FLY follows the honey.**
Non è miele senza mosche.

792 **He changes a FLY into an elephant.**
Fare d'una mosca un elefante.

Sim. *To make a mountain out of a molehill.*

793 **The FLY has her spleen and the ant her gall.**
Anche la mosca ha la sua collera.

Var. *Even a fly hath its spleen.*
Cf. *Even a WORM will turn.*

794 **The FLY that plays too long in the candle, singes his wings at last.**
Tanto vola il parpaglione intorno al fuoco, che vi s'abbrucia.

795 **No FLYING without wings.**
Non si può volare senz'ale.

796 **No FOE to a flatterer.**
Chi ti adula, ti tradisce.

797 **Short FOLLIES are best.**
È meglio corta follia che lunga.

798 **If FOLLY were grief every house would weep.**
Se le pazzie fossero dolori, il mondo sarebbe in pianto.

799 **The first degree of FOLLY is to hold one's self wise, the second to profess it, the third to despise counsel.**
Il primo grado di pazzia è tenersi savio, il secondo farne professione, il terzo sprezzare il consiglio.

800 **A FOOL and his money are soon parted.**
Il pazzo e il suo denaro son presto separati.
La roba dei matti è la prima a andarsene.

801 **A FOOL believes everything.**
È troppo folle, chi crede a tutte le parole.

o Proverbs 14, 15 / Proverbi 14, 15

802 **A FOOL knows more in his own house than a wise man in another's.**
Più ne sa un pazzo a casa sua che un savio a casa d'altri.
Sa meglio il matto i fatti suoi che il savio quelli degli altri.

803 **A FOOL may give a wise man counsel.**
Anche il pazzo dice talvolta parole da savio.

Sim. *A fool may sometimes speak to the purpose.*

804 **A FOOL may throw a stone into a well, which a hundred wise men cannot pull out.**
Un pazzo getta una pietra nel pozzo, che poi ci voglion cento savi a cavarla fuori.

805 **A FOOL, unless he knows Latin, is never a great fool.**
I pazzi per lettera sono i maggiori pazzi.

806 **Every FOOL likes his own bauble best.**
Ad ogni pazzo piace il suon del suo sonaglio.

807 **Every one has a FOOL in his sleeve.**
Ciascuno ha un pazzo nella manica.

Sim. *Every man is a fool sometimes and none at all times.*
Cf. *Every man is MAD on some point / No man is WISE at all times.*

808 **He is a FOOL that makes a wedge of his fist.**
Folle è chi del suo pugno fa un cugno.

809 **He is a FOOL that thinks not that another thinks.**
Sciocco è chi pensa che altri non pensa.

810 **He is a FOOL who makes his physician his heir.**
È follia di far il suo medico erede.

811 **He that is born a FOOL is never cured.**
Chi nasce matto, non guarisce mai.
Chi nasce tondo non muore quadro.

Sim. *Once a fool, always a fool.*

812 **He that sends a FOOL expects one.**
Chi matto manda, matto aspetta.

Sim. *Send a fool to the market (far, to France) and a fool he will return again / How much the fool who goes to Rome excels the fool who stays at home.*
Cf. *If an ASS goes a-travelling, he'll not come home a horse.*

813 **He that teaches himself has a FOOL for his master.**
Chi si fa maestro di se stesso, si fa discepolo d'un pazzo.

814 **Make not a FOOL of thyself to make others merry.**
Pazzo è colui che strazia sé per compiacer altrui.

815 **One FOOL makes a hundred.**
Un matto ne fa cento.

Var. *One fool makes many.*

816 **One FOOL praises another.**
Uno sciocco trova sempre un altro che l'ammira.
Un asino trova sempre un altr'asino che lo ammira.

817 **Praise a FOOL, and you water his folly.**
Loda il matto e fal saltare; se non è matto il farai diventare.

818 **To promise and give nothing is comfort to a FOOL.**
Promettere non è per dare, ma per matti contentare.

819 **FOOLS are wise as long as silent.**
Ogni pazzo è savio quando tace.
Quando non dice niente, non è dal savio il pazzo differente.

o Proverbs 17, 28 / Proverbi 17, 28

820 **FOOLS ask questions that wise men cannot answer.**
Un matto sa più domandare che sette savi rispondere.

Var. *A fool may ask more questions in an hour than a wise man can answer in seven years.*

821 **FOOLS grow without watering.**
I pazzi crescono senza innaffiarli.

822 **FOOLS live poor to die rich.**
È gran pazzia il viver poco per morir ricco.

823 **FOOLS make feasts, and wise men eat them.**
I matti fanno le feste ed i savi le godono.

Sim. *Set a fool to roast eggs, and a wise man to eat them / Fools build houses, and wise men live in them.*

824 **If all FOOLS wore white caps we should seem a flock of geese.**
Se tutti i pazzi portassero la berretta bianca, il mondo parrebbe un branco d'oche.

825 **If FOOLS should not fool it, they shall lose their season.**
Se i matti non matteggiano, perdono la stagione.

826 **If FOOLS went not to market, bad wares would not be sold.**
Quando gli sciocchi vanno al mercato, i furbi fanno buoni affari.

827 **Two FOOLS in one house are too many.**
Basta un matto per casa.

828 **Who has neither FOOLS nor beggars nor whores among his kindred, was born of a stroke of thunder.**
Chi non ha poveri o matti nel parentato, è nato o di lampo o di tuono.

829 **Better the FOOT slip than the tongue.**
È meglio sdrucciolare coi piedi che colla lingua.

o Ecclesiasticus 20, 18 / Siràcide 20, 18

830 **He that has one FOOT in the straw, has another in the spittle.**
Chi ha un piè in bordello, ha l'altro all'ospedale.

831 **The FOOT on the cradle and hand on the distaff is the sign of a good housewife.**
Piede alla culla e mano al fuso, mostrano la buona massaia.

832 **The master's FOOTSTEPS fatten the soil.**
Il piede del padrone ingrassa il campo.

Var. *The master's footsteps fattens the soil, and his foot the ground.*

833 **In the FOREHEAD and the eye, the lecture of the mind doth lie.**
Nella fronte e negli occhi si legge la lettera del cuore.

Cf. *The HEART's letter is read in the eye.*

834 FOREWARNED is forearmed.
Uomo avvisato è mezzo salvato.
Uomo avvertito, mezzo munito.
Var. *A man forewarned is a man forearmed.*

835 FORGIVE all but thyself.
Perdona a tutti, ma niente a te.

836 A man's best FORTUNE or his worst is a wife.
La maggior sventura o ventura dell'uomo è la moglie.

837 FORTUNE can take from us nothing but what she gave us.
La fortuna non ci può togliere se non quello che ci ha dato.

838 FORTUNE favours fools.
La fortuna aiuta i pazzi.
La fortuna aiuta i matti e i fanciulli.

839 FORTUNE favours the brave.
La fortuna aiuta gli audaci.
Var. *Fortune favours the bold.*

840 FORTUNE is blind.
La fortuna è cieca.
Cf. *FORTUNE is blind and makes blind.*

841 FORTUNE is blind and makes blind.
Fortuna cieca, i suoi accieca.
Cf. *FORTUNE is blind.*

842 FORTUNE is made of glass.
La fortuna ha i piedi di vetro.
Var. *Fortune is like glass.*

843 FORTUNE is variant.
Non sempre la fortuna un luogo tiene.

844 FORTUNE knocks once at least at every man's gate.
La fortuna non arriva mai due volte.
Var. *Opportunity never knocks twice at any man's door.*

845 FORTUNE to one is mother, to another is stepmother.
La fortuna un dì è madre, l'altro matrigna.

846 He dances well to whom FORTUNE pipes.
Assai ben balla, a chi fortuna suona.

847 He gains enough whom FORTUNE loses.
Assai avanza chi fortuna passa.

848 **When FORTUNE knocks, open the door.**
Quando viene la fortuna, apri le porte.
La fortuna non vuol fare anticamera.

Var. *When fortune smiles, embrace her.*
Cf. *Take OCCASION by the forelock.*

849 **Whom FORTUNE wishes to destroy, she first makes mad.**
Fortuna istupidisce colui ch'ella troppo favorisce.

Cf. *When GOD will punish, he will first take away the understanding.*

850 **FORTUNE's wheel is never stopped.**
La ruota della fortuna non è sempre una.

Var. *Not only ought fortune to be pictured on a wheel, but every thing else in the world.*

851 **FOUL in the cradle, and fair in the saddle.**
Brutto in fascia, bello in piazza.

Cf. *FAIR in the cradle, and foul in the saddle.*

852 **Count not FOUR, except you have them in a wallet.**
Non dir quattro se non l'hai nel sacco.

Sim. *Don't cross the bridge till you come to it / Do not count your chickens before they are hatched / Never fry fish till it's caught / It is not good praising a ford till a man be over / Do not halloo till you are out of the wood.*
Cf. *Don't sell the BEAR's skin before you have caught him.*

853 **He that has but FOUR and spends five, has no need of a purse.**
Chi ha quattro e spende sette, non ha bisogno di borsette.

854 **An old FOX is not easily snared.**
Malamente si piglia la volpe col laccio.

Cf. *You cannot catch old BIRDS with chaff.*

855 **At length the FOX is brought to the furrier.**
Tutte le volpi alla fine si riveggono in pellicceria.
Le vecchie volpi finiscono in pellicceria.

Sim. *Every fox must pay his own skin to the flayer / The smartest fox is caught at last.*

856 **At length the FOX turns monk.**
La volpe vuol farsi romita.

857 **He that has a FOX for his mate has need of a net at his girdle.**
Chi ha la volpe per compagno porti la rete alla cintola.

858 **The FOX is known by his furred tail.**
La volpe si conosce dalla coda.

859 **The FOX may grow grey, but never good.**
La volpe perde il pelo, ma il vizio mai.

Cf. *The WOLF may lose his teeth, but never his nature.*

860 **The FOX preys farthest from his home.**
La volpe in vicinato non fa mai danno.

Var. *The wolf preys farthest from his home (den).*
Sim. *A good fox does not eat his neighbour's fowls.*

861 **The sleeping FOX catches no poultry.**
Volpe che dorme, vive sempre magra.
Chi dorme non piglia pesci.

Var. *A sleeping fox catches no geese / The sleepy fox has seldom feathered breakfasts.*
Sim. *When the fox sleeps, no grapes fall in his mouth.*

862 **Though the FOX run, the chicken has wings.**
Benché la volpe corra, i polli hanno le ali.

863 **When the FOX preaches, beware of your geese.**
Quando la volpe predica, guardatevi galline.
Consiglio di volpi, tribolo di galline.

Var. *When the fox preaches, then beware your geese.*

864 **With FOXES you must play the fox.**
Con la volpe convien volpeggiare.

865 **A FRIAR who asks alms for God's sake begs for two.**
Frate che chiede per Dio, chiede per due.

Sim. *He who begs for others is contriving for himself.*

866 **The FRIAR preached against stealing, and had a goose in his sleeve.**
Il frate predicava che non si dovea rubare, e lui avea l'oca nello scapolare.

867 **FRIARS observant spare their own and eat other men's.**
Frati osservanti risparmiano il suo e mangiano quel degli altri.

868 **A faithful FRIEND is hard to find, remember man and keep in mind.**
I veri amici son come le mosche bianche.

869 **A FRIEND in need is a friend indeed.**
Al bisogno si conosce l'amico.
Nei pericoli si vede, chi d'amico ha vera fede.
Amico certo si conosce nell'incerto.

Var. *A friend is never known till a man have need.*

870 **A FRIEND in the market is better than money in the chest.**
Val più avere amici in piazza che danari nella cassa.
Gli amici sono buoni in ogni piazza.

> Sim. *A friend in a way is better than a penny in the purse.*

871 **A FRIEND is easier lost than found.**
Per fare un amico basta un bicchier di vino; per conservarlo è poca una botte.

> Sim. *A friend is not so soon gotten as lost.*

872 **A FRIEND to everybody is a friend to nobody.**
Amico d'ognuno, amico di nessuno.
Amico di tutti e di nessuno, è tutt'uno.

873 **A good FRIEND is a treasure.**
Chi trova un amico, trova un tesoro.
Trova un amico e troverai un tesoro, dice la Bibbia, e son parole d'oro.

> o Ecclesiasticus 6, 14 / Siràcide 6, 14

874 **A good FRIEND is my nearest relation.**
Val più un amico che cento parenti.

> Cf. *A near NEIGHBOUR is better than a far-dwelling kinsman.*

> o Proverbs 18, 24 / Proverbi 18, 24

875 **A true FRIEND is forever our friend.**
Le amicizie devono essere immortali.

876 **Before you make a FRIEND eat a bushel of salt with him.**
Prima di scegliere l'amico bisogna averci mangiato il sale sett'anni.

> Sim. *You should know a man seven years before you stir his fire.*

877 **Better lose a FRIEND than a jest.**
Meglio perdere l'amico che un bel detto.

878 **He is a FRIEND at a sneeze; the most you can get out of him is a "God bless you".**
Amici da starnuti, il più che ne cavi è un "Dio t'aiuti".

879 **He is my FRIEND that grinds at my mill.**
Colui è mio zio che vuole il bene mio.

> Cf. *He LOVES me well that makes my belly swell.*

880 **It is a good FRIEND that is always giving, though it be never so little.**
Se vuoi che l'amicizia si mantenga, fa che un paniere vada e l'altro venga.
Piccoli regali mantengono l'amicizia.

> Sim. *Small gifts keep friendship alive / Giff-gaffe makes good friends.*

881 **Love your FRIEND with his fault.**
Ama l'amico tuo con il difetto suo.

882 **Treat your FRIEND as if he might become an enemy.**
Parla all'amico come se avesse a diventar nemico.

883 **Fair-weather FRIENDS are not worth having.**
Amico di buon tempo mutasi col vento.
Amico di ventura molto briga e poco dura.

   Sim. *When good cheer is lacking, our friends will be packing.*
   Cf. *Eaten BREAD is soon forgotten.*

884 **FRIENDS may meet, but mountains never greet.**
I monti stan fermi e le persone camminano.
S'incontrano gli uomini e non le montagne.

885 **FRIENDS tie their purse with a cobweb thread.**
Gli amici hanno la borsa legata con un filo di ragnatela.

886 **Old FRIENDS and old wine and old gold are best.**
Amici, oro e vino vecchio sono buoni per tutto.
Amico e vino vogliono esser vecchi.

   Var. *Old friends and old wine are best.*

   o Ecclesiasticus, 9, 10 / Siràcide, 9, 10

887 **The FRIENDS of my friends are also my friends.**
Gli amici dei miei amici sono miei amici.

888 **A broken FRIENDSHIP may be soldered, but will never be sound.**
Amicizia riconciliata è una piaga mal saldata.

   Sim. *Take heed of reconciled enemies and of meat twice boiled.*
   Cf. *CABBAGE twice cooked is death.*

889 **Perfect FRIENDSHIP cannot be without equality.**
Ove non è ugualità, mai perfetto amor sarà.

890 **The FROG cannot out of her bog.**
Mal si può cavar la ranocchia dal pantano.

891 **A white FROST never lasts more than three days.**
Bianco gelo, d'acqua è messaggero.

892 **Forbidden FRUIT is sweet.**
Frutto proibito, più saporito.

   Var. *Stolen fruit is sweet.*
   Cf. *Stolen WATERS are sweet.*

   o Genesis 3, 6 / Genesi, 3, 6

893 **Don't jump from the FRYING-PAN into the fire.**
Cadere dalla padella nella brace.

894 **The FRYING-PAN said to the kettle, "Avaunt, black brows!"**
La padella dice al paiuolo: Fatti in là che mi tingi.
Tirati in là, paiolo, che la padella non ti tinga.

Sim. *The kettle calls the pot black-brows (burnt-arse) / The kiln calls the oven burnt-hearth / The pot calls the kettle black.*
Cf. *Thou art a bitter BIRD, said the raven to the starling.*

G

895 **To GAIN teaches how to spend.**
Il guadagnare insegna a spendere.

896 **Fair GAININGS make fair spendings.**
Il bel guadagnare fa il bello spendere.

897 **The GAME is not worth the candle.**
Il gioco non vale la candela.
È più la spesa che l'impresa.

898 **At the GAME's end we shall see who gains.**
Al fin del giuoco si vede chi guadagna.
Alla fin del gioco si vede chi ha vinto.

899 **GAMESTERS and race-horses never last long.**
A caval corridor e felice giocator, poco dura l'onor.

900 **GAMING, women and wine, while they laugh, they make men pine.**
Fuggi donne, vino, dado; se no, il tuo fato è spacciato.

Sim. *Dicing, drabbing and drinking bring men to destruction / Play, women, and wine undo men laughing.*
Cf. *Three things drive a man out of his house - SMOKE, rain and a scolding wife.*

901 **Our last GARMENT is made without pockets.**
L'ultimo vestito ce lo fanno senza tasche.
Il ricco non si porta all'altro mondo che un lenzuolo.

Sim. *Shrouds have no pockets / To the grave a pall, and that's all.*

902 **None says his GARNER is full.**
Nessuno dice che il suo granaio è pieno.

903 **All his GEESE are swans.**
La gallina del vicino par un'oca.

Cf. *The GRASS is always greener on the other side of the fence / Our NEIGHBOUR's ground yields better corn than ours.*

904 **One GENERATION passeth away, and another generation cometh: but the earth abideth for ever.**
Una età va via, e un'altra età viene; e la terra resta in perpetuo.

o Ecclesiastes 1, 4 / Qoèlet 1, 4

905 **GENOA has mountains without wood, sea without fish, women without shame, and men without conscience.**
Genova, aria senza uccelli, mare senza pesce, monti senza legna, uomini senza rispetti.

906 **A GENTLEMAN without an estate is like a pudding without suet.**
Conte senza terra, fiasco senza vino.

    Cf. *A man without MONEY is no man at all.*

907 **The GERMAN's wit is in his fingers.**
I Tedeschi hanno l'ingegno nella mano.

908 **After a great GETTER comes a great spender.**
Dopo uno scarso e un avaro, viene un prodigo.

    Cf. *After a thrifty FATHER, a prodigal son.*

909 **A GIFT much expected is paid, not given.**
Dono molto aspettato è venduto e non donato.

    Var. *A gift long waited for is sold, not given.*
    Cf. *He that is long GIVING knows not how to give / PLEASURE long expected is dear enough sold.*

910 **Don't look a GIFT horse in the mouth.**
A caval donato non si guarda in bocca.
A caval donato non si guarda il pelo.

    Var. *A gift horse should not be looked in the mouth / Never look a gift horse in the mouth / No man ought to look a gift horse in the mouth.*

911 **Every man has his proper GIFT.**
Ciascuno ha il proprio dono da Dio.

    o I Corinthians 7, 7 / I Corinzi 7, 7

912 **Who receives a GIFT sells his liberty.**
Chi dono prende, libertà vende.

    Var. *Bound is he that gifts taketh.*

913 **GIFTS blind the eyes.**
Il regalo acceca gli occhi.

    o Exodus 23, 8 / Esodo 23, 8

914 **GIFTS from enemies are dangerous.**
Spesso i doni sono danni.
Da chi ti dona, guardati.

    Var. *Fear the Greeks bearing gifts.*

915 **She that takes GIFTS, herself she sells, and she that gives, does not else.**
Donna che piglia è nell'altrui artiglia.

916 **A man cannot GIVE what he hasn't got.**
Nessuno può dar quel che non ha.

    Sim. *Where nothing is, nothing can be had / It is hard to get a stocking off a bare leg.*
    Cf. *Where nothing is the KING must lose his right / He that has NOTHING need fear to lose nothing.*

917 **It is better to GIVE than to receive.**
Meglio donare che pigliare.
Più felice cosa è il dare che il ricevere.

    Var. *Better give than take / It is more blessed to give than to receive.*

    o Acts 20, 35 / Atti 20, 35

918 **He GIVES twice who gives quickly.**
Chi dà presto dà due volte.
Chi dà presto raddoppia il dono.

919 **Who GIVES to all, denies all.**
Chi tutto dona, tutto abbandona.

920 **GIVING is dead, restoring very sick.**
Donato è morto e Ristoro sta male.

921 **He that is long GIVING knows not how to give.**
Non sa donare chi tarda a dare.

    Cf. *A GIFT much expected is paid, not given.*

922 **Those who live in GLASS houses shouldn't throw stones.**
Chi ha tegoli di vetro, non tiri sassi al vicino.

    Var. *Don't throw stones at your neighbours if your own windows are of glass / He that has a house of glass must not throw stones at another.*
    Cf. *He that has a HEAD of glass must not throw stones at another / He that has a HEAD of wax must not walk in the sun.*

923 **What your GLASS tells you will not be told by counsel.**
Quel che ti dirà lo specchio non te lo dirà il consiglio.

924 **GLUTTONY kills more than the sword.**
Ne uccide più la gola che la spada.

    Sim. *To dig one's grave with one's teeth / By suppers more have been killed than Galen ever cured.*

925 **To strain at a GNAT and swallow a camel.**
Colare la zanzara, e inghiottire il cammello.

    o Matthew 23, 24 / Matteo 23, 24

926 **All must be as GOD will.**
Quel ch'è disposto in cielo convien che sia.

    o Job 2, 10 / Giobbe 2, 10

927 **All things are possible with GOD.**
Dio può tutto.
Dio solo non può fallire.

Var. *With God all things are possible.*
Sim. *God doth what he will.*

    o Matthew 19, 26 / Matteo 19, 26; Mark 10, 27 / Marco 10, 27; Luke 18, 27 / Luca 18, 27

928 **Beware of him whom GOD hath marked.**
Guardati dai segnati da Dio.

Var. *Take care of that man whom God has set his mark upon.*

929 **GOD defend me from my friends; from my enemies I can defend myself.**
Dagli amici mi guardi Dio, che dai nemici mi guardo io.

Var. *Save us from our friends.*

    o Ecclesiasticus 6, 13 / Siràcide, 6, 13

930 **GOD heals, and the doctor takes the fee.**
Dio è quello che guarisce, e il medico ne porta via i denari.

Cf. *GOD heals, and the physician has the thanks.*

931 **GOD heals, and the physician has the thanks.**
Dio guarisce, e il medico è ringraziato.

Cf. *GOD heals, and the doctor takes the fee.*

932 **GOD helps those who help themselves.**
Aiutati che Dio t'aiuta.
Aiutati che il ciel t'aiuta.
Chi s'aiuta, Dio l'aiuta.

Var. *God helps him who helps himself.*
Cf. *Get thy SPINDLE and thy distaff ready and God will send thee flax.*

933 **GOD is still in heaven.**
Non peccare, Dio ti vede.

934 GOD keep me from the man that has but one thing to mind.
Dio ti guardi da chi non ha altro che una faccenda sola.

Cf. *Beware of the man of one BOOK.*

935 GOD make me great and big, for white and red I can make myself.
Grande e grossa mi faccia Dio, ché bianca e rossa mi farò io.

936 GOD never sends mouth but He sends meat.
Dio non manda mai bocca, che non mandi cibo.

937 GOD provides for him that trusts.
A chi ben crede, Dio provvede.

938 GOD sends cold after clothes.
Dio manda il freddo secondo i panni.

Cf. *GOD tempers the wind to the shorn lamb.*

939 GOD sends corn and the devil mars the sack.
Quando Dio ci dà la farina, il diavolo ci toglie il sacco.

940 GOD sends meat and the devil sends cooks.
Dio ci manda la carne, e il diavolo i cuochi.

941 GOD shapes the back to the burden.
Dio non manda se non quel che si può portare.

942 GOD stays long, but strikes at last.
La vendetta di Dio non piomba in fretta.

Sim. *God hath leaden feet, but iron hands.*

943 GOD tempers the wind to the shorn lamb.
Dio misura il vento all'agnello tosato.

Cf. *GOD sends cold after clothes.*

944 He that speaks not, GOD hears not.
Chi non parla, Dio non l'ode.

Sim. *He that cannot ask, cannot live / Dumb men get no land.*
Cf. *The lame TONGUE gets nothing.*

945 He to whom GOD gave no sons, the devil gives nephews.
A chi Dio non dà i figliuoli, il diavolo gli manda nipoti.

946 He who serves GOD serves a good master.
Chi serve Dio ha buon padrone.

947 What GOD hath joined together, let not man put asunder.
Quel che Iddio congiunse, uom non divida.
Ciò che Iddio ha congiunto l'uomo nol separi.

o Matthew 19, 6 / Matteo 19, 6; Mark 10, 9 / Marco 10, 9

948 **When GOD will, no wind but brings rain.**
Quando Iddio vuole, con tutti i venti piove.
Non muove foglia, che Dio non voglia.

949 **When GOD will punish, he will first take away the understanding.**
Quando Dio ci vuol punire, dal vero senno ci fa uscire.
A chi vuole il male, Dio toglie il senno.
A chi Dio vuol castigare, leva il cervello.

Var. *Whom the Gods would destroy, they first make mad.*
Cf. *Whom FORTUNE wishes to destroy, she first makes mad.*

950 **When it pleases not GOD, the saint can do little.**
Quando Dio non vuole, i santi non possono.

951 **Where GOD has his church, the devil will have his chapel.**
Dio non fa mai chiesa, che il diavolo non ci voglia la sua cappella.

952 **Whom GOD loves, his bitch brings forth pigs.**
A chi ha fortuna, il bue gli fa un vitello.

Cf. *GOOD things come to some when they are asleep.*

953 **Whom GOD will help, nothing does harm.**
A chi Dio aiutar vuole, niente nuocer gli puole.

Sim. *He is no loser who keeps God for his friend.*

954 **You cannot serve GOD and Mammon.**
Non si può servire insieme a Dio e a Mammona.

Cf. *No man can serve two MASTERS.*

o Matthew 6, 24 / Matteo 6, 24; Luke 16, 13 / Luca 16, 13

955 **GOD's help is better than early rising.**
Non vale levarsi a buon'ora, bisogna aver ventura.

956 **Whom the GODS love die young.**
Muor giovane colui che al cielo è caro.
Muor giovane chi è caro agli dei.

957 **He that GOES softly goes safely.**
Chi va piano, va sano e va lontano.

Sim. *Fair and softly goes far.*
Cf. *Soft pace GOES far / SLOW but sure.*

958 **Soft pace GOES far.**
Pian piano si va lontano.
Passo a passo si va lontano.

Sim. *Fair and softly goes far.*
Cf. *He that GOES softly goes safely / SLOW but sure.*

959 **All that glitters is not GOLD.**
Non è tutt'oro quel che riluce.
Var. *All is not gold that glitters / All that glistens is not gold.*

960 **GOLD goes in at any gate except heaven's.**
Martello d'oro non rompe le porte del cielo.

961 **GOLD is tried in the fire.**
L'oro si prova nel fuoco.
Sim. *Fire is the test of gold.*
Cf. *FIRE is the test of gold; adversity of friendship.*
o I Peter 1, 7 / I Pietro 1, 7; Revelation 3, 18 / Apocalisse 3, 18

962 **That is GOLD which is worth gold.**
Oro è che oro vale.

963 **When we have GOLD we are in fear; when we have none we are in danger.**
L'oro presente cagiona timore, e assente dà dolore.

964 **Where GOLD speaks every tongue is silent.**
Dove l'oro parla, la lingua tace.
Sim. *You may speak with your gold and make other tongues dumb.*

965 **A GOOD thing lost is a good thing valued.**
Ben perduto è conosciuto.
Non si conosce il bene, se non quando s'è perso.
Cf. *The COW knows not what her tail is worth till she has lost it / We never know the worth of WATER till the well is dry.*

966 **Better GOOD afar off than evil at hand.**
Bene lontano è meglio di male vicino.

967 **GOOD and quickly seldom meet.**
Presto e bene raro avviene.
Presto e bene non stanno assieme.

968 **GOOD cheap is dear.**
Buon mercato diventa qualche volta caro.
Cf. *A good BARGAIN is a pick-purse.*

969 **GOOD finds good.**
Il bene trova il bene.
Sim. *Do good: thou doest it for thyself / One good turn deserves another / One never loses by doing a good turn.*
Cf. *A good DEED is never lost / DO well and have well.*

970 **GOOD is good, but better carries it.**
Il buono è buono, ma il migliore è meglio.

971 **GOOD things come to some when they are asleep.**
Chi ha d'aver bene, dormendo gli viene.
La fortuna viene dormendo.

> Var. *Fortune come to some when they are asleep.*
> Cf. *Whom GOD loves, his bitch brings forth pigs.*

972 **He knows best what GOOD is that has endured evil.**
Chi ha provato il male, gusta meglio il bene.

> Var. *No man better knows what good is than he who has endured evil.*

973 **Nothing so GOOD but it might have been better.**
Non si sta mai tanto bene che non si possa star meglio, né tanto male che non si possa star peggio.

> Var. *Nothing so bad but it might have been worse.*

974 **GOODS are theirs that enjoy them.**
La roba non è di chi se la fa, ma di chi se la gode.

975 **He that gives his GOODS before he be dead, take up a mallet and knock him on the head.**
Chi del suo si spodesta, un maglio gli sia dato sulla testa.
Chi dà il suo avanti di morire, si prepari pure a ben soffrire.

976 **Ill-gotten GOODS never prosper.**
La roba mal acquistata non arricchisce.
I beni mal acquistati non arricchiscono.

> Var. *Ill-gotten (Evil-gotten) gains seldom prosper.*
> Cf. *What is got over the DEVIL's back is spent under his belly.*
>
>   o Proverbs 10, 2 / Proverbi 10, 2

977 **Ill-gotten GOODS thrive not to the third heir.**
Della roba di mal acquisto non ne gode il terzo erede.

978 **Stolen GOODS never thrive.**
Roba rubata non fa frutto.
Roba rubata ha poca durata.
Il rubare non fa fruttare.

979 **GOOSE and gander and gosling are three sounds but one thing.**
Se non è zuppa è pan bagnato.

980 **He that eats the king's GOOSE shall be choked with the feathers.**
Chi mangia l'oca alla corte, in capo all'anno caca le penne.
Chi mangia la vacca del re, a cent'anni di là ne paga le ossa.

981 **GOSLINGS lead the geese to water.**
I paperi vogliono menare a bere le oche.

Sim. *Teach your Grandmother to suck eggs.*

982 **With the GOSPEL one becomes heretic.**
Col Vangelo si può diventare eretici.

983 **So GOT, so gone.**
La roba va secondo la viene.

Cf. *EASY come, easy go.*

984 **To the GOUT all physicians are blind.**
Nella gotta il medico non vede gotta.

985 **Divine GRACE was never slow.**
A tempo viene quel che Dio manda.

986 **Every GRAIN has its bran.**
Ogni grano ha la sua semola.
Ogni farina ha crusca.

Sim. *In much corn is some cockle.*

987 **Though one GRAIN fills not the sack, it helps.**
A granello a granello s'empie lo staio e si fa il monte.

Sim. *Grain by grain, and the hen fills her belly.*
Cf. *LITTLE and often fills the purse.*

988 **"Sour GRAPES" said the fox when he could not reach them.**
La volpe dice che l'uva è agresta.
Quando la gatta non può arrivare al lardo dice che sa di rancido.

Var. *Fie upon hens! quoth the fox, because he could not reach them / Foxes, when they cannot reach the grapes, say they are not ripe / The grapes are sour.*

989 **GRASS grows not upon the highway.**
L'erba non cresce sulla strada maestra.

990 **If you see GRASS in January, lock your grain in your granary.**
Quando gennaio mette erba, se tu hai grano, e tu lo serba.

991 **The GRASS is always greener on the other side of the fence.**
L'erba del vicino è sempre più verde.

Cf. *All his GEESE are swans / Our NEIGHBOUR's ground yields better corn than ours.*

992 **While the GRASS grows, the horse starves.**
Mentre l'erba cresce, il cavallo muore di fame.

Cf. *Live, HORSE, and you'll get grass.*

993 There would be no GREAT ones if there were no little ones.
Il piccolo fa il grande, e il grande fa il piccolo.

994 The GREATER embraces the less.
Nel più c'è il meno.

995 Go not for every GRIEF to the physician, nor for every quarrel to the lawyer, nor for every thirst to the pot.
Né per ogni male al medico, né per ogni lite all'avvocato, né per ogni sete al boccale.

996 To weep is to make less the depth of GRIEF.
Il pianto è sollievo.

997 All GRIEFS with bread are less.
Tutti i dolori col pane son buoni.
Col pane tutti i guai sono dolci.

998 Great GRIEFS are mute.
I gran dolori sono muti.

Var. *Great griefs are silent / Little griefs are loud, great griefs are silent / Little cares speak, great ones are dumb / Small sorrows speak; great ones are silent.*

999 A constant GUEST is never welcome.
Ospite raro, ospite caro.
Chi raro viene, ben viene.

Cf. *FISH and guests stink after three days.*

1000 An unbidden GUEST knows not where to sit.
Chi va alla festa e non è invitato, ben gli sta se n'è scacciato.

Var. *An unbidden guest must bring his stool with him.*
Sim. *He who comes uncalled sits unserved.*

H

1001 **A holy HABIT cleanses not a foul soul.**
Non lava abito santo anima lorda.

1002 **A HAIR of the dog that bit you.**
Con il pelo del cane si sana la morditura.

1003 **Long HAIR, little brains.**
Capelli lunghi e cervello corto.
Le donne hanno lunghi i capelli e corti i cervelli.

> Var. *Bush natural; more hair than wit / Long hair and short sense / Long hair and short wit.*

1004 **No HAIR so small but has his shadow.**
Ogni pelo ha la sua ombra.

1005 **Red HAIR; devil's hair.**
Rosso mal pelo.

> Cf. *A red BEARD and a black head, catch him with a good trick and take him dead.*

1006 **Grey HAIRS are death blossoms.**
I capelli grigi sono i fiori dell'albero della morte.

1007 **The HALF is more than the whole.**
La metà è più dell'intero.

> Var. *The half is better than the whole.*

1008 **Between the HAMMER and the anvil.**
Essere tra l'incudine ed il martello.

> Cf. *Put not your HAND between the bark and the tree.*

1009 **An iron HAND in a velvet glove.**
Mano di ferro e guanto di velluto.

1010 **Between the HAND and the lip the morsel may slip.**
Dalla mano alla bocca spesso si perde la zuppa.
Tra la bocca e il boccone mille cose accadono.

> Sim. *Many a slip between the cup and the lip.*

1011 **He that is fed at another's HAND may stay long ere he be full.**
Chi per l'altrui man s'imbocca, tardi si satolla.

> Sim. *He that waits upon another's trencher, makes many a little dinner / Who depends upon another man's table often dines late.*

1012 **Many kiss the HAND they wish cut off.**
V'è chi bacia tal mano che vorrebbe veder mozza.
Tal mano si bacia che si vorrebbe veder tagliata.

1013 **One HAND washes the other.**
Una mano lava l'altra.

> Cf. *One HAND washes another and both the face.*

1014 **One HAND washes another and both the face.**
Una mano lava l'altra, e tutt'e due lavano il viso.

> Cf. *One HAND washes the other.*

1015 **Put not your HAND between the bark and the tree.**
Tra l'incudine e il martello, man non metta chi ha cervello.
Tra moglie e marito, non mettere il dito.

> Cf. *Between the HAMMER and the anvil.*

1016 **The HAND that gives gathers.**
La mano che dà raccoglie.

1017 **Cold HANDS, warm heart.**
Mani fredde, cuore caldo.
Freddo di mano, caldo di cuore.

> Var. *A cold hand and a warm heart.*

1018 **Many HANDS make light work.**
Molte mani fanno l'opera leggera.

1019 **HANDSOME is that handsome does.**
Bello è chi bello fa.

1020 **He that is not HANDSOME at twenty, nor strong at thirty, nor rich at forty, nor wise at fifty, will never be handsome, strong, rich, or wise.**
Chi di venti non è, di trenta non sa e di quaranta non ha, né mai sarà, né mai saprà, né mai avrà.

1021 **He that is born to be HANGED shall never be drowned.**
Chi ha d'esser impiccato non sarà mai annegato.
Chi ha da morir di forca può ballare sul fiume.

Var. *Born to be hanged, never be drowned / You can never hang a man if he is born to be drowned.*
Cf. *There is no flying from FATE / What MUST be, must be.*

1022 **HANGING and wiving go by destiny.**
Il maritare e l'impiccare è destinato.
Cf. *MARRIAGES are made in heaven.*

1023 **Call no man HAPPY till he dies.**
Avanti la morte non lice chiamar alcun felice.
Cf. *PRAISE no man till he is dead.*

1024 **If you would be HAPPY for a week take a wife; if you would be happy for a month kill a pig; but if you would be happy all your life plant a garden.**
Chi vuol aver bene un dì, faccia un buon pasto; chi una settimana, ammazzi il porco; chi un mese, pigli moglie; chi tutta la vita, si faccia prete.

1025 **HARD with hard makes not the stone wall.**
Duro con duro non fa buon muro.

1026 **He who eats the HARD shall eat the ripe.**
Chi mangia le dure, mangerà le mature.

1027 **First catch your HARE, then cook him.**
Mal si mangia la lepre, se prima non si piglia.
Var. *First catch your hare.*

1028 **The HARE always returns to her form.**
La lepre sta volentieri dove è nata.

1029 **To hunt for a HARE with a tabor.**
La lepre mal si piglia al suon di tamburo.
Le lepri non si pigliano col tamburo.
Var. *Drumming is not the way to catch a hare / To catch a hare with a tabor.*
Sim. *To fright a BIRD is not the way to catch her.*

1030 **Where we least think, there goeth the HARE away.**
Di dove men si pensa, si leva la lepre.
Sim. *The hare starts when a man least expects it.*

1031 **HARES may pull dead lions by the beard.**
Morto il leone, fino le lepri gli fanno il salto.
Cf. *He that is DOWN, down with him.*

1032 **If you run after two HARES, you will catch neither.**
Chi due lepri caccia, l'una non piglia, e l'altra lascia.

> Var. *He who chases two hares catches neither.*
> Sim. *Dogs that put up many hares kill none.*

1033 **HARM watch, harm catch.**
Chi cerca mal, mal trova.

> Cf. *He that seeks TROUBLE, never misses.*

1034 **HASTE makes waste.**
Troppa fretta nuoce.
La fretta fa romper la pentola.

> Cf. *The hasty BITCH brings forth blind whelps / Too HASTY burned his lips.*

1035 **Make HASTE slowly.**
Chi ha fretta, indugi.

1036 **Nothing should be done in HASTE but gripping a flea.**
Non far nulla in fretta se non che pigliar le pulci.

1037 **Too HASTY burned his lips.**
Chi fa in fretta, ha disdetta.

> Cf. *The hasty BITCH brings forth blind whelps / HASTE makes waste.*

1038 **A man's HAT in his hand never did him any harm.**
Berretta in mano non fece mai danno.
Cortesia di bocca, mano al cappello, poco costa, ed è buono e bello.

> Sim. *Civility costs nothing / Good words cost nought.*
> Cf. *LIP-HONOUR costs little, yet may bring in much / Kind WORDS go a long way.*

1039 **The greatest HATE springs from the greatest love.**
Niun odio è maggiore di quel che nasce d'amore.

1040 **HATRED is blind, as well as love.**
L'odio è cieco come l'amore.

1041 **HATRED stirreth up strife.**
L'odio muove contese.
L'odio suscita litigi.

> o Proverbs 10, 12 / Proverbi 10, 12

1042 **HATRED with friends is succour to foes.**
Odio fra amici è soccorso ai nemici.

1043 Better to HAVE than wish.
È meglio posseder che desiare.
È meglio avere in borsa che stare in speranza.

  Var. *Better is possession than desiring.*
  Cf. *One "TAKE IT" is more worth than two "Thow shalt have it" / One TODAY is worth two tomorrows.*

1044 Make HAY while the sun shines.
Bisogna tagliare il fieno finché non piove.

  Cf. *Strike while the IRON is hot.*

1045 A bald HEAD is soon shaven.
Dove non son capelli, mal si pettina.

1046 A forgetful HEAD makes a weary pair of heels.
Chi non ha testa, abbia gambe.
Chi non ha cervello, abbia gambe.
Chi non ha buona memoria, deve avere buone gambe.

  Sim. *If you don't use your head, you must use your legs / Little wit in the head makes much work for the feet / Who has not understanding, let him have legs / What you haven't got in your head, you have in your feet.*

1047 Better be the HEAD of a dog than the tail of a lion.
È meglio essere capo di gatto che coda di leone.

  Sim. *Better be the head of an ass than the tail of a lion / Better be the head of a mouse than the tail of a lion.*
  Cf. *Better be the HEAD of a lizard than the tail of a lion / Better be the HEAD of a pike than the tail of a sturgeon.*

1048 Better be the HEAD of a lizard than the tail of a lion.
È meglio essere capo di lucertola che coda di dragone.

  Sim. *Better be the head of an ass than the tail of a lion / Better be the head of a mouse than the tail of a lion.*
  Cf. *Better be the HEAD of a dog than the tail of a lion / Better be the HEAD of a pike than the tail of a sturgeon.*

1049 Better be the HEAD of a pike than the tail of a sturgeon.
È meglio essere capo di luccio che coda di storione.

  Sim. *Better be the head of an ass than the tail of a lion / Better be the head of a mouse than the tail of a lion.*
  Cf. *Better be the HEAD of a dog than the tail of a lion / Better be the HEAD of a lizard than the tail of a lion.*

1050 **Cover your HEAD by day as much as you will, by night as much as you can.**
Di giorno quando vuoi, di notte quando puoi.

1051 **He that has a HEAD of glass must not throw stones at another.**
Chi ha la testa di vetro, non faccia a sassi.

Var. *He that has a house of glass must not throw stones at another.*
Cf. *Those who live in GLASS houses shouldn't throw stones / He that has a HEAD of wax must not walk in the sun.*

1052 **He that has a HEAD of wax must not walk in the sun.**
Chi ha il capo di cera, non vada al sole.

Sim. *Be not a baker if your head be of butter.*
Cf. *Those who live in GLASS houses shouldn't throw stones / He that has a HEAD of glass must not throw stones at another / Who has skirts of STRAW needs fear the fire.*

1053 **He that has no HEAD needs no hat.**
Chi non ha testa non ha che far di cappello.

1054 **Mickle HEAD, little wit.**
Capo grosso, cervello magro.
Grossa testa non fa buon cervello.

1055 **The HEAD grey, and no brains yet.**
A testa bianca, spesso cervello manca.

Sim. *No fool to the old fool.*

1056 **The wiser HEAD gives in.**
Al più potente cede il più prudente.

1057 **When the HEAD aches all the body is the worse.**
Quando la testa duole, tutte le membra languono.

o I Corinthians 12, 26 / I Corinzi 12, 26

1058 **Scabby HEADS love not the comb.**
Il tignoso non ama il pettine.

1059 **So many HEADS, so many minds.**
Tante teste, tante idee.
Tante teste, tante sentenze.

Cf. *So many MEN, so many opinions.*

1060 **Two HEADS are better than one.**
Ne sanno più due villani che un dottore.
Sa più il papa e un contadino, che il papa solo.
Ne sa più un papa e un contadino che un papa solo.

1061 HEALTH is better than wealth.
La maggior ricchezza che sia è la sanità.
La salute non si paga con valuta.
Chi ha sanità è ricco e non lo sa.

Sim. *Health is great riches.*

o Ecclesiasticus 30, 15 / Siràcide 30, 15

1062 HEALTH is not valued till sickness comes.
Nell'infermità si conosce la sanità.

1063 HEALTH without money is half an ague.
Sanità senza quattrini è mezza malattia.
La salute senza ricchezza è mezzo male.

1064 HEAR all parties.
Chi vuol ben giudicare, le parti deve ascoltare.
A sentire una campana sola si giudica male.

Sim. *He has a good judgement that relies not wholly on his own.*

1065 HEAR much, speak little.
Parla poco e ascolta assai, e giammai non fallirai.

Sim. *Hear and see and say nothing.*
Cf. *He that would live in PEACE and rest, must hear, and see, and say the best.*

1066 A gentle HEART is tied with an easy thread.
Un cuor gentile con poco canape s'allaccia.

1067 A good HEART cannot lie.
Il cuor non mente.

1068 A good HEART conquers ill fortune.
Cuor forte rompe cattiva sorte.

Sim. *Nothing is impossible to a willing heart.*

1069 Every HEART has its own ache.
Ogni cuore ha il suo dolore.
Ogni magione ha la sua passione.

Cf. *Every man has his CROSS to bear.*

1070 Faint HEART never won fair lady.
Amante non sia chi coraggio non ha.

1071 What the HEART thinks, the tongue speaks.
Cuor sulla bocca, la bocca nel cuore.

Sim. *He wears his heart upon his sleeve / His heart is in his mouth.*
Cf. *Out of the ABUNDANCE of the heart the mouth speaketh.*

1072 **The HEART's letter is read in the eye.**
Gli occhi sono la spia del cuore.
Gli occhi sono lo specchio dell'anima.

Cf. *The EYE lets in love / In the FOREHEAD and the eye, the lecture of the mind doth lie.*

1073 **One's own HEARTH is gold's worth.**
Casa propria non c'è oro che la paghi.

Sim. *East, west, home's best / Home is home, though it be never so homely / There is no place like home.*
Cf. *An ENGLISHMAN's home is his castle.*

1074 **Neither HEAT nor cold abides always in the sky.**
Né caldo né gelo restò mai in cielo.

1075 **Better go to HEAVEN in rags than to hell in embroidery.**
È meglio andare in paradiso stracciato, che all'inferno in abito ricamato.

1076 **There is no going to HEAVEN in a sedan.**
In paradiso non ci si va in carrozza.

Var. *To go to heaven in a featherbed.*

1077 **A HEDGE between keeps friendship green.**
Vicinanza senza siepe porta nimicizia in casa.

Cf. *Love your NEIGHBOUR, yet pull not down the hedge / A WALL between preserves love.*

1078 **Where the HEDGE is lowest, men may soonest over.**
Dove la siepe è bassa, ognun vuol passare.

Var. *A low hedge is easily leaped over / Men leap over where the hedge is lowest.*

1079 **HELL and destruction are never full.**
Il sepolcro e il luogo della perdizione non son giammai satolli.

o Proverbs 27, 20 / Proverbi 27, 20

1080 **HELL is paved with good intentions.**
Di buone intenzioni è lastricato l'inferno.
L'inferno è lastricato di buone intenzioni.

Var. *The road to hell is paved with good intentions.*

1081 **There is no redemption from HELL.**
Chi scende all'inferno, più non risale.

1082 **They that be in HELL ween there is none other heaven.**
Chi è nell'inferno non sa ciò che sia nel cielo.

1083 **A black HEN lays a white egg.**
La gallina nera fa l'uovo bianco.
Anche le mucche nere danno il latte bianco.

1084 **A HEN that does not cackle doesn't lay.**
La gallina che canta ha fatto l'uovo.

   Sim. *The hen that cackles is she that has laid.*

1085 **He that comes of a HEN must scrape.**
Chi di gallina nasce, convien che razzoli.

   Cf. *That that comes of a CAT will catch mice / Who is born of a CAT will run after mice.*

1086 **Not even HERCULES could contend against two.**
Contro due non la potrebbe Orlando.

1087 **Praise a HILL, but keep below.**
Loda il monte e tienti al piano.

1088 **HISTORY repeats itself.**
La storia si ripete.

1089 **Every HOG has its Martinmas.**
Ad ogni porcello il suo San Martino.

1090 **He that has one HOG makes him fat; and he that has one son makes him a fool.**
Chi ha un figliolo solo, lo fa matto; chi un porco, lo fa grasso.

1091 **The worst HOG often gets the best pear.**
Al più tristo porco vien la miglior pera.

   Cf. *Into the mouth of a bad DOG often falls a good bone.*

1092 **To steal a HOG and give the feet in alms.**
Rubar il porco e dar i piedi per l'amor di Dio.

1093 **Every day is HOLIDAY with sluggards.**
Per i poltroni è sempre festa.

   Sim. *He that does nothing always finds helpers.*

1094 **HOMER sometimes nods.**
Qualche volta anche Omero sonnecchia.

1095 **HONESTY is the best policy.**
L'onestà è la miglior moneta.

1096 **Dear bought is the HONEY that is licked from the thorn.**
Caro è quel miele che bisogna leccar sulle spine.

1097 **He has HONEY in the mouth and a razor at the girdle.**
Avere il miele in bocca e il rasoio alla cintola.

1098 **He that handles HONEY shall feel it cling to his fingers.**
Chi maneggia il miele, si lecca le dita.

    Cf. *He that measures OIL shall anoint his fingers / He that touches PITCH shall be defiled.*

1099 **He who shares HONEY with the bear, has the least part of it.**
Chi divide il miele coll'orso, n'ha sempre men che parte.

1100 **HONEY is not for the ass's mouth.**
Il miele non è fatto per gli asini.

    Var. *Honey is not for asses.*

1101 **Make yourself all HONEY and the flies will devour you.**
Fatti di miele, e ti mangeranno le mosche.

    Var. *Daub yourself with honey and you will have plenty of flies.*
    Cf. *He that makes himself a SHEEP shall be eaten by the wolf.*

1102 **Too much HONEY cloys the stomach.**
Il troppo dolce stomaca.

    o Proverbs 25, 16 / Proverbi 25, 16

1103 **HONOUR is the reward of virtue.**
Onor, pasto e premio della virtù.

1104 **HONOUR to whom honour is due.**
Onore a chi onore è dovuto.

1105 **HONOUR without profit is a ring on the finger.**
Anello in mano, un onor vano.

1106 **We cannot come to HONOUR under coverlet.**
A tavola e a letto, né vergogna né rispetto.

1107 **Where there is no HONOUR, there is no grief.**
Dove non c'è onore, non c'è dolore.
Dove non è vergogna, non è virtù.

1108 **Great HONOURS are great burdens.**
Chi ha gli onori ne porta i pesi.
L'onore è onere.
Non c'è dignità senza obbligo.

    Sim. *The more cost, the more honour.*

1109 **HONOURS change manners.**
Gli onori mutano i costumi.
Gli onori cambiano i costumi e le maniere.

1110 **HONOURS nourish arts.**
L'onore nutrisce le arti.

1111 **He that lives in HOPE dances without music.**
Chi vive con speranza, magra fa la danza.

Var. *He that lives in hope dances to an ill tune.*

1112 **HOPE deferred maketh the heart sick.**
Speranza lunga, infermità di cuore.

o Proverbs 13, 12 / Proverbi 13, 12

1113 **HOPE is a good breakfast but a bad supper.**
La speranza è una buona colazione, ma una cattiva cena.

1114 **HOPE is but the dream of those that wake.**
La speranza è un sogno nella veglia.

1115 **HOPE is the poor man's bread.**
La speranza è il pane dei poveri.

1116 **HOPE maketh not ashamed.**
La speranza non confonde.

o Romans 5, 5 / Romani 5, 5

1117 **Too much HOPE deceives.**
La speranza è fallace.

Sim. *Hope often deludes the foolish man.*

1118 **Who lives by HOPE will die by hunger.**
Chi si pasce di speranza muore di fame.
Chi vive nella speranza muore a stento.

Var. *He that lives on hope has a slender diet / He that lives upon hope will die fasting.*

1119 **He that HOPES not for good, fears not evil.**
Chi non ha speranza del bene, non teme il male.

1120 **He that has HORNS in his bosom, let him not put them on his head.**
Chi ha le corna in seno, non se le metta in capo.

1121 **A hired HORSE tired never.**
Sproni propri e cavallo altrui fanno corte le miglia.

1122 **A HORSE, a wife, and a sword may be shown, but not lent.**
Moglie, schioppo e cavallo, non li prestare a nessuno.
La moglie, il fucile e il cane non si prestano a nessuno.
La moglie, lo schioppo e il cane non si prestano a nessuno.
Moglie e pipa non si prestano a nessuno.

Sim. *Four things cannot be lent: a good horse, a wise woman, a faithful servant and a good sword.*

1123 **A HORSE may stumble that has four legs.**
E cade anche un cavallo che ha quattro gambe.

> Cf. *It is a good HORSE that never stumbles.*

1124 **A HORSE that will not carry a saddle must have no oats.**
A cavallo che non porta sella, biada non si crivella.

> Cf. *No PAINS, no gains / No SWEET without some sweat / He that will not WORK shall not eat.*

1125 **A running HORSE is an open grave.**
Uomo a cavallo, sepoltura aperta.

1126 **A running HORSE needs no spur.**
Caval che corre non ha bisogno di sprone.
A caval che corre non abbisognano sproni.

> Var. *Do not spur a free horse / A good horse should be seldom spurred.*
> Sim. *The beast that goes always never wants blows.*

1127 **He that cannot beat the HORSE, beats the saddle.**
Chi non può battere il cavallo, batte la sella.

> Cf. *He that cannot beat the ASS, beats the saddle.*

1128 **He that has a white HORSE and a fair wife never wants trouble.**
Chi ha cavallo bianco e bella moglie, non è mai senza doglie.

1129 **He that lets his HORSE drink at every lake, and his wife go to every wake, shall never be without a whore and a jade.**
Chi lascia andar sua moglie ad ogni festa e bere il cavallo a ogni fontana, in capo all'anno il cavallo è bolso, e la moglie puttana.

1130 **It is a good HORSE that never stumbles.**
Cavallo che inciampa e non cade, è buon segnale.

> Var. *It is a good horse that never stumbles, and a good wife that never grumbles.*
> Cf. *A HORSE may stumble that has four legs.*

1131 **It is a proud HORSE that will not bear his own provender.**
Superbo è quel cavallo che non si vuol portar la biada.

1132 **It is good walking with a HORSE in one's hand.**
Chi ha buon cavallo in stalla può andare a piedi.
È facile andar a piedi quando si ha il caval per la briglia.

1133 **Live, HORSE, and you'll get grass.**
Campa cavallo che l'erba cresce.
Cavallo non stare a morire, che l'erba ha da venire.

Cf. *While the GRASS grows, the horse starves.*

1134 **One thing thinks the HORSE, and another he that saddles him.**
L'asino e'l mulattiero non hanno lo stesso pensiero.

Var. *The horse thinks one thing and he that rides him another.*
Sim. *One thing thinketh the bear, and another he that leadeth him.*

1135 **Ride a HORSE and mare on the shoulders, an ass and mule on the buttocks.**
Cavallo e cavalla, cavalcali sulla spalla; asino e mulo, cavalcali sul culo.

1136 **Scabbed HORSE cannot abide the comb.**
Caval rognoso non vuol né briglia né striglia.

1137 **The common HORSE is worst shod.**
L'asino del comune porta una grave soma.
Asino di molti, i lupi lo mangiano.

1138 **The HORSE that draws after him his halter is not altogether escaped.**
Cavallo scappato, da sé si castiga.

Cf. *He is not free that draws his CHAIN.*

1139 **The HORSE that draws most is most whipped.**
Il cavallo che meglio tira, tocca le peggio scudisciate.

1140 **To a greedy eating HORSE, a short halter.**
A cavallo mangiatore, capestro corto.

1141 **Who hath no HORSE may ride on a staff.**
Chi non ha letto, dorma sulla paglia.

1142 **You can take a HORSE to the water, but you can't make him drink.**
Si può portare il cavallo all'acqua, ma non costringerlo a bere.
Trenta monaci ed un abate non farebbero bere un asino per forza.
Non si fa ber l'asino quando non ha sete.
Quando il bue non vuole arare, tu puoi cantare, tu puoi cantare.

Var. *You may lead a mule to water, but you can't make him drink / One man can lead a horse to water, but ten men can't make him drink.*

1143 **You look for the HORSE you ride on.**
Cerca l'asino e ci va a cavallo.
Fare come colui che cercava l'asino e c'era sopra.

Sim. *You are like the man that sought his mare, and he riding on her.*
Cf. *The BUTCHER looked for his knife and it was in his mouth.*

HOST

1144 **Ask mine HOST whether he have good wine.**
Non domandare all'oste se ha buon vino.
Domanda all'oste s'egli ha buon vino.

1145 **He that reckons without his HOST must reckon twice.**
Chi fa il conto senza l'oste, gli convien farlo due volte.

1146 **An HOST's invitation is expensive.**
Invito d'oste non è senza costo.

Cf. *Three things COST dear: the caresses of a dog, the love of a whore, and the invitation of a host.*

1147 **The fairer the HOSTESS, the fouler the reckoning.**
Bella ostessa, brutti conti.

1148 **It happens in an HOUR that happens not in seven years.**
Accade in un'ora quel che non avviene in mill'anni.

Var. *It may come in an hour that will not come in a year.*

1149 **The morning HOUR has gold in its mouth.**
Le ore del mattino hanno l'oro in bocca.
L'aurora ha l'oro in bocca.
Dal mattino si vede il giorno.

Sim. *The Muses love the morning.*

1150 **Six HOURS' sleep for a man, seven for a woman, and eight for a fool.**
Sei ore un corpo, sette un pigro, otto un porco.

1151 **A HOUSE built by the wayside is either too high or too low.**
Chi fa la casa in piazza, o è troppo alta, o è troppo bassa.

Sim. *He who builds by the roadside has many masters.*

1152 **Choose not a HOUSE near an inn, or in a corner.**
Né casa in un canto, né vigna in un campo.

1153 **He that burns his HOUSE warms himself for once.**
Poichè la casa brucia, io mi scalderò.
Quando la casa brucia tutti si scaldano.

1154 **If you put nothing into your HOUSE, you can take nothing out.**
Casa nuova, chi non ve ne porta, non ve ne trova.

1155 **It is a sad HOUSE where the hen crows louder than the cock.**
In casa non c'è pace, quando gallina canta e gallo tace.
Triste quella casa dove gallina canta e gallo tace.

1156 **The HOUSE shows the owner.**
Dalla casa si conosce il padrone.

1157 **When the HOUSE is burned down, you bring water.**
Tardi si vien con l'acqua, quando la casa è arsa.

Cf. *When a thing is done, ADVICE comes too late / It's too late to shut the STABLE-DOOR after the horse has bolted / It is easy to be WISE after the event.*

1158 **Woe to the HOUSE where there is no chiding.**
Guai a quella casa dove la famiglia s'accorda.

1159 **The HUNCHBACK does not see his own hump, but sees his companion's.**
Il gobbo non vede la sua gobba, ma quella del suo compagno.
Chi ha la gobba non se la vede.

Var. *A hunchback cannot see his hunch.*
Cf. *You can see a mote in another's EYE, but cannot see a beam in your own.*

1160 **HUNGER and cold deliver a man up to his enemy.**
Città affamata, città espugnata.

1161 **HUNGER drives the wolf out of the woods.**
La fame caccia il lupo dal bosco.

1162 **HUNGER finds no fault with the cookery.**
La fame è il miglior cuoco che vi sia.

Sim. *The cat is hungry when a crust contents her / Hungry dogs will eat dirty puddings.*
Cf. *HUNGER is the best sauce / HUNGER makes hard beans sweet.*

1163 **HUNGER is the best sauce.**
Buon appetito non vuol salsa.
La fame è il miglior condimento.
La fame è il miglior intingolo.

Sim. *The cat is hungry when a crust contents her / Hungry dogs will eat dirty puddings.*
Cf. *HUNGER finds no fault with the cookery / HUNGER makes hard beans sweet.*

1164 **HUNGER is the teacher of the arts.**
La fame insegna tutte le arti.
La fame, gran maestra, anche le bestie addestra.

Cf. *The BELLY teaches all arts / NECESSITY is the mother of invention / POVERTY is the mother of all arts.*

1165 **HUNGER makes hard beans sweet.**
La fame muta le fave in mandorle.

Sim. *The cat is hungry when a crust contents her / Hungry dogs will eat dirty puddings.*
Cf. *HUNGER finds no fault with the cookery / HUNGER is the best sauce.*

1166 **A HUNGRY man, an angry man.**
Villano affamato è mezzo arrabbiato.

1167 **Don't HUNT with unwilling hounds.**
Mal si caccia coi cani svogliati.

1168 **All are not HUNTERS that blow the horn.**
Non tutti sono cacciatori, quelli che suonano il corno.

Cf. *All are not SAINTS that go to church.*

1169 **He that HURTS another hurts himself.**
Chi fa danno agli altri, fa danno a sé.
Chi fa male, aspetti male.
Chi male fa, male aspetta.
A chi mal fa, mal va.

Cf. *He that MISCHIEF hatches, mischief catches.*

1170 **A deaf HUSBAND and a blind wife always make a happy couple.**
Il marito vuol esser sordo e la moglie cieca per aver pace.

Var. *To make a happy couple the husband must be deaf, and the wife blind / A husband must be deaf and the wife blind to have quietness.*

1171 **In the HUSBAND wisdom, in the wife gentleness.**
Nel marito prudenza, nella moglie pazienza.

1172 **The HUSBAND is always the last to know.**
Chi le porta è l'ultimo a saperlo.

Var. *The cuckold is the last that knows of it.*

1173 **The HUSBAND is the head of the wife.**
Il marito sia capo della donna.

o Ephesians 5, 23 / Efesini 5, 23; I Corinthians 11, 3 / I Corinzi 11, 3

I

1174 An IDLE person is the devil's cushion.
Un uomo ozioso è il capezzale del diavolo.

1175 IDLE people have the least leisure.
Uomo lento non ha mai tempo.

　Cf. *A SLUGGARD takes an hundred steps because he would not take one in due time.*

1176 IDLENESS is the key of poverty.
La pigrizia è la chiave della povertà.
L'ozioso è sempre bisognoso.
Il pigro è sempre in bisogno.
Nella casa dov'è un buon dottore o un ricco prete, non si sente né la fame né la sete.

　Var. *Idleness is the key of beggary / Sloth is the key to poverty.*
　Cf. *The SLOTHFUL man is the beggar's brother.*

1177 IDLENESS is the mother of all vice.
L'ozio è il padre di tutti i vizi.

　Var. *Idleness is the root (mother) of all evil.*

　　o Ecclesiasticus 33, 27 / Siràcide 33, 27

1178 Of IDLENESS comes no goodness.
Non fece mai prodezze la pigrizia.

　Cf. *By DOING nothing we learn to do ill.*

1179 If IFS and ANs were pots and pans, there'd be no trade for tinkers.
Se non ci fosse il se e il ma, si sarebbe ricchi.

1180 By IGNORANCE we mistake, and by mistakes we learn.
Sbagliando s'impara.

　Sim. *Failure teaches success / Mistakes are often the best teachers.*

1181 IGNORANCE is the mother of impudence.
La presunzione è figlia dell'ignoranza.

1182 IGNORANCE of the law is no excuse.
L'ignoranza della legge non scusa nessuno.
La legge non ammette scuse.

1183 He that does ILL hates the light.
Chi fa male, odia il lume.

    o John 3, 20 / Giovanni 3, 20

1184 ILL be to him that thinks ill.
Chi mal pensa, mal abbia.

1185 ILL gotten, ill spent.
La roba di mal acquisto se la porta il vento.

Var. *Evil gotten, evil spent.*

1186 Of one ILL come many.
Un male tira l'altro.
Da colpa nasce colpa.

Sim. *One misfortune comes on the neck of another.*
Cf. *DISGRACES are like cherries, one draws another / MISFORTUNES never come singly.*

1187 So great is the ILL that does not hurt me as is the good that does not help me.
Tanto è il male che non mi nuoce quanto il bene che non mi giova.

1188 ILL LUCK is good for something.
Non c'è male che per ben non venga.

Cf. *Nothing so BAD in which there is not something of good.*

1189 An ILL TURN is soon done.
A gran mal fare poco tempo basta.

1190 No one is bound to do IMPOSSIBILITIES.
All'impossibile nessuno è tenuto.
Nessuno è tenuto a fare l'impossibile.
Chi fa quel che può, non è tenuto a far di più.

Var. *No one is bound by the impossible.*

1191 First IMPRESSIONS are most lasting.
La prima impressione mal si cancella.

1192 To do good to an INGRATEFUL man is to throw rose-water in the sea.
Chi fa del bene agli ingrati, fa onta a Dio.
Chi fa del bene al villano, si sputa in mano.

    o Ecclesiasticus 12, 5-7 / Siràcide 12, 5-7

1193 **Not all the INSANE are in lunatic asylums.**
Non tutti i matti sono al manicomio.
Non tutti i matti stanno all'ospedale.

   Sim. *Not all the monkeys are in the zoo.*

1194 **IRON whets iron.**
Il ferro lima il ferro.

   Cf. *One KNIFE whets another.*

   o Proverbs 27, 17 / Proverbi 27, 17

1195 **Strike while the IRON is hot.**
Bisogna battere il ferro finché è caldo.
Batti il ferro finché è caldo.

   Sim. *Hoist your sail when the wind is fair.*
   Cf. *Make HAY while the sun shines.*

1196 **It IS not what is he, but what has he.**
L'essere sta nell'avere.
Un gran proverbio, caro al Potere, dice che l'essere sta nell'avere.

   Cf. *MONEY makes the man.*

1197 **In settling an ISLAND the first building erected by a Spaniard will be a church; by a Frenchman, a fort; by a Dutchman, a warehouse; and by an Englishman, an alehouse.**
Nel colonizzare un'isola, la prima fabbrica eretta da uno Spagnolo sarebbe una chiesa, da un Francese un forte, da un Olandese un magazzino, e da un Inglese una bottega di birra.

1198 **The ITALIANS are wise before the deed, the Germans in the deed, the French after the deed.**
L'Italiano è saggio prima di fare una cosa, il Tedesco quando la fa, e il Francese quando è bell'e fatta.

J

1199 A JADE eats as much as a good horse.
Tanto mangia una rozza quanto un buon cavallo.

1200 JANUARY commits the fault, and May bears the blame.
Gennaio fa il peccato e maggio ne è incolpato.

1201 JEALOUSY is cruel as the grave.
La gelosia è dura come l'inferno.

> o Song of Solomon 8, 6 / Cantico dei Cantici 8, 6

1202 Better lose a JEST than a friend.
Meglio perdere un bel detto che un amico.
Per un bel detto si perde un amico.

1203 If you make a JEST, you must take a jest.
Chi scherza con altrui, non si sdegni se altri scherza con lui.

1204 Leave a JEST when it pleases you best.
Ogni bel gioco dura poco.
Lascia la burla quando più piace.

Var. *Leave a jest when it pleases lest it turn to earnest.*
Sim. *Leave off while the play is good.*
Cf. *Long JESTING was never good.*

1205 Long JESTING was never good.
Scherzo lungo non fu mai buono.

Cf. *Leave a JEST when it pleases you best.*

1206 Good JESTS bite like lambs, not like dogs.
Lo scherzo deve mordere come pecora, non come il cane.

1207 The JEWS spend at Easter, the Moors at marriages, the Christians in suits.
I Giudei in Pasqua, i Mori in nozze, i Cristiani in piatire, sanno impoverire.

1208 To make the best of a bad JOB.
Fare buon viso a cattivo gioco.

Var. *To put a good face on a bad business.*
Cf. *Make a VIRTUE of necessity.*

1209 **In a long JOURNEY straw weighs.**
In lungo viaggio anche una paglia pesa.
A lungo andar la paglia pesa.

Sim. *Light burdens far heavy.*

1210 **JOVE laughs at lovers' perjuries.**
Giuramento d'amante poco conta e meno vale.
I giuramenti degli innamorati sono come quelli dei marinai.

1211 **No JOY without annoy.**
Non v'è gioia senza noia.

Cf. *Every WHITE hath its black, and every sweet its sour.*

1212 **Sudden JOY kills sooner than excessive grief.**
Di dolore non si muore, ma d'allegrezza sì.

1213 **The JOY of the heart makes the face fair.**
Cuor gioioso, volto allegro.
L'allegria fa il viso bello.

o Proverbs 15, 13 / Proverbi 15, 13

1214 **A good JUDGE conceives quickly, judges slowly.**
Il buon giudice tosto intende, e tardi giudica.

1215 **From a foolish JUDGE, a quick sentence.**
Da giudice folle, breve sentenza.

1216 **JUDGE not, that ye be not judged.**
Non giudicar, se non vuoi esser giudicato.

o Matthew 7, 1 / Matteo 7, 1

1217 **JUDGE nothing before the time.**
Non giudicate di nulla innanzi al tempo.
Non giudicare troppo in fretta.

o I Corinthians 4, 5 / I Corinzi 4, 5

1218 **No one should be JUDGE in his own cause.**
Non si può essere giudice e parte.

Sim. *Men are blind in their own cause.*

1219 **The JUST shall live by faith.**
Il giusto vivrà per fede.

o Romans 1, 17 / Romani 1, 17

1220 **Extreme JUSTICE is extreme injustice.**
Gran giustizia, grande offesa.
Var. *Extreme law is extreme wrong / Much law, little justice.*

1221 **JUSTICE pleases few in their own house.**
A nessuno piace la giustizia a casa sua.
Ognuno ama la giustizia a casa d'altri.

K

1222 **He that will eat the KERNEL must crack the nut.**
Bisogna rompere la noce, se si vuol mangiare il nocciolo.

    Sim. *He that would eat the fruit must climb the tree.*
    Cf. *You cannot make an OMELETTE without breaking eggs.*

1223 **A golden KEY can open any door.**
La chiave d'oro apre ogni porta.
Colle chiavi d'oro s'apre ogni porta.
Vuoi tu aprire qualunque porta? Chiavi d'oro teco porta.

    Sim. *There is no lock but a golden key will open it / No lock will hold against the power of gold.*

1224 **A silver KEY can open an iron lock.**
Il martello d'argento spezza le porte di ferro.

1225 **All the KEYS hang not at one man's girdle.**
Tutte le chiavi non pendono a una cintura.

1226 **The KICK of the dam hurts not the colt.**
Calcio di cavalla non fece mai male a puledro.
Calcio di stallone non fa male alla cavalla.

1227 **Every man is a KING in his own house.**
In casa sua ciascuno è re.
Ognuno è padrone in casa sua.

    Var. *Every groom is a king at home.*
    Cf. *Every COCK is bold on his own dunghill / Every DOG is a lion at home.*

1228 **Like KING, like people.**
Qual re, tal popolo.
Il popolo è simile al signore.
Tal è il gregge, qual è chi lo regge.

    Var. *Like prince, like people.*

1229 **The KING is dead. Long live the King!**
Morto un papa, se ne fa un altro.

1230 **The KING reigns, but does not govern.**
Il re regna, ma non governa.

1231 Where nothing is, the KING must lose his right.
Dove non c'è nulla, il re non ha ragione.
Quando non c'è, perde la Chiesa.
Dove non n'è, non ne toglie neanche la piena.

Var. *Where nought's to be got, kings lose their scot.*
Cf. *A man cannot GIVE what he hasn't got / He that has NOTHING need fear to lose nothing.*

1232 KINGDOMS divided soon fall.
Nemico diviso, mezzo vinto.

Cf. *DIVIDE and rule.*

o Mark 3, 24 / Marco 3, 24

1233 KINGS have long arms.
I principi hanno le mani lunghe.
I principi hanno le braccia lunghe.

Var. *Kings have many ears and many eyes.*

1234 Two KINGS in one kingdom do not agree well together.
Non stanno bene due galli in un pollaio.

Sim. *Two sparrows on one ear of corn make an ill agreement.*

1235 A fat KITCHEN is near to poverty.
Grassa cucina, povertà vicina.
Cucina grassa, borsa magra.
Ricca cucina, miseria vicina.

1236 A little KITCHEN makes a large house.
La cucina piccola fa la casa grande.

1237 Wanton KITTENS make sober cats.
Gattini sventati fanno gatti posati.

Cf. *Many a shabby COLT makes a good horse.*

1238 Once a KNAVE, and ever a knave.
Una volta furfante, e sempre furfante.

Cf. *Once a THIEF, always a thief.*

1239 The more KNAVE, the better luck.
Più briccone, più fortunato.
Gli sfacciati son sempre fortunati.

Sim. *The more wicked, the more fortunate.*

1240 When a KNAVE is in a plum-tree, he has neither friend nor kin.
Il villan nobilitato non conosce il parentado.
Quando il villano è sul fico, non conosce parente né amico.

Cf. *Set a BEGGAR on horseback, and he'll ride to the Devil / No PRIDE like that of an enriched beggar.*

1241 One KNIFE whets another.
Un coltello aguzza l'altro.

Cf. *IRON whets iron.*

1242 He gives one KNOCK on the hoop, and another on the barrel.
Dare un colpo al cerchio e uno alla botte.

1243 He that would KNOW what shall be must consider what has been.
Chi vuol vedere quel che sarà, guardi quello che è stato.
Se vuoi saper quel che ha da essere, guarda a quel che è stato.

1244 KNOW thyself.
Conosci te stesso.

1245 He that increaseth KNOWLEDGE increaseth sorrow.
Chi acquista sapere, acquista dolere.
Chi aggiunge sapere, aggiunge dolere.
Chi più capisce, più patisce.

Cf. *Much science, much sorrow.*

o Ecclesiastes 1, 18 / Qoèlet 1, 18

1246 KNOWLEDGE is folly, except grace guide it.
La scienza è follia, se senno non la governa.

1247 KNOWLEDGE is power.
Intendere è potere.

o Proverbs 24, 5 / Proverbi 24, 5

1248 He KNOWS enough that knows nothing if he knows how to hold his peace.
Assai sa chi non sa, se tacer sa.

1249 He KNOWS most who speaks least.
Chi più sa, meno parla.
Chi più sa, più tace.

1250 He that KNOWS nothing, doubts nothing.
Chi niente sa, di niente dubita.
Chi non sa, non dubita.

Var. *He who doubts nothing, knows nothing.*

1251 He who KNOWS little soon tells it.
Chi sa poco, presto lo dice.
Chi poco sa, presto parla.

Var. *He that knows little soon repeats it.*

L

1252 **He that will not endure LABOUR in this world, let him not be born.**
Chi non vuol durar fatica in questo mondo, non ci nasca.
Chi non vuol affaticarsi in questo mondo, non ci nasca.

1253 **LABOUR as long lived, pray as ever dying.**
Lavora come avessi a campare ognora, adora come avessi a morire allora.

1254 **LABOUR overcomes all things.**
Il lavoro tutto vince.

1255 **The LABOURER is worthy of his hire.**
L'operaio ha diritto alla sua mercede.
Ogni fatica merita ricompensa.

    o Luke 10, 7 / Luca 10, 7

1256 **He that LABOURS and thrives spins gold.**
Il laoro cava fuoco dalla pietra.

1257 **The LAME goes as far as your staggerer.**
Tanto cammina lo zoppo, quanto lo sciancato.

1258 **Every LAND has its own law.**
Paese che vai, usanza che trovi.

    Cf. *So many COUNTRIES, so many customs.*

1259 **Good LAND: evil way.**
Buona terra, cattiva strada.

1260 **No LAND without stones, or meat without bones.**
Non si può avere la carne senz'osso.

1261 **Woe to thee, O LAND, when thy King is a child!**
Guai a te, o paese, il cui re è fanciullo!

    o Ecclesiastes 10, 16 / Qoèlet 10, 16

1262 **He that has LANDS has war.**
Chi ha terra ha guerra.

1263 **To think that LARKS will fall into one's mouth ready roasted.**
A nessuno piovono le lasagne in bocca.

Var. *He thinks that roasted larks will fall into his mouth.*
Sim. *You may gape long enough ere a bird fall in your mouth.*
Cf. *If the SKY falls we shall catch larks.*

1264 He that comes LAST to the pot is soonest wroth.
All'ultimo tocca il peggio.

1265 The LAST shall be the first.
Gli ultimi saranno i primi.

o Matthew 19, 30 / Matteo 19, 30

1266 Better LATE than never.
Meglio tardi che mai.

Sim. *It is not lost that comes at last.*

1267 Never too LATE to mend.
Non è mai troppo tardi per ravvedersi.

1268 Who comes LATE lodges ill.
Chi tardi arriva, male alloggia.

Sim. *Last come, last served.*

1269 With LATIN, a horse and money, you may travel the world.
Col latino, con un ronzino e con un fiorino si gira il mondo.

1270 LAUGH before breakfast, you'll cry before supper.
Spesso chi ride la mattina, piange la sera.

Var. *He that laughs in the morning, weeps at night / If you sing before breakfast, you'll cry before night.*
Cf. *After LAUGHTER, tears / SADNESS and gladness succeed each other / He that SINGS on Friday, will weep on Sunday / SORROW treads upon the heels of mirth.*

1271 He LAUGHS best who laughs last.
Ride bene chi ride ultimo.

Var. *He who laughs last, laughs longest.*
Sim. *Let them laugh that win / He laughs who wins / Better the last smile than the first laughter.*

1272 After LAUGHTER, tears.
La fine del riso è il pianto.

Cf. *LAUGH before breakfast, you'll cry before supper / SADNESS and gladness succeed each other / He that SINGS on Friday, will weep on Sunday / SORROW treads upon the heels of mirth.*

1273 LAUGHTER is the best medicine.
L'allegria è d'ogni male il rimedio universale.

1274 Too much LAUGHTER discovers folly.
Il riso abbonda sulla bocca degli stolti.
Chi troppo ride ha natura di matto.
I matti si conoscono dal molto ridere.
Dal riso molto conosci lo stolto.

Sim. *A loud laugh bespeaks the vacant mind / The louder the laugh, the more empty the head.*

o Ecclesiasticus 21, 20 / Siràcide 21, 20; Ecclesiastes 7, 6; 2, 2 / Qoèlet 7, 6; 2,2

1275 Every LAW has a loophole.
Fatta la legge, trovato l'inganno.
Fatta la legge, pensata la malizia.

1276 LAW makers should not be law breakers.
Chi fa la legge, servarla deve.

1277 The LAW grows of sin, and chastises it.
La legge nasce dal peccato e lo castiga.

Cf. *Of evil MANNERS spring good laws.*

1278 The LAW is good, if a man use it lawfully.
La legge è buona, se alcuno l'usa legittimamente.

o I Timothy 1, 8 / I Timoteo 1, 8

1279 LAWS catch flies but let hornets go free.
Le leggi sono come i ragnateli.
Le leggi sono come le tele di ragno.

Cf. *Little THIEVES are hanged, but great ones escape.*

1280 LAWS go as kings like.
Le leggi si volgono dove i regi vogliono.

Sim. *What the kings wills, that the law wills.*

1281 A good LAWYER, a bad neighbour.
Buon avvocato, cattivo vicino.
Buoni avvocati sono cattivi vicini.

Var. *A good lawyer makes an evil neighbour.*

1282 A LAWYER never goes to law himself.
Nessun buono avvocato piatisce mai.

1283 LAWYERS' gowns are lined with the wilfulness of their clients.
La veste dei dottori è foderata dell'ostinazione dei clienti.
Temete, litiganti sventurati, più delle liti stesse, gli avvocati.
Gli sciocchi e gli ostinati fanno ricchi i laureati.

1284 **LEARN weeping, and you shall gain laughing.**
Impara piangendo e riderai guadagnando.

o Psalms 126, 5 / Salmi 126, 5

1285 **What we first LEARN we best know.**
Quel che si impara in gioventù, non si dimentica mai più.

Sim. *Whoso learneth young forgets not when he is old.*
Cf. *What YOUTH is used to, age remembers.*

1286 **Much LEARNING makes men mad.**
Chi troppo studia matto diventa, chi niente studia mangia polenta.

o Acts 26, 24 / Atti 26, 24

1287 **There is no royal road to LEARNING.**
Chi studia molto impara poco; chi studia poco impara nulla.

Sim. *There is no short cut to master a valuable art.*

1288 **Better LEAVE than lack.**
È meglio lasciare che mancare.

1289 **He that fears LEAVES, let him not go into the wood.**
Chi ha paura d'ogni foglia, non vada al bosco.

Sim. *He that fears every grass must not walk in a meadow / He that is afraid of the wagging of feathers must keep from among wild fowl.*
Cf. *He that is AFRAID of wounds must not come nigh a battle / He that forecasts all PERILS will never sail the sea.*

1290 **Everyone stretches his LEGS according to the length of his coverlet.**
Bisogna stendersi quanto il lenzuolo è lungo.
Chi si stende più del lenzuolo, si scopre da piedi.

Var. *Stretch your legs according to your coverlet.*
Sim. *Stretch your arm no further than your sleeve will reach.*
Cf. *Cut your COAT according to your cloth.*

1291 **He has but a short LENT that must pay money at Easter.**
Chi vuol quaresima corta, faccia debiti da pagare a Pasqua.

Var. *Those have a short Lent who owe money to be paid at Easter / Who desires a short Lent, let him make a debt to be paid at Easter.*

1292 **In a LEOPARD the spots are not observed.**
Nel leopardo non si conoscono le macchie.

1293 **The LEOPARD does not change his spots.**
Il leopardo non muta le macchie.

o Jeremiah 13, 23 / Geremia 13, 23

1294 **Let your LETTER stay for the post, not the post for the letter.**
Bisogna che la lettera aspetti il messo, non il messo la lettera.
Lettera fatta, fante aspetta.

1295 **The LETTER killeth, but the spirit giveth life.**
La lettera uccide, ma lo spirito vivifica.

    o II Corinthians 3, 6 / II Corinzi 3, 6

1296 **A LIAR is not believed when he speaks the truth.**
Al bugiardo non è creduto il vero.

    Sim. *He that once deceives is ever suspected.*

1297 **A LIAR is sooner caught than a cripple.**
Si conosce prima un bugiardo che uno zoppo.

1298 **A LIAR should have a good memory.**
Il bugiardo vuole avere buona memoria
Forza e tenga ben a mente, un bugiardo quando mente.

    Var. *Liars have need of good memories.*

1299 **LIBERALITY is not giving largely, but wisely.**
La liberalità non sta nel dar molto, ma saggiamente.

1300 **LIBERTY is more worth than gold.**
Meglio un'oncia di libertà che dieci libbre d'oro.

    Cf. *A BEAN in liberty is better than a comfit in prison.*

1301 **Who loses his LIBERTY loses all.**
Chi di libertà è privo, ha in odio d'esser vivo.

1302 **He that trusts in a LIE shall perish in truth.**
Chi si fida in bugia, col ver perisce.

1303 **He that will LIE will steal.**
Chi è bugiardo è ladro.

    Sim. *Lying and thieving go together / Show me a liar and I will show you a thief.*

1304 **One LIE makes many.**
Una bugia ne tira dieci.
Una bugia ne fa cento.

    Sim. *One lie leads to another / One seldom finds a lonely lie.*

1305 **Tell a LIE and find a truth.**
Fai parlare un bugiardo, e l'hai colto.

1306 **"They say so" is half a LIE.**
Aver sentito dire è mezza bugia.
Chi parla per udita, aspetti la mentita.

1307　LIES have short legs.
　　　Le bugie hanno le gambe corte.

1308　An ill LIFE, an ill end.
　　　Chi mal vive, mal muore.

1309　He who despises his own LIFE is soon master of another's.
　　　È padron della vita altrui chi la propria sprezza.

1310　LIFE is a battle.
　　　La vita è una continua battaglia.
　　　La vita dell'uom su questa terra, altro non è che una continua guerra.

1311　LIFE is a shuttle.
　　　La vita è un lampo.
　　　La vita è un passaggio.

1312　LIFE is but a dream.
　　　La vita è un sogno.

1313　LIFE is not a bed of roses.
　　　La vita non è tutta rose.

1314　LIFE without a friend is death without a witness.
　　　Chi non ha amico o germano, non ha forza in braccio né mano.

　　　Sim. *Life is death without real friends.*

1315　Such a LIFE, such a death.
　　　Quale è la vita, tale sarà la fine.
　　　Come si vive, così si muore.

　　　Sim. *As a man lives, so shall he die, as a tree falls, so shall it lie.*

1316　While there is LIFE, there is hope.
　　　Finché c'è vita, c'è speranza.

　　　Var. *As long as there is life, there is hope.*

　　　　o Ecclesiastes 9, 4 / Qoèlet 9, 4

1317　The LIGHT is naught for sore eyes.
　　　Ad occhio infermo nuoce la luce.

1318　LIKE cures like.
　　　Simili con simili si curino.

　　　Cf. *One DEVIL drives out another / One NAIL drives out another / One POISON drives out another.*

1319　LIKE will to like.
　　　Ogni simile ama il suo simile.
　　　Ogni simile attrae il simile.
　　　Chi si somiglia si piglia.
　　　Chi s'assomiglia si piglia.

Var. *Like attracts like.*
Sim. *Likeness causes liking.*
Cf. BIRDS *of a feather flock together.*

1320 **There is a LIMIT to everything.**
C'è un limite a ogni cosa.

1321 **There is a LIMIT to one's patience.**
Anche la pazienza ha un limite.

Cf. PATIENCE *provoked turns to fury.*

1322 **One does not wash one's dirty LINEN in public.**
I panni sporchi si lavano in casa.
Lavare i panni sporchi in famiglia.
Lavare il bucato in famiglia.

Var. *Do not wash your dirty linen in public / Dirty linen should be washed at home.*

1323 **A LION may come to be beholden to a mouse.**
Il leone ebbe bisogno del topo.

Var. *A mouse may help a lion.*

1324 **The LION is known by his claws.**
Dall'unghia si conosce il leone.

Sim. *The devil is known by his claws.*

1325 **Who takes the LION when he is absent, fears a mouse present.**
Tal piglia leoni in assenza, che teme un topo in presenza.

1326 **If the LION's skin cannot the fox's shall.**
Se non puoi con la pelle del leone, fa con quella della volpe.
Dove non basta la pelle del leone, bisogna attaccarvi quella della volpe.

Sim. *Either by might or by sleight.*

1327 **The LION's share.**
Far la parte del leone.

1328 **LIP-HONOUR costs little, yet may bring in much.**
Onor di bocca assai giova e poco costa.

Sim. *Civility costs nothing / Good words cost naught.*
Cf. *A man's* HAT *in his hand, never did him any harm /* Kind WORDS *go a long way.*

1329 **Scald not your LIPS in another man's pottage.**
Non metter bocca, dove non ti tocca.
Ciò che non ti scotta, non vi soffiare sopra.

1330 LISTENERS never hear any good of themselves.
Chi sta in ascolteria sente cose che non vorria.
Chi sta alle scolte sente le sue colpe.
Var. *Eavesdroppers never hear any good of themselves.*
Sim. *He who peeps through a hole, may see what will vex him.*

1331 A LITTLE too wise, they say, do never live long.
Fanciullo che presto sa, presto muore.

1332 A LITTLE with peace is a great blessing.
Poco e in pace, molto mi piace.

1333 Every LITTLE helps.
Tutto fa brodo.
Sim. *Where nothing is a little does ease.*

1334 LITTLE and often fills the purse.
Poco e spesso empie il borsellino.
A goccia a goccia si riempie il secchio.
Sim. *Grain by grain, and the hen fills her belly.*
Cf. *Though one GRAIN fills not the sack, it helps.*

1335 That which suffices is not LITTLE.
Quel che basta non è poco.

1336 LIVE and learn.
Vivendo s'impara.
Sin che si vive, sempre s'impara.
Cf. *Never too OLD to learn.*

1337 LIVE and let live.
Vivi e lascia vivere.
Bisogna vivere e lasciar vivere.

1338 We must LIVE by the quick, not by the dead.
Chi muore giace, e chi vive si dà pace.
Var. *We must live by the living, not by the dead.*
Sim. *Let the dead bury their dead.*
Cf. *Let the DEAD bury the dead and the living lead a gay life.*

1339 Good for the LIVER may be bad for the spleen.
Quello che è buono per il fegato può essere cattivo per la milza.

1340 All that LIVES must die.
Tutti siamo nati per morire.
Sim. *It is as natural to die as to be born / Our lives are but our marches to the grave.*
Cf. *As soon as a man is BORN he begins to die / He that is once BORN, once must die / All MEN are mortal.*

1341 **He LIVES long that lives well.**
Chi giustamente vive non muor mai.

1342 **He that LIVES long suffers much.**
Chi più vive più languisce.

1343 **He that LIVES most dies most.**
Chi più vive, più muore.

1344 **Half a LOAF is better than no bread.**
Più val mezzo pan che niente.

Sim. *Better some of a pudding than none of a pie.*
Cf. *SOMETHING is better than nothing.*

1345 **Roll my LOG, and I'll roll yours.**
Tienmi il sacco oggi, e domani lo terrò io a te.

Cf. *Scratch my BACK and I'll scratch yours.*

1346 **Crooked LOGS make straight fires.**
Anche la legna storta dà fuoco diritto.
Il legno contorto lo raddrizza il fuoco.

1347 **LONG and lazy, little and loud; fat and fulsome, pretty and proud.**
Se è grande è oziosa, se è piccola è viziosa, se è bella è vanitosa, se è brutta è fastidiosa.

1348 **LOOK before you leap.**
Guarda innanzi che tu salti.

Var. *Think twice before you leap.*
Cf. *Think on the END before you begin.*

1349 **LOOKERS-ON see more than players.**
Lo spettatore vede più che il giocatore.

Var. *Lookers-on see most of the game / Standers-by see more than gamesters.*

1350 **He that LOOKS not before, finds himself behind.**
Chi non guarda innanzi, rimane indietro.
Chi dinanzi non mira, di dietro sospira.

1351 **A LORD without riches is a soldier without arms.**
Nobiltà poco si prezza, se vi manca la ricchezza.

Sim. *Nothing agreeth worse than a lord's heart and a beggar's purse.*

1352 **Whom the LORD loveth, he chasteneth.**
A chi Dio vuol bene, manda delle pene.
Il Signore corregge colui che egli ama.

o Hebrews 12, 6 / Ebrei 12, 6

1353 New LORDS, new laws.
Nuovo principe, nuove leggi.
Nuovo principe, nuove usanze.

1354 The LOSER is always laughed at.
Chi ha il danno, ha pur le beffe.
Cf. *LOSERS are always in the wrong / LOSS embraces shame.*

1355 LOSERS are always in the wrong.
Chi perde sempre ha torto.
Cf. *The LOSER is always laughed at / LOSS embraces shame.*

1356 One never LOSES by doing a good turn.
Piacere fatto non va perduto.
A far servizio non ci si perde.
Il servizio torna sempre a casa col guadagno.
Cf. *A good DEED is never lost.*

1357 LOSS embraces shame.
Il danno abbraccia la vergogna.
Cf. *The LOSER is always laughed at / LOSERS are always in the wrong.*

1358 One man's LOSS is another man's gain.
Niun perde che altro non guadagni.
Non è mai mal per uno che non sia ben per un altro.
Cf. *One man's BREATH, another's death.*

1359 He would skin a LOUSE, and send the hide to the market.
Scorticherebbe il pidocchio per aver la pelle.

1360 Don't toy with LOVE.
Non si scherza con l'amore.

1361 He that has LOVE in his breast has spurs in his sides.
Chi ha l'amor nel petto ha lo spron nei fianchi.

1362 LOVE and a cough cannot be hid.
Amore e tosse non si nascondono.
Il fuoco, l'amore e la tosse presto si conosce.
Sim. *Love and smoke cannot be hidden.*

1363 LOVE and business teach eloquence.
L'amore, l'inganno e il bisogno insegnano la rettorica.

1364 LOVE and lordship like no fellowship.
Amore e signoria non voglion compagnia.
Amore e signoria non soffron compagnia.

1365 LOVE asks faith, and faith asks firmness.
Amore vuol fede, e fede vuol fermezza.

1366 LOVE begets love.
Amore nasce d'amore.
Chi vuol essere amato convien che ami.
Amato non sarai se a te solo penserai.

Sim. *Show your love to win love.*

1367 LOVE, being jealous, makes a good eye look asquint.
Amor, occhio ben sano fa spesso veder torto.

1368 LOVE can neither be bought nor sold; its only price is love.
Amore con amor si paga.
Amore non si compra né si vende, ma in premio d'amor, amor si rende.

Sim. *Love is the true reward of love.*

1369 LOVE cannot be compelled.
Al cuor non si comanda.
Cosa fatta per forza, non vale una scorza.

Sim. *Fanned fires and forced love never did well yet.*

1370 LOVE covers many infirmities.
L'amore ricopre ogni colpa.
La carità ricopre ogni misfatto.

Sim. *Love sees no faults / Love covers many faults.*

o Proverbs 10, 12 / Proverbi 10, 12

1371 LOVE does much, money does everything.
Amor fa molto, il denaro fa tutto.

Var. *Love does much, but money does more.*
Cf. *MONEY will do anything.*

1372 LOVE is a sweet torment.
Amore non è senza amaro.

Sim. *Love is full of trouble.*
Cf. *The course of true LOVE never did run smooth.*

1373 LOVE is blind.
L'amore è cieco.

Cf. *AFFECTION blinds reason.*

1374 LOVE is full of fear.
Chi ama, teme.
Con l'amore sta il timore.
Non è vero amore quel ch'è senza timore.
Quando si vuole bene si ha sempre paura.

1375 LOVE is lawless.
Amor regge senza legge.

1376 LOVE is never without jealousy.
Non c'è amore senza gelosia.
Amore e gelosia nascono in compagnia.

1377 LOVE is strong as death.
L'amore è forte come la morte.
o Song of Solomon 8, 6 / Cantico dei Cantici 8, 6

1378 LOVE is sweet in the beginning but sour in the ending.
L'amore dinanzi ha il miele, e di dietro si attacca il fiele.
L'amore è come il cetriolo, comincia dolce e finisce amaro.

1379 LOVE is the fruit of idleness.
In amoroso stato non dura l'occupato.

1380 LOVE is the loadstone of love.
L'amor di amor suol esser calamita.

1381 LOVE is without reason.
Quando è alta la passione, è bassa la ragione.

Sim. *No folly like being in love.*

1382 LOVE lives in cottages as well as in courts.
L'amore si trova tanto sotto la lana che sotto la seta.

1383 LOVE makes all equal.
Ogni disuguaglianza amore agguaglia.

1384 LOVE me little, love me long.
Amami poco, ma continua.

1385 LOVE rules his kingdom without a sword.
Amor regge il suo regno senza spada.

1386 LOVE will find a way.
Tutto vince amor.

Cf. *LOVE will go through stone walls.*

1387 LOVE will go through stone walls.
L'amore passa sette muri.

Cf. *LOVE will find a way.*

1388 No LOVE is foul, nor prison fair.
Niuna prigione è bella, e niuna amante è brutta.

1389 No LOVE like the first love.
Il primo amore non si scorda mai.
I primi amori sono i migliori.

Cf. *Old LOVE will not be forgotten / Of SOUP and love, the first is the best.*

1390 **Old LOVE does not rust.**
Amor vecchio non fa ruggine.

1391 **Old LOVE will not be forgotten.**
Amor nuovo va e viene ed il vecchio si mantiene.

Sim. *One always returns to his/her first love / Old love is easily kindled.*
Cf. *No LOVE like the first love / Of SOUP and love, the first is the best.*

1392 **One LOVE expels another.**
Un amore scaccia l'altro.

Cf. *The new LOVE drives out the old love.*

1393 **Perfect LOVE casteth out fear.**
L'amore perfetto scaccia il timore.
La compiuta carità caccia fuori la paura.

o I John 4, 18 / I Giovanni 4, 18

1394 **The course of true LOVE never did run smooth.**
Dov'è grand'amore quivi è gran dolore.
Se ne vanno gli amori e restano i dolori.

Var. *The path of true love never runs smooth.*
Sim. *The road to love is bumpy.*

1395 **The LOVE of money is the root of all evil.**
L'attaccamento al denaro è la radice di tutti i mali.
La radice di tutti i mali è l'avarizia.

Var. *Money is the root of all evil.*

o I Timothy 6, 10 / I Timoteo 6, 10

1396 **The new LOVE drives out the old love.**
Gli amori nuovi fanno dimenticare i vecchi.
Come chiodo scaccia chiodo, così amore scaccia amor.

Cf. *One LOVE expels another.*

1397 **The remedy for LOVE is land between.**
La lontananza ogni gran piaga salda.

Sim. *The only victory over love is flight.*
Cf. *In LOVE's war he who flies is conqueror.*

1398 **Where LOVE is, there is faith.**
Chi ama crede.

1399 Who marries for LOVE without money, has good nights and sorry days.
Chi si marita per amore, di notte ha piacere e di giorno ha dolore.

1400 In LOVE's war he who flies is conqueror.
Nella guerra d'amor vince chi fugge.

Sim. *The only victory over love is flight.*
Cf. *The remedy for LOVE is land between.*

1401 There is nothing worse than an old LOVER.
Non v'è cosa peggiore che in vecchio pizzicor d'amore.

1402 LOVERS think others blind.
Pensano gli innamorati che gli altri siano ciechi.

Var. *Lovers think others have no eyes.*

1403 The falling out of LOVERS is the renewing of love.
Sdegno cresce amore.

Var. Sim. *Love's anger is fuel to love.*
Cf. *LOVERS' tiffs are harmless / SCORN at first makes after-love the more.*

1404 LOVERS' tiffs are harmless.
Chi ti berteggia, ti vagheggia.

Cf. *The falling out of LOVERS is the renewing of love / SCORN at first makes after-love the more.*

1405 He LOVES me well that makes my belly swell.
Chi mi dà da mangiar, tengo da quello.

Cf. *He is my FRIEND that grinds at my mill.*

1406 He that LOVES well sees afar off.
Chi vuol bene vede da lontano.

1407 He who LOVES well will never forget.
Chi ama non oblia.

1408 LUCKY men need no counsel.
Non occorre di consigliar il fortunato.

M

1409 **Every man is MAD on some point.**
Ognuno ha un ramo di pazzia.

Sim. *Every man is a fool sometimes and none at all times.*
Cf. *Every one has a FOOL in his sleeve / No man is WISE at all time.*

1410 **They that buy MAGISTRACY must sell justice.**
Chi compra il magistrato vende la giustizia.

1411 **A MAID that laughs is half taken.**
Donna che ride, ti ha detto di sì.
La donna ridarella, o matta o puttanella.

1412 **While the tall MAID is stooping, the little one hath swept the house.**
Mentre la grande s'abbassa, la piccola scopa la casa.

1413 **A great MAN and a great river are often ill neighbours.**
Né mulo, né mulino, né signore per vicino.
Né mulo, né mulino, né fiume, né forno, né signore per vicino.

Sim. *A great lord is a bad neighbour.*

1414 **A MAN assaulted is half taken.**
Uomo assalito è mezzo perso.
Uomo affrontato è mezzo morto.

1415 **A MAN is as old as he feels, and a woman as old as she looks.**
Gli uomini hanno gli anni che sentono, e le donne quelli che mostrano.

1416 **A MAN is not so soon healed as hurt.**
È più facile far le piaghe che sanarle.

1417 **A MAN may cut himself with his own knife.**
Folle è chi del suo proprio coltello si taglia.

1418 **A MAN of straw is worth a woman of gold.**
Un uomo di paglia vale una donna d'oro.

1419 **A MAN without a wife is but half a man.**
Uomo senza moglie è mosca senza capo.
Senza moglie a lato, l'uom non è beato.

Var. *A man is only half a man without a wife.*
Sim. *A man without a woman is like a ship without a sail.*
Cf. *It is not good that the man should be ALONE.*

1420 **A solitary MAN is either a beast or an angel.**
Uomo solitario, o bestia o angelo.

Var. *Man alone is either a saint or a devil.*

1421 **A valiant MAN esteems every place to be his own country.**
Ogni paese al valentuomo è patria.

Sim. *Go where he will, the wise man is at home, his hearth the earth, his hall the azure dome.*

1422 **Beware of a silent MAN and still water.**
Guardati da can rabbioso e da uomo sospettoso.
Uomo che ghigna, can che ringhia, non te ne fidare.

Var. *Beware of a silent dog and still water.*

1423 **Every MAN after his fashion.**
Ognuno a suo modo, e gli asini all'antica.

1424 **Every MAN as he loves, quoth the good man when he kissed his cow.**
Ad ognuno come piace, diceva colui che baciava la vacca.

1425 **Every MAN for himself and God for us all.**
Ognuno per sè, e Dio per tutti.

1426 **Every MAN has his faults.**
Nessun uomo senza difetti.
Tutti abbiamo i nostri difetti.

Cf. *Shew me a MAN without a spot, and I'll shew you a maid without a fault.*

1427 **Every MAN is best known to himself.**
Ognuno sa sé.
Ognuno sa sé e Dio sa tutti.

1428 **Every MAN is nearest himself.**
Il primo prossimo è se stesso.
L'io sta al numero uno.

Cf. *CHARITY begins at home.*

1429 **Every MAN likes his own thing best.**
A ciascuno piace il suo.
Ogni naso par bello alla sua faccia.

1430 **Every MAN must walk in his own trade.**
Ognuno all'arte sua, e il bue all'aratro.

Var. *Every man must walk in his own calling.*
Sim. *Every man as his business lies.*

o I Corinthians 7, 20 / I Corinzi 7, 20

1431 Every MAN should take his own.
A ciascuno il suo.

Cf. *Render unto CAESAR the things which are Caesar's.*

1432 MAN is a wolf to man.
L'uomo è lupo all'uomo.

1433 MAN is to man a God.
L'uomo è Dio all'uomo.

1434 MAN proposes, God disposes.
L'uomo propone, e Dio dispone.

1435 No MAN is a hero to his valet.
Nessuno è eroe per il suo cameriere.
Davanti al cameriere non v'ha Eccellenza.

Var. *No man is a hero to his wife or his butler.*

1436 No MAN is born into the world, whose work is not born with him.
L'uomo fu creato per lavorare, come l'uccello per volare.

1437 Shew me a MAN without a spot, and I'll shew you a maid without a fault.
Non vi è lino senza resca, né donna senza pecca.
Non c'è uomo che non erri, né cavallo che non sferri.

Cf. *Every MAN has its faults.*

1438 The healthful MAN can give counsel to the sick.
Il sano consiglia bene il malato.

1439 The hurt MAN writes with steel on a marble stone.
Le offese si iscrivono nel marmo, i benefizi tosto si dimenticano.
Chi offende scrive in polvere di paglia, chi è offeso, nei marmi lo sdegno intaglia.

Sim. *Injuries are written in brass.*

1440 When a MAN sleeps his head is in his stomach.
Chi dorme si trova la testa nello stomaco.

1441 Of evil MANNERS spring good laws.
Dai mali costumi nascono le buone leggi.

Cf. *The LAW grows of sin, and chastises it.*

1442 MANY are called, but few are chosen.
Molti sono i chiamati, ma pochi gli eletti.

o Matthew 20, 16; 22, 14 / Matteo 20, 16; 22, 14

1443 MANY small make a great.
Molti pochi fanno un assai.

Sim. *Many a little makes a mickle.*
Cf. *Many DROPS make a shower / PENNY and penny laid up will be many.*

1444 A dry MARCH, wet April and cool May, fill barn and cellar and bring much hay.
April piovoso, maggio ventoso, anno fruttuoso.

Cf. *APRIL rains for men; May, for beasts.*

1445 He that speaks ill of the MARE would buy her.
Chi dice mal della cavalla, la vuol menar via.

Cf. *He that BLAMES would buy.*

1446 A good MARKSMAN may miss.
Sbaglia il prete all'altare e il contadino all'aratro.
Sbaglia anche il prete all'altare.

1447 MARRIAGE is a lottery.
Il matrimonio è un terno al lotto.

1448 MARRIAGE makes or mars a man.
Il matrimonio non è per tutti, chi fa belli e chi fa brutti.

1449 At MARRIAGES and funerals, friends are discerned from kinsfolk.
Alle nozze e alla morte si conoscon gli amici.

1450 MARRIAGES are made in heaven.
Matrimoni e vescovati son dal cielo destinati.
Nozze e magistrato, dal cielo è destinato.

Cf. *HANGING and wiving go by destiny.*

1451 A MARRIED man turns his staff into a stake.
Uomo ammogliato, uccello in gabbia.
Uomo sposato è uomo imprigionato.

1452 He that goes far to be MARRIED will either deceive or be deceived.
Chi di lontano si va a maritare, sarà ingannato o vuol ingannare.

Var. *He that goes a great way for a wife is either cheated or means to cheat.*

1453 He that MARRIES for wealth, sells his liberty.
Dov'entra dote, esce libertà.

1454 Who MARRIES does well, who marries not does better.
Chi si marita fa bene, chi no, meglio.

1455 Before you MARRY, be sure of a house, wherein to tarry.
Innanzi il maritare, abbi l'abitare.

1456 **MARRY in haste, and repent at leisure.**
Chi si marita in fretta, stenta adagio.
Chi mal si marita non esce mai di fatica.

   Sim. *Marriage rides upon the saddle and repentance upon the crupper.*

1457 **MARRY in May, repent alway.**
Nel maggio non si fanno nozze.

1458 **MARRY your equal.**
Il parentato dev'esser pari.

   Var. *Marry your like (match).*
   Cf. *Like BLOOD, like good, and like age, make the happiest marriage.*

1459 **It is better to be a MARTYR than a confessor.**
È meglio esser martire che confessore.

1460 **Better MASTER one than engage with ten.**
È meglio esser padrone di un testone, che servo di un milione.

1461 **Like MASTER, like man.**
Tal padrone, tal servitore.

1462 **MASTER absent and house dead.**
Tristo a quell'avere che il suo signor non vede.

1463 **None is born a MASTER.**
Nessuno nasce maestro.

   Sim. *No man is his craft's master the first day.*

1464 **No man can serve two MASTERS.**
Non si può servire a due padroni.
Chi due padroni ha da servire, ad uno ha da mentire.

   Cf. *You cannot serve GOD and Mammon.*

   o Matthew 6, 24 / Matteo 6, 24; Luke 16, 13 / Luca 16, 13

1465 **St. MATTHIAS breaks the ice; if he finds none, he will make it.**
A San Mattia, la neve per la via.

1466 **A wet MAY brings plenty of hay.**
Maggio fresco e ventoso, rende l'anno copioso.
Maggio molle, lin per le donne.

1467 **Cast ne'er a clout till MAY be out.**
Né di maggio né di maggione, non ti levare il pelliccione.

   Cf. *Till APRIL's dead, change not a thread.*

1468 **He that is not with ME is against me.**
Chi non è con me è contro di me.

   o Matthew 12, 30 / Matteo 12, 30; Luke 11, 23 / Luca 11, 23

1469 **The MEAN is the best.**
La migliore è la via di mezzo.

Sim. *The middle way of measure is ever golden.*

1470 **Use the MEANS, and God will give the blessing.**
Comincia, che Dio provvede al resto.

1471 **And with what MEASURE you meet, it shall be measured to you again.**
Secondo la misura che farai, misurato ancor sarai.

o Matthew 7, 2 / Matteo 7, 2; Luke 6, 38 / Luca 6, 38

1472 **MEASURE thrice what thou buyest; and cut it but once.**
Misura tre volte e taglia una.
Tre misure e un taglio.

Var. *Measure twice, cut but once.*

1473 **There is a MEASURE in all things.**
Ogni cosa vuol misura.
Per fare vita pura, conviene arte e misura.

Sim. *Measure is treasure / Moderation in all things.*

1474 **He that MEASURES not himself is measured.**
Chi non si misura, è misurato.

1475 **After MEAT, mustard.**
Arrivare a piatti lavati.

Var. *After dinner, mustard.*
Cf. *After DEATH the doctor.*

1476 **He who eats the MEAT, let him pick the bone.**
Chi mangia la carne, roda anche le ossa.

1477 **New MEAT begets new appetite.**
Il variar vivande accresce l'appetito.

1478 **Sweet MEAT will have sour sauce.**
Dolce vivanda vuol salsa acerba.

1479 **They that have no other MEAT, bread and butter are glad to eat.**
Quando si ha fame il pane sa di carne.
Chi non può avere la carne, beva il brodo.

Sim. *Acorns were good till bread was found / Better a louse (mouse) in the pot than no flesh at all.*
Cf. *If thou hast not a CAPON, feed on an onion.*

1480 **Every MEDAL has its reverse.**
Ogni medaglia ha il suo rovescio.
Sim. *There are two sides to everything.*

1481 **The MEEK will inherit the earth.**
I miti possederanno la terra.

o Matthew 5, 5 / Matteo 5, 5; Psalms 36, 11,29 / Salmi 37, 11,29

1482 **All MEN are equal before the law.**
Tutti sono uguali dinanzi alla legge.
La legge è uguale per tutti.

1483 **All MEN are free of other men's goods.**
Della roba d'altri si spende senza risparmio.
Sim. *Men are very generous with what costs them nothing.*
Cf. *Men cut large THONGS of other men's leather.*

1484 **All MEN are mortal.**
Gli uomini sono mortali.
Sim. *It is as natural to die as to be born / Our lives are but our marches to the grave.*
Cf. *As soon as a man is BORN he begins to die / He that is once BORN, once must die / All that LIVES must die.*

o II Corinthians, 1, 9 / II Corinzi 1, 9

1485 **Honest MEN marry soon, wise men not at all.**
Gli uomini dabbene si maritano e i savi no.

1486 **MEN are not to be measured by inches.**
Gli uomini non si misurano a canne.

1487 **MEN, not walls, make a city safe.**
Le mura non fanno le città, ma gli uomini.

1488 **So many MEN, so many opinions.**
Tanti uomini, tanti pareri.
Var. *Many men have many minds.*
Cf. *So many HEADS, so many minds.*

1489 **Tall MEN had ever very empty heads.**
Uomo lungo, testa corta.

1490 **There are more MEN threatened than stricken.**
Più sono i minacciati che gli uccisi.
Molte minacce non ammazzano la gente.

1491 **Either MEND or end.**
O mangiare questa minestra o saltare da quella finestra.
Cf. *SINK or swim.*

1492 If every man MEND one, all shall be mended.
Se ciascuno volesse emendare uno, tutti sarebbero emendati.

1493 A MERCHANT that gains not, loses.
Dove non v'è guadagno la perdita è sicura.

1494 He that loses is MERCHANT as well as he that gains.
Tanto è mercante quello che perde che quello che guadagna.

1495 MESSENGERS should neither be headed nor hanged.
Ambasciator non porta pena.

1496 MIGHT is right.
Il più forte ha sempre ragione.
La forza ammazza la ragione.

Var. *Might makes right / Might overcomes right.*

1497 MILK says to wine, Welcome friend.
Latte sopra vino è veleno.
Latte su vino è veleno, ma vino su latte è buono per tutti.

1498 The MILL cannot grind with the water that is past.
Acqua passata non macina più.

Var. *Water that has passed cannot make the mill go.*

1499 Every MILLER draws water to his own mill.
Ognuno tira l'acqua al suo mulino.

1500 MILLS and wives are ever wanting.
Al mulino e alla sposa, manca sempre qualche cosa.

1501 MILLS will not grind if you give them not water.
Il mulino non macina senz'acqua.

1502 The MILLS of God grind slowly, yet they grind exceeding small.
I mulini di Dio macinano adagio, ma tanto più amare sono le semole.

Var. *God's mill grinds slow but sure.*
Cf. *PUNISHMENT is lame, but it comes.*

1503 A contented MIND is a continual feast.
Mente sicura, banchetto continuo.

Cf. *CONTENT is happiness.*

o Proverbs 15, 15 / Proverbi 15, 15

1504 A sound MIND in a sound body.
Mente sana in corpo sano.

1505 **Great MINDS think alike.**
Le grandi menti si assomigliano.

Sim. *Great wits jump.*

1506 **The best MIRROR is an old friend.**
Non c'è miglior specchio, dell'amico vecchio.

1507 **The MIRTH of the world dureth but a while.**
Allegrezza di questo mondo dura poco.

1508 **He that MISCHIEF hatches, mischief catches.**
Chi mal semina, mal raccoglie.
Chi semina malizia, obbrobrio miete.
Chi desidera il male ad altri, al suo sta vicino.

Cf. *He that HURTS another hurts himself.*

1509 **MISCHIEF comes by the pound and goes away by the ounce.**
Il male viene a carrate, e va via a oncie.
Il male viene a cavallo e se ne va a piedi.

Cf. *DISEASES come on horseback, but go away on foot.*

1510 **It is MISERY enough to have once been happy.**
Grave è la tristezza che segue l'allegrezza.

1511 **MISFORTUNES never come singly.**
Un malanno non vien mai solo.

Var. *Misfortunes never come alone.*
Sim. *One misfortune comes on the neck of another / It never rains but it pours.*
Cf. *DISGRACES are like cherries, one draws another / Of one ILL come many.*

1512 **MISRECKONING is no payment.**
Errore non fa pagamento.

1513 **He who makes no MISTAKES makes nothing.**
Solo chi non fa niente è certo di non errare.
Chi non fa mai nulla, di nulla si confessa.
Chi non fa, non falla.

Var. *He who never made a mistake never made anything.*

1514 **Like MISTRESS, like maid.**
Tal padrona, tal serva.

1515 **A man without MONEY is no man at all.**
Uomo senza quattrini è un morto che cammina.
Uomo senza roba è una pecora senza lana.

Sim. *A man without money is a bow without an arrow.*
Cf. *A GENTLEMAN without an estate is like a pudding without suet.*

1516 He that has MONEY and capers is provided for Lent.
Chi ha denari e capperi è fornito per Quaresima.

1517 He that has MONEY has what he wants.
Chi ha quattrini ha tutto.

1518 He that has no MONEY needs no purse.
Chi non ha denari non ha che far di borsa.

1519 If you have no MONEY in your purse, you must have honey in your mouth.
Chi non ha denari in borsa, abbia miele in bocca.

Var. *He that has no honey in his pot, let him have it in his mouth / He that has not silver in his purse, should have silk on his tongue.*

1520 Lend your MONEY and lose your friend.
Amico beneficato, nemico dichiarato.
Se vuoi farti un nemico, prestagli quattrini.
Chi presta, perde l'amico e il denaro.

Sim. *When I lent, I had a friend; but when I asked, he was unkind.*
Cf. *If you would make an ENEMY, lend a man money, and ask it of him again.*

1521 MONEY can't buy happiness.
I soldi non fanno la felicità.

1522 MONEY draws money.
I soldi chiamano soldi.
Il denaro è fratello del denaro.
La roba va alla roba.

Sim. *Money begets money.*
Cf. *MONEY makes money.*

1523 MONEY has no smell.
I soldi non hanno odore.
Il denaro non puzza.

Sim. *Money is welcome, though it come in a dirty clout.*

1524 MONEY is a good servant, but a bad master.
Il denaro è un buon servo ed un cattivo padrone.

1525 MONEY is round, and rolls away.
I denari sono tondi e ruzzolano.

1526 MONEY is the god of the world.
Il denaro è il re del mondo.
L'oro governa il mondo.

1527 MONEY is the sinews of war.
Il denaro è il nervo della guerra.
Il denaro fa la guerra.

1528 MONEY makes money.
I denari fanno denari.
Soldo fa soldo.
Il denaro è fratello del denaro.

Cf. *MONEY draws money.*

1529 MONEY makes the man.
Il danaro fa l'uomo intero.

Cf. *It IS not what is he, but what has he.*

1530 MONEY makes the mare go.
I danari fanno correre i cavalli.
Il quattrino fa cantare il cieco.

1531 MONEY opens all doors.
Il denaro apre tutte le porte.

1532 MONEY talks.
Nulla di più eloquente che il denaro contante.

Sim. *Gold is an orator.*

1533 MONEY will do anything.
Con i soldi si fa tutto.
Coi quattrini si fa tutto.

Sim. *All things are obedient to money / Money commands all.*
Cf. *LOVE does much, money does everything.*

1534 Of MONEY, wisdom, and good faith, there is commonly less than men count upon.
Denari, senno e fede, ce n'è manco l'uom crede.
Quattrini e fede, meno ch'un si crede.

1535 Of MONEY, wit and virtue, believe one-fourth of what you hear.
Denari e santità, credine la metà della metà.
Danari e santità, metà della metà.

1536 Public MONEY is like holy water, everybody helps himself to it.
I denari del comune sono come l'acqua benedetta, ognun ne piglia.

1537 The MONEY you refuse will never do you good.
Denari rifiutati non si spendono.

1538 **A MONK out of his cloister is like a fish out of water.**
Religioso fuor della sua cella, pesce fuor dell'acqua.

1539 **A runaway MONK never praises his convent.**
Monaco vagabondo non disse mai ben del suo convento.

1540 **Pale MOON does rain, red moon does blow: white moon does neither rain nor snow.**
Quando la luna è bianca, il tempo è bello; se è rossa, significa vento; se pallida, pioggia.

1541 **The MOON does not heed the barking of dogs.**
La luna non cura l'abbaiar dei cani.

Var. *The dog (wolf) barks in vain at the moon.*
Sim. *Dogs bark, but the caravan goes on.*

1542 **The MOON is not seen where the sun shines.**
Quando il sol ti splende, non ti curar della luna.

Var. *Stars are not seen where the sun shines.*

1543 **The MORE you get, the more you want.**
Chi più ha, più desidera.

Cf. *MUCH would have more / He that has PLENTY of good shall have more.*

1544 **He who sleeps all the MORNING, may go a begging all the day after.**
Chi dorme grassa mattinata, va mendicando la giornata.
Chi si cava il sonno, non si cava la fame.

1545 **In the MORNING mountains, in the evening fountains.**
La mattina al monte, la sera al fonte.

1546 **A light-heeled MOTHER makes a heavy-heeled daughter.**
La madre da fatti fa la figliuola misera.

1547 **A pitiful MOTHER makes a scabby daughter.**
La madre pietosa fa la figlia tignosa.
La madre pietosa fa la figlia viziosa.

Var. *A tender mother breeds a scalby daughter.*
Cf. *Spare the ROD and spoil the child.*

1548 **Like MOTHER, like daughter.**
Qual è la madre, tal è la figlia.
Quale madre, tale figlia.

Cf. *An APPLE never falls far from the tree / A CHIP off the old block / Like FATHER, like son.*

o Ezekiel 16, 44 / Ezekiele 16, 44

1549 The good MOTHER says not, Will you? but gives.
La buona madre non dice: Vuoi tu? ma dà.

1550 MOTHER-IN-LAW and daughter-in-law are a tempest and hail storm.
Suocera e nuora, tempesta e gragnuola.

1551 Four good MOTHERS have four bad daughters: truth, hatred; prosperity, pride; security, peril; familiarity, contempt.
Quattro madri buone fanno figliuoli cattivi: la Verità l'Odio, la Prosperità il Fasto, la Sicurtà il Pericolo, la Famigliarità il Dispregio.

1552 A MOUNTAIN and a river are good neighbours.
Monte, porto, città, bosco o torrente, abbi se puoi per vicino o parente.

1553 If the MOUNTAIN will not come to Mahomed, Mahomed must go to the mountain.
Se la montagna non va a Maometto, Maometto andrà alla montagna.

Var. *If the mountain will not go to Mahomet, Mahomet must go to the mountain.*

1554 The higher the MOUNTAIN, the greater descent.
Quanto più alto il monte, tanto più profonda la valle.
A gran salita, gran discesa.

Var. *The higher the mountain, the lower the vale.*
Sim. *The bigger they are, the harder they fall.*
Cf. *Hasty CLIMBERS have sudden falls / The higher STANDING, the lower fall.*

1555 Behind the MOUNTAINS there are people to be found.
Al di là del monte c'è gente anche.

1556 The MOUNTAINS have brought forth a mouse.
Partoriscono i monti e nasce un topo.

1557 A MOUSE in time may bite in two a cable.
Col tempo il sorcio rode la fune.

1558 The MOUSE that has but one hole is soon caught.
Tristo quel sorcio che ha un buco solo.
Guai a quel topo che ha un sol buco per salvarsi!

1559 What may the MOUSE do against the cat.
Molto sa il topo, ma però più il gatto.

1560 A close MOUTH catches no flies.
In bocca chiusa non entrano mosche.
In bocca chiusa non entrò mai mosca.

Var. *Into a shut mouth flies fly not.*

1561 A cool MOUTH, and warm feet, live long.
Bocca umida, e piede asciutto.

1562 A man cannot have his MOUTH full of flour and also blow the fire.
Non si può tenere la farina in bocca e soffiare.

Sim. *No man can sup and blow together.*
Cf. *A man cannot WHISTLE and drink at the same time.*

1563 It's by the MOUTH of the cow that the milk comes.
Le galline fanno l'uova dal becco.
Dal becco vien l'uovo.

1564 Keep your MOUTH shut and your eyes open.
Bocca chiusa e occhi aperti.

1565 Ask MUCH to have a little.
Chi vuole assai, non domandi poco.

1566 MUCH would have more.
Chi più ne ha, più ne vorrebbe.

Cf. *The MORE you get, the more you want / He that has PLENTY of good shall have more.*

1567 Nought is that MUSE that finds no excuse.
Triste quella musa che non sa trovar una scusa.

1568 MUSIC helps not the toothache.
A dolor di dente non aiuta strumento.

1569 MUSIC is the eye of the ear.
La musica è l'occhio dell'orecchio.

1570 What MUST be, must be.
Quel che ha da essere, sarà.
Che sarà, sarà.

Sim. *Whatever happens, all happens as it should.*
Cf. *There is no flying from FATE / He that is born to be HANGED shall be never drowned.*

N

1571 **For want of a NAIL the shoe was lost; for want of a shoe the horse was lost; for want of a horse the rider was lost.**
Per un chiodo si perde un ferro, e per un ferro si perde un cavallo, e per un cavallo si perde un cavaliere.
Per un punto Martin perse la cappa.

 Sim. *Oft times for sparing of a little cost a man has lost the large coat for the hood.*

1572 **One NAIL drives out another.**
Chiodo scaccia chiodo.

 Cf. *One DEVIL drives out another / LIKE cures like / One POISON drives out another.*

1573 **No NAKED man is sought after to be rifled.**
Non si può spogliar il nudo.
Cento ladri non possono spogliare un uomo nudo.

 Cf. *The BEGGAR may sing before the thief.*

1574 **A good NAME is better than riches.**
È meglio aver buon nome che molte ricchezze.
Val più un'oncia di reputazione che mille libbre d'oro.
Meglio povertà onorata che ricchezza svergognata.

Var. *A good name is better than gold.*
Sim. *A good name is better than a good face.*

 o Proverbs 22, 1 / Proverbi 22, 1

1575 **Get a good NAME and go to bed.**
Acquista buona fama, e mettiti a dormire.
Fatti buon nome e piscia a letto, e diranno che hai sudato.
Fatti fama e coricati.

Var. *Get a good name of early rising and you may lie abed / He who gets a name of early rising may sleep al day.*

1576 **He that has an ill NAME is half hanged.**
Chi ha cattivo nome è mezzo impiccato.
Chi ha persa la fama è morto al mondo.

Sim. *An ill wound is cured, not an ill name.*
Cf. *Ill DEEMED, half hanged.*

1577 **See NAPLES and die.**
Vedi Napoli e poi muori.

1578 **NATURE draws more than ten oxen.**
Natura tira più che cento cavalli.
Cf. *BEAUTY draws more than oxen.*

1579 **NATURE is content with a little.**
Di poco si contenta la natura.

1580 **NATURE is the true law.**
La vera legge è la natura.

1581 **NATURE passes art.**
La natura può più dell'arte.

1582 **NATURE, time and patience are the three great physicians.**
La natura, il tempo e la pazienza, tre medici principali.

1583 **NECESSITY and opportunity may make a coward valiant.**
Il bisogno fa l'uomo bravo.

1584 **NECESSITY has no law.**
Necessità non ha legge.

1585 **NECESSITY is the mother of invention.**
Necessità è madre dell'invenzione.
La necessità aguzza l'ingegno.
Il bisogno aguzza l'ingegno.
Il bisogno fa l'uomo ingegnoso.

Cf. *The BELLY teaches all arts / HUNGER is the teacher of the arts / POVERTY is the mother of all arts.*

1586 **NEED makes the old wife trot.**
Il bisogno fa trottar la vecchia.

Sim. *Need makes the naked man run and sorrow makes websters spin.*

1587 **NEED makes virtue.**
La necessità conduce a Dio.

1588 **When NEED is highest, God's help is nighest.**
Quando è maggiore il bisogno, l'aiuto di Dio è più vicino.
Quando il caso par disperato, la provvidenza è vicina.

Sim. *When the night's darkest, the dawn's nearest.*

1589 NEEDLES and pins, needles and pins: when a man marries his trouble begins.
Chi non sa quel che sia malanno e doglie, se non è maritato, prenda moglie.

1590 Two NEGATIVES make an affirmative.
Due negazioni affermano.

1591 A good NEIGHBOUR, a good morrow.
Chi ha il buon vicino, ha il buon mattutino.

    Sim. *All is well with him who is beloved of his neighbours / You must ask your neighbour if you shall live in peace.*
    Cf. A near NEIGHBOUR is better than a far-dwelling kinsman.

1592 A near NEIGHBOUR is better than a far-dwelling kinsman.
Meglio un prossimo vicino che un lontano cugino.
La vicinanza è mezza parentela.

    Var. *Better is a neighbour that is near than a brother far off.*
    Sim. *All is well with him who is beloved of his neighbours.*
    Cf. A good FRIEND is my nearest relation / A good NEIGHBOUR, a good morrow.

    o Proverbs 27, 10 / Proverbi 27, 10

1593 An ill NEIGHBOUR is an ill thing.
Chi ha il mal vicino, ha il mattutino.

1594 Love thy NEIGHBOUR as thyself.
Amerai il prossimo tuo come te stesso.

    o Leviticus 19, 18 / Levitico 19, 18; Matthew 19, 19; 22, 39 / Matteo 19, 19; 22, 39; Mark 12, 31,33 / Marco 12, 31,33; Luke 12, 27 / Luca 12, 27; Romans 13, 9 / Romani 13, 9; Galatians 5, 14 / Galati 5, 14

1595 Love your NEIGHBOUR, yet pull not down your hedge.
Amate i vicini, senza togliere i confini.

    Sim. *Good fences make good neighbours.*
    Cf. A HEDGE between keeps friendship green / A WALL between preserves love.

1596 Our NEIGHBOUR's ground yields better corn than ours.
Sempre par più grande la parte del compagno.

    Sim. *Our neighbour's cow yields more milk than ours.*
    Cf. All his GEESE are swans / The GRASS is always greener on the other side of the fence.

1597 **When your NEIGHBOUR's house is on fire, beware of your own.**
Quando l'incendio è nel vicinato, porta l'acqua a casa tua.
Quando brucia nel vicinato, porta l'acqua a casa tua.
Var. *Look to thyself when thy neighbour's house is on fire.*

1598 **He dwells far from NEIGHBOURS that is fain to praise himself.**
Chi loda se stesso ha cattivi vicini.

1599 **In vain the NET is spread in the sight of any bird.**
Indarno si tende la rete in vista degli uccelli.

    o Proverbs 1, 17 / Proverbi 1, 17

1600 **It is in vain to cast your NET where there is no fish.**
In fiume senza pesce non si gettan le reti.

1601 **Everything NEW is fine.**
Di novello, tutto è bello.

Sim. *New things are fair.*

1602 **Bad NEWS has wings.**
Le cattive nuove volano.

Var. *Bad news travels fast.*
Sim. *Ill news comes apace.*

1603 **He that brings good NEWS knocks hard.**
Arditamente batte alla porta, chi buone nuove apporta.

Var. *He knocks boldly who brings good news.*

1604 **Ill NEWS is too often true.**
Le male nuove son sempre vere.

1605 **No NEWS is good news.**
Nessuna nuova, buona nuova.
Nulla nuova, buona nuova.

1606 **NIGHT is the mother of counsel.**
La notte porta consiglio.

Sim. *To take counsel of (consult with) one's pillow.*

1607 **The NIGHT comes when no man can work.**
Viene la notte quando nessuno può più operare.

    o John 9, 4 / Giovanni 9, 4

1608 **To a great NIGHT, a great lanthorn.**
A gran notte, gran lanterna.

1609 **What is done by NIGHT appears by day.**
Quel che si fa all'oscuro, apparisce al sole.

o Luke 12, 3 / Luca 12, 3

1610 **NO and yes causes long disputes.**
Il sì e il no governano il mondo.

1611 **He that has NOTHING need fear to lose nothing.**
Chi non ha niente, non teme niente.

Sim. *You cannot lose what you never had.*
Cf. *A man cannot GIVE what he hasn't got / Where nothing is, the KING must lose his right.*

1612 **NOTHING comes of nothing.**
Con niente non si fa niente.
Col nulla non si fa nulla.

Var. *From nothing nothing can come.*
Sim. *Nought lay down, nought take up.*

1613 **NOUGHT will be nought.**
Zero via zero fa zero.

1614 **NURTURE passes nature.**
Nutritura passa natura.

Cf. *ART improves nature.*

O

1615 **An OAK is not felled at one stroke.**
Al primo colpo non cade un albero.
D'un solo colpo non s'abbatte la quercia.

Sim. *Little (Many) strokes fell great (tall) oaks.*

1616 **Great OAKS from little acorns grow.**
La quercia cresce da piccola ghianda.

Var. *Every oak has been an acorn.*

1617 **An unlawful OATH is better broken than kept.**
Promessa ingiusta, tener non è giusto.

1618 **OBEDIENCE is the first duty of a soldier.**
L'obbedienza è il primo dovere del soldato.

1619 **He that cannot OBEY cannot command.**
Chi non sa ubbidire non sa comandare.

Sim. *He commands enough that obeys a wise man / He can ill be a master that never was a scholar / No man can be a good ruler unless he has first been ruled.*

1620 **An OCCASION lost cannot be redeemed.**
Occasione perduta non si ritrova più.
Occasione perduta non si riacquista mai più.

Sim. *A lost opportunity never returns.*
Cf. *TIME lost cannot be won again.*

1621 **Take OCCASION by the forelock.**
La fortuna va afferrata per i capelli.
Bisogna afferrare l'occasione per i capelli.
Bisogna afferrare l'occasione al volo.

Var. *Take occasion by the forelock, for she is bald behind.*
Cf. *When FORTUNE knocks, open the door.*

1622 **An OCCUPATION is as good as land.**
Il miglior podere è un buon mestiere.

1623 **The OFFENDER never pardons.**
Chi offende non perdona.

1624 He has a good OFFICE, he must needs thrive.
Chi ha mestiere non può perire.

1625 OFFICES may well be given, but not discretion.
Donasi l'ufficio e la promozione, e non la prudenza né la discrezione.

1626 He that measures OIL shall anoint his fingers.
Chi misura l'olio, s'unge le mani.

> Cf. *He that handles HONEY shall feel it cling to his fingers / He that touches PITCH shall be defiled.*

1627 An OLD man in a house is a good sign.
Beata quella casa che di vecchio sa.

1628 An OLD man never wants a tale to tell.
Al vecchio non manca mai da raccontare, né al sole né al focolare.
Il vecchio ha l'almanacco in corpo.

1629 If you would not live to be OLD, you must be hanged when you are young.
Se non vuoi viver vecchio appiccati giovane.

1630 Never too OLD to learn.
Non è mai troppo tardi per imparare.
Non si è mai vecchi per imparare.

> Cf. *LIVE and learn.*

1631 OLD age should have honour.
Onora il senno antico.

1632 OLD men are twice children.
I vecchi son due volte fanciulli.

1633 OLD men, when they marry young women, make much of death.
Quando i vecchi pigliano moglie, le campane suonano a morto.

1634 OLD young, young old.
Se vuoi viver sano e lesto, fatti vecchio un po' più presto.

Var. *If you want to be old long, be old young.*

1635 When an OLD man will not drink, go to see him in another world.
Quando il vecchio non vuol bere, nell'altro mondo vallo a vedere.

1636 OLDER and wiser.
Gli anni dan senno.
Il tempo e l'esperienza generano la prudenza.

1637 Call me not an OLIVE till thou see me gathered.
Non mi dir oliva prima d'avermi colta.

1638 You cannot make an OMELETTE without breaking eggs.
Non si può far la frittata senza rompere le uova.
Chi non rompe le uova, non fa la frittata.

  Var. *Omelets are not made without breaking of eggs.*
  Cf. *He that will eat the KERNEL must crack the nut.*

1639 ONE and none is all one.
Uno e nessuno è tutt'uno.
Uno non fa numero.

  Sim. *One is no number.*

1640 ONE man is worth a hundred and a hundred is not worth one.
Un uomo ne val cento e cento non ne valgono uno.

1641 Our own OPINION is never wrong.
Il parer proprio non ha mai torto.

1642 OPPORTUNITY makes the thief.
L'occasione fa l'uomo ladro.

  Sim. *The hole calls the thief.*
  Cf. *An open DOOR may tempt a saint / The back DOOR robs the house / EASE makes thief.*

1643 He is a good ORATOR who convinces himself.
È buon oratore chi a sé persuade.

1644 An OUNCE of fortune is worth a pound of forecast.
Val più un'oncia di fortuna che una libbra di sapere.
È meglio essere fortunato che savio.

  Var. *An ounce of good fortune is worth a pound of discretion.*

1645 An OUNCE of mirth is worth a pound of sorrow.
Un'oncia di allegrezza vale più che una libbra di malinconia.

1646 He who OWES is in all the wrong.
Chi deve ha tutti i torti.

1647 The OWL thinks her own young fairest.
All'orsa paion belli i suoi orsacchini.
Ogni rospo ama i suoi rospetti.
Ogni scimmia trova belli i suoi scimmiotti.
Ad ogni civetta piace il suo civettino.

  Cf. *The CROW thinks her own bird fairest / FAIR is not fair, but that which pleases.*

1648 An old OX makes a straight furrow.
Bue vecchio, solco diritto.

1649 **An OX is taken by the horns, and a man by the tongue.**
L'uomo per la parola e il bue per le corna.
Gli uomini si legano per la lingua, e i buoi per le corna.
Il bue per le corna, e l'uomo per la parola.
Le parole legano gli uomini, e le funi le corna ai buoi.

Sim. *Words bind men.*

1650 **An OX when he is loose licks himself at pleasure.**
Bue sciolto lecca per tutto.

1651 **Take heed of an OX before, of a horse behind, of a monk on all sides.**
Dal bue, dinanzi; dal mulo, di dietro; e dalla donna, da tutte le parti.
Guardati dal davanti della donna, dal di dietro d'un mulo e da tutti i lati dal frate.

1652 **The OX when weariest treads surest.**
Bue fiacco stampa più forte il piè in terra.

1653 **Muzzle not the OXEN's mouth.**
Non metterai la museruola al bue, mentre sta trebbiando.

o Deuteronomy 25, 4 / Deuteronomio 25, 4

P

1654 **No PAIN, no gain.**
Non c'è pane senza pena.
Nessun bene senza pene.

    Var. *No pains, no gains.*
    Sim. *Nothing to be got without pains.*
    Cf. *A HORSE that will not carry a saddle must have no oats / No SWEET without some sweat / He that will not WORK shall not eat.*

1655 **Of all PAINS, the greatest pain, is to love, but love in vain.**
Amare e non essere amato è tempo perso.
Tanto è amare e non essere amato, quanto rispondere senz'esser chiamato.

1656 **PAINTERS and poets have leave to lie.**
Poeti, pittori e pellegrini a fare e a dire sono indovini.

1657 **On PAINTING and fighting look aloof.**
Le pitture e le battaglie si veggon meglio da lontano.

1658 **The PALENESS of the pilot is a sign of a storm.**
Pallidezza nel nocchiero, di burrasca segno vero.

1659 **PAPER endures all.**
Carta canta e villan dorme.

    Sim. *Pens may blot, but they cannot blush.*
    Cf. *PAPER won't blush.*

1660 **PAPER won't blush.**
La carta non diventa rossa.
La carta non arrossisce.

    Cf. *PAPER endures all.*

1661 **He that will enter into PARADISE must have a good key.**
Bisogna aver buona chiave per entrare in Paradiso.

1662 **PARDONING the bad is injuring the good.**
Chi perdona ai tristi, nuoce ai buoni.
Col perdonar troppo a chi falla, si fa ingiuria a chi non falla.

    Var. *Who pardons the bad, injures the good.*
    Sim. *He that helps the evil hurts the good / Mercy to the criminal may be cruelty to the people.*

1663 A mad PARISH must have a mad priest.
A popolo pazzo, prete spiritato.

1664 The end of PASSION is the beginning of repentance.
La fine dell'ira è il principio del pentimento.

1665 No PATH of flowers leads to glory.
A gloria non si va senza fatica.

1666 He that has PATIENCE has fat thrushes for a farthing.
Chi ha pazienza, ha i tordi grassi a un quattrin l'uno.

1667 PATIENCE is a flower that grows not in every one's garden.
La pazienza è una buon'erba, ma non nasce in tutti gli orti.

1668 PATIENCE is a remedy for every grief.
D'ogni dolor rimedio è la pazienza.
Non v'è mal che non finisca se si soffre con pazienza.
Quel che sarebbe grave, fa pazienza lieve.

Var. *Patience is a plaster for all sores / Patience is the best remedy.*

1669 PATIENCE is a virtue.
La pazienza è la virtù dei Santi.

1670 PATIENCE overcomes all things.
Colla pazienza si vince tutto.

Sim. *Patient men win the day.*

1671 PATIENCE provoked turns to fury.
Pazienza spinta all'estremo, furia diventa.

Var. *Abused patience turns to fury / Beware the fury of a patient man.*
Cf. *There is a LIMIT to one's patience.*

1672 PATIENCE, time, and money accommodate all things.
Pazienza, tempo e denari acconciano ogni cosa.

1673 As the PAY, so the work.
Secondo la paga, il lavoro.

1674 Better to PAY and have little than have much and to be in debt.
È meglio pagare e poco avere, che molto avere e sempre dovere.

1675 He that cannot PAY, let him pray.
Chi non può pagare, preghi.

1676 PAY beforehand was never well served.
Chi paga innanzi tratto, trova il lavoro mal fatto.
Chi vuol lavor mal fatto, lo paghi innanzi tratto.
Chi paga innanzi è servito dopo.

Var. *He that pays beforehand shall have his work ill done.*

1677 **PAY what you owe and you'll know what you're worth.**
Se vuoi saper ciò che hai, paga prima quel che devi.

1678 **A good PAYER is master of another's purse.**
Buon pagatore, dell'altrui borsa è signore.
Chi paga debiti è padrone degli altri.

1679 **A good PAYMASTER needs no surety.**
Buon pagatore non si cura di dar buon pegno.

1680 **A disarmed PEACE is weak.**
La pace non armata è debole.

1681 **He that will not have PEACE, God gives him war.**
Chi la pace non vuol, abbia la guerra.

1682 **He that would live in PEACE and rest, must hear, and see, and say the best.**
Ascolta, vede e tace, chi vuol vivere in pace.

Sim. *Wide ears and a short tongue / Hear and see and say nothing.*
Cf. *HEAR much, speak little.*

1683 **If you want PEACE, you must prepare for war.**
Se vuoi la pace, preparati alla guerra.
Chi vuol la pace, guerra apparecchi.

Var. *In time of peace, prepare for war / If you wish for peace, be prepared for war.*

1684 **PEACE and patience, and death with repentance.**
Pace e pazienza, e morte con penitenza.

1685 **PEACE makes plenty.**
La pace nutre, la discordia consuma.
Dalla prudenza viene la pace, e dalla pace l'abbondanza.

Sim. *By wisdom peace, and by peace plenty.*

1686 **Where there is PEACE God is.**
Dove c'è la pace c'è Dio.

1687 **When the PEAR is ripe, it falls.**
Quando la pera è matura, casca da sé.

1688 **Do not throw PEARLS to swine.**
Non gettare le perle ai porci.
Buone ragioni male intese sono perle ai porci stese.

Var. *To cast pearls before swine.*

o Matthew 7, 6 / Matteo 7, 6

1689 Share not PEARS with your master, either in jest or in earnest.
Chi mangia peri col suo signore, non sceglie i migliori.

Cf. *Those that eat CHERRIES with great persons shall have their eyes squirted out with the stones.*

1690 Every PEDLAR praises his needles.
Ogni mercante loda la sua mercanzia.

1691 Let every PEDLAR carry his own burden.
Ognuno va al mulino col suo sacco.

Var. *Let every pedlar carry his own pack.*

1692 The PEN is mightier than the sword.
Ne uccide più la penna che la spada.

1693 A PENNY saved is a penny gained.
Quattrino risparmiato, due volte guadagnato.

Var. *He who saves a penny earns a penny.*
Cf. *SPARING is the first gaining.*

1694 He has never a PENNY to bless himself with.
Non avere un quattrino da far cantare un cieco.

1695 In for a PENNY, in for a pound.
Chi fa trenta può far trentuno.

1696 No PENNY, no paternoster.
Senza denari non si hanno i paternoster.
Per nulla non canta un cieco.

Sim. *No money, no Swiss.*

1697 PENNY and penny laid up will be many.
A quattrino a quattrino si fa il fiorino.

Cf. *Many DROPS make a shower / MANY small make a great.*

1698 Who will not keep a PENNY, never shall have many.
Chi non tien conto del poco, non acquista l'assai.

1699 PENSION never enriched a young man.
Salario non arricchì mai giovane.

1700 He that builds on the PEOPLE, builds on the dirt.
Chi fonda sul popolo, fonda sull'arena.

1701 He who serves the PEOPLE serves nothing.
Chi serve al comune, non serve a nessuno.

Sim. *A common servant is no man's servant / He that serves everybody is paid by nobody / He that serves the public, obliges nobody.*

1702 **He who has plenty of PEPPER will pepper his cabbage.**
Chi ha del pepe, ne mette anche sul cavolo.
Chi ha molto pepe ne condisce anche gli erbaggi.

1703 **He that forecasts all PERILS will never sail the sea.**
Chi guarda a ogni nuvolo, non fa mai viaggio.
Chi teme acqua e vento, non si metta in mare.
   Var. *He that forecasts all perils will win no worship.*
   Sim. *He that will sail without danger must never come upon the main sea /*
       He that counts all costs will never put plough in the earth.
   Cf. *He that is AFRAID of wounds must not come nigh a battle / He that*
       fears LEAVES, let him not go into the wood.

1704 **One hates not the PERSON, but the vice.**
Non la persona, ma il vizio si odia.

1705 **PERSUASION of the fortunate sways the doubtful.**
La persuasione del fortunato può assai nel dubbioso.

1706 **PERVERSENESS makes one squint-eyed.**
La perversità fa l'uomo guercio.

1707 **A young PHYSICIAN fattens the churchyard.**
Medico giovane ingrassa il sagrato.

1708 **PHYSICIAN, heal thyself!**
Medico, cura te stesso!

   o Luke 4, 23 / Luca 4, 23

1709 **Piss clear, and defy the PHYSICIAN.**
Piscia chiaro, e abbi in tasca il medico.

1710 **They that be whole need not a PHYSICIAN, but they that are sick.**
Coloro che stanno bene non han bisogno di medico, ma i malati.

   o Matthew 9, 12 / Matteo 9, 12; Mark 2, 17 / Marco 2, 17; Luke 5, 31 /
   Luca 5, 31

1711 **The best PHYSICIANS are Dr. Diet, Dr. Quiet, and Dr. Merryman.**
Dottor Acqua, Dottor Dieta e Dottor Quiete sono i migliori medici.
Vita quieta, mente lieta, moderata dieta.

1712 **PHYSICIANS' faults are covered with earth.**
Gli errori dei medici la terra li copre.

   Sim. *Doctors bury their mistakes / If the doctor cures, the sun sees it; but if*
       he kills, the earth hides it.
   Cf. *DOCTORS' faults are covered with earth, and rich men's with money.*

1713 They agree like PICKPOCKETS in a fair.
Intendersi come i tiraborse alla fiera.
Essere come i ladri di Pisa, che di giorno si leticano, e la notte vanno a rubare assieme.

1714 The first PIG, but the last whelp of the litter, is the best.
Primo porco, ultimo cane.

1715 The PIG dreams of acorns, and the goose of maize.
Il porco sogna ghiande.
Scrofa magra, ghianda s'insogna.

1716 When the PIG has had a belly full, it upsets the trough.
L'asino, quando ha mangiato la biada, tira calci al corbello.

1717 When the PIG is proffered, hold up the poke.
Se ti gettano la fune, tu lega la vacca.

1718 PIGEONS and priests make foul houses.
Chi vuol la casa monda, non tenga mai colomba.

1719 Bitter PILLS may have blessed effects.
Amaro, tienlo caro.

1720 If the PILLS were pleasant, they would not want gilding.
Se la pillola avesse buon sapore, dorata non sarebbe per di fuore.

1721 He that will steal a PIN will steal a better thing.
Chi ruba una spilla, ruba una libbra.
Ladroncello di stringhetta, alfin viene alla borsetta.

Cf. *He that will steal an EGG will steal an ox.*

1722 No longer PIPE, no longer dance.
Senza suono non si balla.

1723 Give the PIPER a penny to play and two pence to leave off.
Dare un soldo al cieco che canti, e dargliene poi due perché si cheti.

1724 He who pays the PIPER calls the tune.
Chi fa le spese ha il diritto di scelta.

Var. *He who calls the tune must pay the piper.*

1725 One PIRATE gets nothing of another but his cask.
Tra corsale e corsale non si guadagna se non barili vuoti.

1726 He who digs a PIT for others falls in himself.
Chi scava la fossa agli altri, vi cade dentro egli stesso.

Cf. *To make a SNARE for another and fall into it oneself.*

o Proverbs 26, 27 / Proverbi 26, 27

1727 **He that touches PITCH shall be defiled.**
Chi tocca la pece s'imbratta.

Cf. *He that handles HONEY shall feel it cling to his fingers / He that measures OIL shall anoint his fingers.*

o Ecclesiasticus 13, 1 / Siràcide 13, 1

1728 **The PITCHER goes so often to the well that it is broken at last.**
Tanto va la secchia al pozzo che ci lascia il manico.
Tante volte al pozzo va la secchia ch'ella vi lascia il manico o l'orecchia.
Vaso che va spesso al fonte, ci lascia il manico o la fronte.

Var. *The pitcher can go to the well too often / A pitcher that goes to the well too often is liable to be broken.*

1729 **Foolish PITY mars a city.**
La troppa pietà guasta molte città.

1730 **One may change PLACE but not change the mind.**
Col mutar paese non si muta cervello.

1731 **Hand PLAY, churls' play.**
Gioco di mano, gioco di villano.

1732 **You can't PLEASE everyone.**
Non si può piacer a tutti.
Non si può accontentare tutti.

Sim. *It is hard to please all parties / He that all men will please shall never find ease / He who pleased everybody died before he was born / He has need rise betimes that would please everybody.*

1733 **A PLEASURE long expected is dear enough sold.**
Piacere molto aspettato è mezzo pagato.

Cf. *A GIFT much expected is paid, not given.*

1734 **After PLEASURE comes pain.**
Dopo il contento vien il tormento.

Var. *No pleasure without pain.*
Sim. *After your fling, watch for the sting.*

1735 **Fly the PLEASURE which pains afterwards.**
Fuggi il piacer presente che prepara il dolor futuro.

1736 **PLEASURE that comes too thick, grows fulsome.**
Piacer preso in fretta, riesce in disdetta.
Il troppo piacere fa dispiacere.
Troppa gioia diventa dolore.
Lungo piacer fa piangere.

1737 **Short PLEASURE, long pain.**
Per un breve piacer, mille tormenti.

Cf. *In WAR, hunting, and love men for one pleasure a thousand griefs prove.*

1738 **The PLEASURES of the mighty are the tears of the poor.**
Dei peccati dei signori fanno penitenza i poveri.
Il peccato del signore fa piangere il vassallo.

Var. *Dainties of the great are the tears of the poor.*

1739 **He that has PLENTY of good shall have more.**
La roba va alla roba.
La roba va alla roba e i pidocchi alle costure.

Cf. *The MORE you get, the more you want / MUCH would have more.*

1740 **PLENTY brings pride.**
Abbondanza genera baldanza.
L'abbondanza, foriera è d'arroganza.

1741 **PLENTY makes poor.**
Superfluità fa povertà.
Ricchezza mal disposta, a povertà s'accosta.
Ricchezza poco vale, a chi l'usa male.

1742 **POETS are born, but orators are made.**
Poeta si nasce, oratore si diventa.

Var. *A poet is born not made.*

1743 **One POISON drives out another.**
Il veleno si spegne col veleno.

Cf. *One DEVIL drives out another / LIKE cures like / One NAIL drives out another.*

1744 **What does not POISON, fattens.**
Quel che non ammazza, ingrassa.

1745 **It is kindly that the POKE savour of the herring.**
Il mortaio sa sempre d'aglio.

Sim. *The cask savours of the first fill.*

1746 **All our POMP the earth covers.**
Tutte le nostre pompe al fin copre la terra.

1747 **Standing POOLS gather filth.**
Acqua che stagna, o puzza o magagna.
Acqua cheta vermini mena.

1748 A POOR man has no friends.
I poveri non hanno parenti.

Sim. *Poverty has no kin.*

1749 A POOR man's tale cannot be heard.
Le parole del povero non son ascoltate.

Cf. *The REASONS of the poor weigh not.*

1750 Giving much to the POOR doth enrich a man's store.
Mai più è povero, chi dona ai poveri.
Dare al povero è ricevere.

1751 He is not POOR that has little, but he that desires much.
Non è povero chi ha poco, ma quel che desidera molto.

1752 He that hath pity upon the POOR lendeth unto the Lord.
Chi dà ai poveri, presta al Signore.
Chi fa elemosina presta, non dona.

Var. *He who gives to the poor lends to the Lord / Who gives to the poor lends to God.*

o Proverbs 19, 17 / Proverbi 19, 17

1753 POOR men seek meat for their stomach; rich men stomach for their meat.
I poveri cercano il mangiare per lo stomaco, ed i ricchi lo stomaco per il cibo.

1754 There are God's POOR and the devil's poor.
C'è il povero di Dio e quello del diavolo.

1755 A POPE by voice, a king by nature, an emperor by force.
Papa per voce, Re per natura, Imperatore per forza.

1756 Any PORT in a storm.
In tempo di tempesta ogni buco è porto.

1757 A little POT is soon hot.
Le piccole pignatte bollono facilmente.
Picciola pentola si scalda presto.

1758 A watched POT never boils.
Pentola guardata non bolle mai.

1759 Every POT has his cover.
Non vi è pentola sì brutta che non trovi il suo coperchio.

Sim. *Every Jack has his Jill.*

1760 To a boiling POT flies come not.
A miele che bolle le mosche non si accostano.

1761 **Who boils his POT with chips makes his broth smell of smoke.**
Chi cucina colle frasche, la minestra sa di fumo.

1762 **A hundred POUNDS of sorrow pays not one ounce of debt.**
Cento libbre di pensieri non pagano un'oncia di debito.

Sim. *A pound of care will not pay an ounce of debt.*

1763 **He that is in POVERTY is still in suspicion.**
In povertà è sospetta la lealtà.

Sim. *It is a hard task to be poor and leal.*

1764 **It is easier to commend POVERTY than to endure it.**
È più facile di lodar la povertà che di sopportarla.

1765 **POVERTY is hateful good.**
Povertà, odiato bene.

1766 **POVERTY is no vice but an inconvenience.**
Povertà non è vizio, ma solo incomodità.

Sim. *Poverty is no sin (crime).*

1767 **POVERTY is not a shame; but the being ashamed of it is.**
La povertà non è vergogna.
La povertà non è colpa.

Sim. *Poverty is no disgrace.*

1768 **POVERTY is the mother of all arts.**
La povertà insegna tutte le arti.

Cf. *The BELLY teaches all arts / HUNGER is the teacher of all arts / NECESSITY is the mother of invention.*

1769 **POVERTY is the mother of health.**
Povertà, madre di sanità.

1770 **POVERTY parts fellowship.**
Chi cade in povertà, perde ogni amico.
Chi è povero ognun lo fugge.
Dove non è roba, anche i cani se ne vanno.

Var. *Poverty parts friends (good company).*
Cf. *A POOR man has no friends / In time of PROSPERITY friends will be plenty; in time of adversity not one amongst twenty / PROSPERITY makes friends, adversity tries them.*

1771 **POVERTY wants many things, and avarice all.**
Alla povertà manca molto, all'avarizia tutto.
L'avarizia è la maggiore delle povertà.

Var. *Poverty is in want of much, avarice of everything.*
Sim. *A poor man wants some things, a covetous man all things.*

1772 When POVERTY comes in at the door, love flies out of the window.
Quando la fame entra dalla porta, l'amore se ne va dalla finestra.

Sim. *Love lasts as long as money endures.*

1773 An ounce of PRACTICE is worth a pound of precept.
Val più la pratica della grammatica.
Val più la pratica che la grammatica.

Cf. *EXPERIENCE is the mother of knowledge.*

1774 PRACTICE makes perfect.
L'esercizio è un buon maestro.

Sim. *Use makes mastery.*

1775 A man's PRAISE in his own mouth stinks.
La lode propria puzza.

Sim. *Self-praise is no recommendation.*
Cf. *He that PRAISES himself spatters himself.*

1776 PRAISE makes good men better, and bad men worse.
La lode giova al savio e nuoce al matto.
Se lodi il buono, diviene migliore; se biasimi il tristo, diviene peggiore.

Cf. *CHASTISE the good and he will mend; chastise the bad and he will grow worse / Show a good man his ERROR and he turns it to virtue; but an ill it doubles his fault.*

1777 PRAISE no man till he is dead.
La vera lode vien dopo la morte.

Cf. *Call no man HAPPY till he dies.*

o Ecclesiasticus 11, 28 / Siràcide 11, 28

1778 PRAISE to the face is open disgrace.
Chi ti loda in presenza, ti biasima in assenza.

1779 He that PRAISES himself spatters himself.
Chi si loda s'imbroda.

Sim. *Self-praise is no recommendation.*
Cf. *A man's PRAISE in his own mouth stinks.*

o Proverbs 27, 2 / Proverbi 27, 2

1780 He that would learn to PRAY, let him go to sea.
Chi non sa orare, vada in mare a navigare.

Var. *Let him who knows not how to pray go to sea.*

1781 **A short PRAYER penetrates heaven.**
Corta preghiera penetra in cielo.
La breve orazione è quella che sale al cielo.

    Var. *Short prayers reach heaven.*

1782 **He PREACHES well that lives well.**
Chi ben vive, ben predica.

1783 **PREVENTION is better than cure.**
Prevenire è meglio che curare.

1784 **No PRIDE like that of an enriched beggar.**
Non è superbia alla superbia eguale, d'uomo basso e vil che in alto sale.
Prima ricco, e poi borioso.

    Cf. *Set a BEGGAR on horseback, and he'll ride to the Devil / When a KNAVE is in a plum-tree, he has neither friend nor kin.*

1785 **PRIDE goes before a fall.**
La superbia andò a cavallo e tornò a piedi.
La superbia viene davanti alla ruina.

    Sim. *Pride never left his master without a fall.*

    o Proverbs 16, 18 / Proverbi 16, 18

1786 **PRIDE goes before, and shame follows after.**
Quando la superbia galoppa, la vergogna siede in groppa.

1787 **PRIDE must be pinched.**
L'orgoglio va adoperato come il pepe.

1788 **PRIDE that apes humility.**
La troppa umiltà vien da superbia.

1789 **There are those who despise PRIDE with a greater pride.**
Tal sprezza la superbia con maggior superbia.

1790 **Each PRIEST praises his own relics.**
Ogni prete loda le sue reliquie.

1791 **Like PRIEST, like people.**
Quale il cappellano, tale il sacrestano.
Tal abate, tali i monaci.

1792 **The parish PRIEST forgets ever he has been holy water clerk.**
La suocera non pensa mai che la fu nuora.

1793 **A thousand PROBABILITIES do not make one truth.**
Mille probabilità non fanno una verità.

1794 It is an ill PROCESSION where the devil bears the cross.
Quando i furbi vanno in processione, il diavolo porta la croce.

1795 PROMISE is debt.
Ogni promessa è debito.
Chi promette, in debito si mette.

1796 Great PROMISES and small performances.
Chi molto promette, poco attende.

Sim. *He promises mountains and performs molehills.*

1797 He that PROMISES too much means nothing.
Promettere certo e venir meno sicuro.

1798 PROMISING and performing are two things.
Altro è promettere, altro è mantenere.
Promettere e mantenere non vanno bene insieme.

Sim. *It is one thing to promise, another to perform / Between promising and performing a man may marry his daughter.*

1799 PROMISING is the eve of giving.
Il promettere è la vigilia del dare.

1800 A PROPHET is not without honour save in his own country.
Nessuno è profeta in patria.

Var. *A prophet has no honour in his own country.*

o Luke 4, 24 / Luca 4, 24; Matthew 13, 57 / Matteo 13, 57; Mark 6, 4 / Marco 6, 4; John 4, 44 / Giovanni 4, 44

1801 Beware of false PROPHETS.
Guardatevi da' falsi profeti.

o Matthew 7, 15; 24, 11,24 / Matteo 7, 15; 24, 11,24; Mark 13, 22 / Marco 13, 22; II Peter 2, 1 / II Pietro 2, 1; I John 4, 1 / I Giovanni 4, 1; Revelation 16, 13 / Apocalisse 16, 13

1802 In PROSPERITY no altars smoke.
Nella prosperità non fumano gli altari.
Nella felicità gli altari non fumano.

1803 In time of PROSPERITY friends will be plenty; in time of adversity not one amongst twenty.
Amici molti avrai, finché ricco sarai.

Cf. *A POOR man has no friends / POVERTY parts fellowship / PROSPERITY makes friends, adversity tries them.*

o Ecclesiasticus, 37, 4-5; 6, 8 / Siràcide 37, 4-5; 6, 8

1804 **PROSPERITY lets go the bridle.**
Il buon tempo fa scavezzare il collo.

1805 **PROSPERITY makes friends, adversity tries them.**
La prosperità acquista amici, la verità li prova.

    Cf. *In time of PROSPERITY friends will be plenty; in time of adversity not one amongst twenty.*

1806 **PROVERBS are the wisdom of nations.**
I proverbi sono la saggezza dei popoli.
I proverbi sono la sapienza dei secoli.

1807 **That which PROVES too much proves nothing.**
Chi vuol troppo provare nulla prova.

1808 **PROVIDENCE is better than rent.**
La Provvidenza val più delle rendite.

1809 **Make ample PROVISION for old age.**
In gioventù devi acquistare quel che in vecchiaia ti può giovare.
È gran saviezza di risparmiar per la vecchiezza.

    Sim. *Keep something for him that rides on the white horse / Spare when you're young and spend when you're old.*
    Cf. *For AGE and want save while you may: no morning sun lasts a whole day / Keep SOMETHING for a rainy day.*

1810 **The PUBLIC pays with ingratitude.**
Il mondo paga d'ingratitudine.

    Sim. *Ingratitude is the way of the world / The world's coin is ingratitude.*

1811 **It is easier to PULL DOWN than to build.**
È più facile lo sfare che il fare.

1812 **PUNISHMENT is lame, but it comes.**
La pena è zoppa, ma pure arriva.

    Cf. *The MILLS of God grind slowly, yet they grind exceeding small.*

1813 **To the PURE all things are pure.**
Tutto è puro per i puri.

    o Titus 1, 15 / Tito 1, 15

1814 **He that cannot pay in PURSE must pay in person.**
Chi non può di borsa, paghi di bocca.

Q

1815 It takes two to make a QUARREL.
Bisogna essere in due per fare una lite.

1816 Ask a silly QUESTION, you'll get a silly answer.
Sciocca proposta non vuol risposta.

>Var. *Silly question, silly answer.*

1817 Every QUESTION requires not an answer.
Ogni parola non vuol risposta.

1818 Like QUESTION, like answer.
Qual proposta, tal risposta.

1819 He that nothing QUESTIONS, nothing learns.
Quando non sai, frequenta in domandare.

R

1820 **The RACE is not to the swift, nor the battle to the strong.**
Non è degli agili la corsa, né dei forti la guerra.

    o Ecclesiastes 9, 11 / Qoèlet 9, 11

1821 **RAGE is without reason.**
L'ira turba la mente ed accieca la ragione.
L'ira è cattiva consigliera.

1822 **Small RAIN lays great winds.**
Piccola pioggia fa cessar gran vento.

  Var. *Small rain lays great dust.*

1823 **A RAINBOW in the morning is the shepherd's warning; a rainbow at night is the shepherd's delight.**
Arco da sera, buon tempo ne mena; arco da mattina, riempie la marina.

1824 **RATS desert a falling house.**
Quando la casa crolla i topi scappano.

  Cf. *RATS desert a sinking ship.*

1825 **RATS desert a sinking ship.**
I topi abbandonano la nave che affonda.

  Cf. *RATS desert a falling house.*

1826 **To READ and not to understand is to pursue and not take.**
Leggere e non intendere è come cacciare e non prendere.
Non tutti quelli che leggono intendono.

  Sim. *What a man does not understand, he does not possess.*

1827 **REASON governs the wise man and cudgels the fool.**
Al savio la ragione, al matto il bastone.

  Sim. *A nod for the wise man and a rod for a fool.*

1828 **REASON lies between the spur and the bridle.**
Tra la briglia e lo sprone consiste la ragione.

1829 **The REASONS of the poor weigh not.**
Le ragioni del povero non pesano.
Uomo senza denaro, di ragione sempre avaro.

  Cf. *A POOR man's tale cannot be heard.*

1830 **The RECEIVER is as bad as the thief.**
Ladro è chi ruba e chi tiene il sacco.
Tanto è ladro chi ruba quanto chi tiene il sacco.

1831 **Short RECKONINGS make long friends.**
Conti spessi, amicizia lunga.
Patti chiari, amicizia lunga.
Patti chiari, amici cari.
Var. *Even reckoning makes long friends.*

1832 **We must RECOIL a little to the end we may leap the better.**
Chi vuol spiccar un bel salto si ritira indietro.

1833 **RELIGION, credit, and the eye are not to be touched.**
L'occhio, la fede e l'onore non toccar mai di signore.

1834 **The REMEDY may be worse than the disease.**
Spesso è peggiore il rimedio che il male.
Sim. *The doctor is often more to be feared than the disease.*

1835 **There is a REMEDY for everything but death.**
A ogni cosa è rimedio fuorché alla morte.
Contro la morte non v'è cosa forte.
Sim. *There is no medicine against death.*
Cf. *A deadly DISEASE neither physician nor physic can ease.*

1836 **Who REPAIRS not his gutter repairs his whole house.**
Chi non rassetta buchino, rassetta bucone.
Chi non tura bucolin, tura bucone.
Sim. *He that repairs not a part builds all.*
Cf. *A STITCH in time saves nine / The TAILOR that makes not a knot loses a stitch.*

1837 **Never too late to REPENT.**
Un buon pentirsi non fu mai tardi.

1838 **He that RESPECTS not is not respected.**
Chi non rispetta non è rispettato.

1839 **Living well is the best REVENGE.**
Vuoi vendicarti dei tuoi nemici? Governati bene.

1840 **REVENGE is a dish that can be eaten cold.**
La vendetta è un piatto da mangiar freddo.

1841 **REVENGE is a morsel for God.**
Vendetta, boccon di Dio.

1842 REVENGE is sweet.
Dolce cosa è lo vendicar giust'onta.

1843 REVENGE of a hundred years has still its sucking teeth.
Vendetta di cent'anni ha ancora i lattaioli.

1844 REWARD and punishment are the walls of a city.
Due cose governano il mondo, il premio e il castigo.

1845 As long as I am RICH reputed, with solemn voice I am saluted.
Scienza senza denar cosa è da sciocchi, per aver fama, basta aver baiocchi.
È più dotto oggidì chi più possiede.

1846 He is RICH enough that wants nothing.
Assai è ricco chi di nulla manca.
Chi non ha gran voglie è ricco.

Sim. *He is rich enough who lacks not bread.*
Cf. *The greatest WEALTH is contentment with a little.*

1847 He is RICH who owes nothing.
È ricco chi non ha debiti.

Sim. *It is better poor and free than to be rich and a slave.*

1848 He who wants to be RICH in a year comes to the gallows in half a year.
Chi vuol arricchire in un anno, è impiccato in sei mesi.
Chi arricchisce in un anno, è impiccato in un mese.

Sim. *He that will be rich before night, may be hanged before noon.*

1849 RICH folk have many friends.
Chi ha quattrini ha amici.
Molti son gli amici del ricco.

Sim. *He that has a full purse never wanted a friend / Everyone is akin to the rich man.*

    o Proverbs 14, 20; 19, 4 / Proverbi 14, 20; 19, 4

1850 RICH man may dine when he will, the poor man when he may.
Il ricco quando vuole, il povero quando può.
L'ora del desinare, pei ricchi quand'hanno appetito, pei poveri quand'hanno da mangiare.

1851 RICH men may have what they will.
Chi è ricco, ha ciò che vuole.

1852 The RICH knows not who is his friend.
Il ricco non sa chi amico gli sia.

1853 **RICHES are like muck, which stink in a heap, but spread abroad make the earth fruitful.**
Le ricchezze son come il concime, ammassato puzza, e sparso fertilizza il campo.

1854 **RICHES bring care and fears.**
Grandi ricchezze, mille pensieri.
Sim. *Much coin, much care.*

1855 **RICHES have wings.**
Le ricchezze hanno l'ali.

1856 **He that has RIGHT, fears; he that has wrong, hopes.**
Chi ha ragione teme, chi ha torto spera.

1857 **The RIVER past and God forgotten.**
Passato il fiume è scordato il santo.
Sim. *Call the bear 'uncle' till you are safe across the bridge / Once on shore, we pray no more.*
Cf. *The DANGER past and God forgotten.*

1858 **All RIVERS run to the sea.**
Tutti i fiumi vanno al mare.
L'acqua va al mare.
Sim. *Follow the river and you will get to the sea.*
    o Ecclesiastes 1, 7 / Qoèlet 1, 7

1859 **He keeps his ROAD well enough who gets rid of bad company.**
Chi fugge un matto, ha fatto buona giornata.

1860 **All ROADS lead to Rome.**
Tutte le strade conducono a Roma.
Tutte le strade portano a Roma.

1861 **Who loves the ROAM may lose his home.**
Chi va via perde il posto all'osteria.

1862 **He that does not ROB makes not a robe or garment.**
Chi non ruba non ha roba.

1863 **ROB Peter to pay Paul.**
Spogliar Pietro per vestir Paolo.
Non bisogna spogliar San Pietro per vestir San Paolo.
Scoprire un altare per ricoprirne un altro.
Var. *Give not St. Peter so much to leave St. Paul nothing.*

1864 Spare the ROD and spoil the child.
Chi ben ama, ben castiga.
Figlio troppo accarezzato non fu mai bene allevato.

    Sim. *He loves well who chastises well / The man who has not been flogged is not educated.*
    Cf. *Better CHILDREN weep than old men / A pitiful MOTHER makes a scabby daughter.*

    o Proverbs 13, 24 / Proverbi 13, 24; Ecclesiasticus 30, 1 / Siràcide 30, 1

1865 ROME was not built in a day.
Roma non fu fatta in un giorno.
Il mondo non fu fatto in un giorno.

1866 When in ROME, do as the Romans do.
Quando a Roma vai, fa come vedrai.
Ovunque vai, fa come vedrai.

    Var. *When you are at Rome, do as the Romans do.*
    Sim. *When you go through the country of the one-eyed, be one-eyed.*

1867 He pulls with a long ROPE that waits for another's death.
A lunga corda tira, chi morte altrui desira.

    Sim. *He that waits for dead men's shoes may go long enough barefoot.*

1868 Never mention ROPE in the house of a man who has been hanged.
Non nominar la fune in casa dell'impiccato.

    Var. *Name not a rope in his house that hanged himself.*

1869 No ROSE without a thorn.
Non c'è rosa senza spine.
Ogni rosa ha la sua spina.

1870 The fairest ROSE at last is withered.
Niuna rosa così bella, che da ultimo non avvizzisca.

1871 Who will not be ruled by the RUDDER must be ruled by the rock.
La nave che non vuol timone avrà lo scoglio.

1872 RUST eats up iron.
La ruggine mangia il ferro.

S

1873 **A broken SACK will hold no corn.**
Sacco rotto non tien miglio.

1874 **An empty SACK cannot stand upright.**
Sacco vuoto non sta in piedi.

   Var. *Empty sacks will never stand upright.*

1875 **An old SACK asks much patching.**
Panno vecchio presto schiantato.

   Var. *Old sacks ask much patching.*

1876 **Bind the SACK before it be full.**
Lega il sacco quantunque non sia pieno.

1877 **It is a bad SACK that will abide no clouting.**
Cattivo è quel sacco che non si può rappezzare.

1878 **There comes nought out of the SACK, but what was there.**
Dal sacco non può uscir se non quel che vi è.

   Cf. *Every CASK smells of the wine it contains.*

1879 **SADNESS and gladness succeed each other.**
Dopo il contento vien il tormento.

   Cf. *After LAUGHTER, tears / LAUGH before breakfast, you'll cry before supper / He that SINGS on Friday will weep on Sunday / SORROW treads upon the heels of mirth.*

   o Proverbs 14, 13 / Proverbi 14, 13

1880 **No sooner SAID than done.**
Detto, fatto.

1881 **There is nothing SAID which has not been said before.**
Non si può dire nulla che non sia già stato detto.

1882 **Hoist your SAIL when the wind is fair.**
Infin che il vento è in poppa, bisogna saper navigare.

1883 **Like SAINT, like offering.**
A tal santo, tal offerta.

   Var. *Such a saint, such an offering.*

1884 Young SAINT, old devil.
Fanciulli, angeli; in età son diavoli.

1885 All are not SAINTS that go to church.
Non son tutti santi quelli che vanno in chiesa.

Sim. *All are not merry that dance lightly / They are not all saints that use holy water.*
Cf. *All are not HUNTERS that blow the horn.*

1886 The old SAINTS are forgotten in the new.
Ai santi vecchi non gli si dà più incenso.

1887 A good SALAD may be the prologue to a bad supper.
Una buona insalata è principio d'una cattiva cena.

1888 Do not offer SALT or brains.
A tavola non si presenti né sale né testa d'animale.

Var. *Help you to salt, help you to sorrow.*

1889 SALT seasons all things.
Il sale condisce le vivande, o anco le guasta.

1890 Seek your SALVE where you get your sore.
Le ferite d'amor non le può sanare che chi le ha fatte.

1891 There is never a SATURDAY without some sunshine.
Non c'è sabato senza sole.

1892 The SAUCE is better than the fish.
È più la giunta della carne.

1893 SAYING and doing are two things.
Fare e dire son due cose.

Cf. *SAYING is one thing, and doing another / From WORD to deed is a great space.*

1894 SAYING is one thing, and doing another.
Il dire è una cosa, il fare è un'altra.
Altro è dire, altro è fare.
Altra cosa è il dire, altra il fare.

Cf. *SAYING and doing are two things / From WORD to deed is a great space.*

1895 Who SAYS A must say B.
Chi dice A, bisogna che dica B.

Var. *You cannot say A without saying B.*

1896 **SCORN at first makes after-love the more.**
Sdegno cresce amore.
Sdegno d'amante poco dura.
Cf. *The falling out of LOVERS is the renewing of love / LOVERS' tiffs are harmless.*

1897 **There is a SCORPION under every stone.**
Lo scorpione dorme sotto ogni lastra.
Cf. *SNAKE in the grass.*

1898 **Being on SEA, sail; being on land, settle.**
Chi è in mare navica, chi è in terra radica.

1899 **He complains wrongfully on the SEA that twice suffers shipwreck.**
A torto si lagna del mare, chi due volte ci vuol tornare.

1900 **He who travels not by SEA knows not what the fear of God is.**
Chi non naviga, non sa cosa sia timor di Dio.

1901 **Praise the SEA, but keep on land.**
Loda il mare e tieniti alla terra.

1902 **Everything is good in its SEASON.**
Ogni cosa ha la sua stagione.

1903 **A SECRET is too little for one, enough for two, too much for three.**
Segreto di due, segreto di Dio; segreto di tre, segreto d'ognuno.
Segreto confidato non è più segreto.

Sim. *Three may keep a secret if two of them are dead / Three may keep counsel if two be away.*
Cf. *It is no SECRET that is known to three.*

1904 **It is no SECRET that is known to three.**
Quel che tre sanno tutti sanno.

Sim. *Three may keep a secret if two of them are dead / Three may keep counsel if two be away.*
Cf. *A SECRET is too little for one, enough for two, too much for three.*

1905 **Tell your SECRET to your servant and you make him your master.**
Servo d'altri si fa, chi dice il suo segreto a chi nol sa.
Dì all'amico il tuo segreto e ti terrà il piè sul collo.

Var. *He that tells a secret is another's servant.*
Sim. *Thy secret is thy prisoner; if thou let it go, thou art a prisoner to it.*
Cf. *To whom you reveal your SECRET you yield your liberty.*

1906 **To whom you reveal your SECRET you yield your liberty.**
A chi dici il tuo segreto, doni la tua libertà.

Sim. *Thy secret is thy prisoner; if thou let it go, thou art a prisoner to it.*
Cf. *Tell your SECRET to your servant and you make him your master.*

1907 SEEING is believing.
Vedere per credere.
Chi con l'occhio vede, col cuor crede.

Cf. *One EYEWITNESS is better than ten hear-so's.*

o John 20, 29 / Giovanni 20, 29

1908 SEEK and you shall find.
Chi cerca, trova.

Var. *He that seeks finds.*
Sim. *The dog that trots finds a bone.*
Cf. *Take heed you FIND not that you do not seek.*

o Matthew 7, 7-8 / Matteo 7, 7-8; Luke 11, 10 / Luca 11, 10

1909 A SERPENT, unless it has devoured a serpent, does not become a dragon.
Se la serpe non mangiasse la serpe non si farebbe drago.

1910 Whom a SERPENT has bitten, a lizard alarms.
Chi è morsicato dalla serpe, teme la lucertola.

Sim. *Once bitten twice shy / A scalded dog fears cold water / He that has been bitten by a serpent is afraid of a rope.*
Cf. *A scalded CAT fears cold water / A burnt CHILD dreads the fire.*

1911 Be ye therefore wise as SERPENTS, and harmless as doves.
Siate prudenti come i serpenti, e semplici come le colombe.

o Matthew 10, 16 / Matteo 10, 16

1912 A good SERVANT should have the back of an ass, the tongue of a sheep, and the snout of a swine.
Muso di porco, schiena d'asino e gambe di cervo vuol avere il buon servitore.

1913 A SERVANT and a cock must be kept but a year.
Il gallo e il servitore in un anno perdon vigore.

1914 A SERVANT is known by his master's absence.
Nell'assenza del signore si conosce il servitore.

1915 He can give little to his SERVANT, that licks his trencher.
Poco può dare al suo scudiere, chi lecca il suo tagliere.

1916 He that has one SERVANT has two, he that has two has but half a one, and he that has three has none.
Chi mette un servo ad un servizio l'ha intero, chi due n'ha un mezzo, chi tre n'ha nessuno.

1917 **If you would have a good SERVANT, take neither a kinsman nor a friend.**
Servitor pregato, parente né amico non torrai mai, se vuoi esser ben servito.

1918 **One must be a SERVANT before one can be a master.**
Prima servitore e poi padrone.
Cf. *He that has not SERVED knoweth not how to command.*

1919 **He that would be well served must know when to change his SERVANTS.**
Chi vuol esser ben servito sappia mutar di servitù.

1920 **So many SERVANTS, so many enemies.**
Tanti servitori, tanti nemici.

1921 **SERVE a great man, and you will know what sorrow is.**
Servi a principe e a signore, e saprai cos'è dolore.

1922 **SERVE a noble disposition, though poor, the time comes that he will repay thee.**
Servi il nobile ancorché sia povero, perché verrà tempo che ti pagherà.

1923 **He that has not SERVED, knoweth not how to command.**
Chi servito non ha, comandar non sa.
Cf. *One must be a SERVANT before one can be a master.*

1924 **He that SERVES, must serve.**
Chi ti serve, ha da servire.

1925 **He that SERVES well needs not ask his wages.**
Chi ben serve, bene è provvisto.
Assai domanda chi ben serve e tace.

1926 **SERVICE is no inheritance.**
Servizio dei grandi non è eredità.
Servizio dei grandi non è retaggio, chi troppo se ne fida non è saggio.

1927 **SERVICE without reward is punishment.**
Servizio senza ricompensa, supplizio.

1928 **The first SERVICE a child does his father is to make him foolish.**
Il primo servigio che faccia il figliuolo al padre, è il farlo disperare.

1929 **All that SHAKES falls not.**
Tutto quel che ciondola non cade.
Cf. *Better BEND than break.*

1930 **A bleating SHEEP loses her bit.**
Pecora che bela perde il boccone.
La pecora per far bè, perde il boccone.

Sim. *Every time the sheep bleats, it loses a mouthful.*
Cf. *The ASS that brays most eats least.*

1931 **As soon goes the young SHEEP to the pot as the old.**
Così presto muoion le pecore giovani come le vecchie.
Non ha più carta l'agnello che la pecora.

Sim. *Death devours lambs as well as sheep.*

1932 **He that makes himself a SHEEP shall be eaten by the wolf.**
Chi pecora si fa, il lupo se lo mangia.

Sim. *Make yourself a sheep and the wolves will eat you.*
Cf. *Make yourself all HONEY and the flies will devour you.*

1933 **It is a foolish SHEEP that makes the wolf his confessor.**
Matta è quella pecora che si confessa al lupo.

1934 **One scabbed SHEEP will mar a whole flock.**
Una pecora rognosa ne guasta un branco.
Una pecora marcia ne guasta un branco.
Una pecora infetta n'ammorba una setta.

1935 **One SHEEP follows another.**
Far come le pecore: ove va una, andar tutte.

1936 **The lone SHEEP is in danger of the wolf.**
La pecora che si sbranca, la fiera la mangia.

Var. *The lone man is in danger of the wolf.*

1937 **There are black SHEEP in every flock.**
In ogni gregge c'è una pecora nera.

1938 **A good SHEPHERD must fleece his sheep, not flay them.**
Il buon pastore tosa, ma non scortica.

Sim. *Where every hand fleeceth, the sheep goes naked.*

1939 **Better give a SHILLING than lend and lose half a crown.**
È meglio di dar un soldo che prestarne venti.

1940 **A great SHIP asks deep waters.**
Gran nave vuol grand'acqua.

1941 **SHIPS fear fire more than water.**
Le navi temono più il fuoco che l'acqua.

1942 **If my SHIRT knew my design I'd burn it.**
Ogni tua guisa non sappia la tua camicia.
La tua camicia non sappia il tuo secreto.

Var. *If my skirt knew my design I'd burn it.*

1943 Near is my SHIRT, but nearer is my skin.
Sta più vicino la pelle che la camicia.

Sim. *Near is my doublet (kirtle, petticoat), but nearer is my smock.*
Cf. *Near is my COAT, but nearer is my shirt.*

1944 Everyone knows best where his own SHOE pinches.
Ognuno sa dove la scarpa lo stringe.

Cf. *No one but the wearer knows where the SHOE pinches.*

1945 No one but the wearer knows where the SHOE pinches.
Nessuno sente da che parte preme la scarpa, se non chi se la calza.
Dove stringe la scarpa, non lo sa altro che chi l'ha in piede.

Cf. *Everyone knows best where his own SHOE pinches.*

1946 One SHOE will not fit all feet.
Una scarpa non è buona per ogni piede.

Var. *Every shoe fits not every foot.*
Cf. *All FEET tread not in one shoe.*

1947 None more bare than the SHOEMAKER's wife and the smith's mare.
In casa di calzolaio non si hanno scarpe.

Var. *Cobblers' children never wear shoes / He who makes shoes goes barefoot.*

1948 Better wear out SHOES than sheets.
È meglio consumar le scarpe che le lenzuola.

1949 The SICKNESS of the body may prove the health of the soul.
Infermità del corpo, sanità dell'anima.

1950 You cannot make a SIEVE of an ass's tail.
Di coda d'asino non si può fare staccio.

Sim. *You cannot make a horn of a pig's tail / You cannot make a silk purse of a sow's ear.*

1951 Out of SIGHT, out of mind.
Lontan dagli occhi, lontan dal cuore.
Se occhio non mira, cuor non sospira.
Assenza nemica d'amore, quanto lontan dall'occhio, tanto dal cuore.

Sim. *Long absent, soon forgotten / Far from eye, far from heart / Seldom seen, soon forgotten / Salt water and absence wash away love.*
Cf. *What the EYE doesn't see, the heart doesn't grieve over.*

1952 The SIGN invites you in, but your money redeem you out.
All'entrar ci vuol ingegno, all'uscir denari o pegno.

1953 **SILENCE does seldom harm.**
Nessuno si pentì mai d'aver taciuto.

    Cf. *More have repented SPEECH than silence / Be STILL, and have thy will.*

1954 **SILENCE is often the best answer.**
Un bel tacer non fu mai scritto.

    Cf. *SPEAK fitly, or be silent wisely / No WISDOM to silence.*

1955 **SILENCE means consent.**
Chi tace acconsente.

    Var. *Silence gives consent.*

1956 **Every SIN brings its punishment with it.**
Ogni fallo aspetta il suo laccio.

1957 **Let him that is without SIN cast the first stone.**
Chi è senza peccato scagli la prima pietra.

    o John 8, 7 / Giovanni 8, 7

1958 **Old SIN makes new shame.**
Peccato vecchio, penitenza nuova.

1959 **SIN plucks on sin.**
Un vizio chiama l'altro.

1960 **SIN that is hidden is half forgiven.**
Peccato celato, mezzo perdonato.

1961 **To fall into SIN is human, to remain in sin is devilish.**
Peccare è umano, perseverare diabolico.

    Cf. *To ERR is human / To ERR is human; to forgive, divine.*

1962 **The SINGING man keeps his shop in his throat.**
Il cantante ha la sua bottega nella gola.

1963 **He that SINGS on Friday will weep on Sunday.**
Chi ride il venerdì, piange la domenica.
Chi ride il sabato, piange la domenica.

    Cf. *After LAUGHTER, tears / LAUGH before breakfast, you'll cry before supper / SADNESS and gladness succeed each other / SORROW treads upon the heels of mirth.*

1964 **He who SINGS drives away his cares.**
Chi canta, i suoi mali spaventa.

1965 **SINK or swim.**
O bere o affogare.

    Cf. *Either MEND or end.*

1966 As a man SINNETH, so is his punishment.
Con quel che uno pecca, è castigato.

1967 Our SINS and our debts are often more than we think.
I peccati e i debiti son sempre più di quelli che si crede.
I debiti e i peccati crescon sempre.

1968 When all SINS grow old, covetousness is young.
Quando tutti i peccati sono vecchi, l'avarizia è ancora giovane.

1969 It is as cheap SITTING as standing.
A chi rincresce lo stare, pongasi a sedere.

1970 He that SITS well, thinks ill.
Chi ben siede, mal pensa.

1971 If the SKY falls we shall catch larks.
Se il cielo rovinasse, si piglierebbero molti uccelli.

Sim. *You may gape long enough ere a bird fall in your mouth.*
Cf. *To think that LARKS will fall into one's mouth ready roasted.*

1972 Red SKY at night, shepherd's delight; red sky in the morning, shepherd's warning.
Rosso di sera, bel tempo si spera, rosso di mattina, la pioggia s'avvicina.

1973 SLANDER leaves a score behind it.
Calunnia, calunnia, che a tirar dell'acqua, al muro sempre se n'attacca.

Sim. *If the ball does not stick to the wall, it will at least leave a mark.*

1974 SLEEP is the brother of death.
Il sonno è parente della morte.

Sim. *Sleep is the image of death.*

1975 A SLEEPING man is not hungry.
Chi dorme, non sente la fame.
Chi dorme, desina.

1976 The SLOTHFUL man is the beggar's brother.
Uomo poltrone, uomo poverone.

Cf. *IDLENESS is the key to poverty.*

1977 SLOW but sure.
Chi va piano, va sano.

Sim. *Fair and softly goes far.*
Cf. *He that GOES softly goes safely / Soft pace GOES far.*

1978 A SLUGGARD takes an hundred steps because he would not take one in due time.
Il pigro per non far un passo ne fa cento.

Sim. *Idle folks have the most labour.*
Cf. *IDLE people have the least leisure.*

1979 One SLUMBER invites another.
Un sonno tira l'altro.
Il sonno mena sonno.

1980 No SMOKE without fire.
Non c'è fumo senza fuoco.
Non si dà fumo senza fuoco.

Var. *Where there is smoke, there is fire.*
Cf. *No FIRE, no smoke.*

1981 Shunning the SMOKE they fall into the fire.
Spesso chi crede fuggir il fumo, cade nel fuoco.
Tal fugge il fumo che casca poi nella bragia.

1982 The SMOKE of a man's own house is better than the fire of another's.
Più vale il fumo di casa mia che l'arrosto dell'altrui.

1983 Three things drive a man out of his house - SMOKE, rain and a scolding wife.
Tre cose cacciano l'uomo di casa: fumo, goccia e femmina arrabbiata.
Acqua, fumo e mala femmina cacciano la gente di casa.
Bacco, tabacco e Venere riducon l'uomo in cenere.
Tre "effe" caccian l'uomo di casa: fame, fumo e mala femmina.
Tre "D" rovinano l'uomo: Diavolo, Danaro, Donna.

Sim. *Dicing, drabbing and drinking bring men to destruction / Play, women, and wine undo men laughing.*
Cf. *GAMING, women and wine, while they laugh, they make men pine.*

o Proverbs 10, 26; 19, 13; 27, 15 / Proverbi 10, 26; 19, 13; 27, 15

1984 SNAKE in the grass.
Il serpe tra i fiori e l'erba giace.

Cf. *There is a SCORPION under every stone.*

1985 To nourish a SNAKE in one's bosom.
Nutri la serpe in seno, ti renderà veleno.
Allevarsi la serpe in seno.

Cf. *Breed up a CROW and he will tear out your eyes.*

1986 To make a SNARE for another and fall into it oneself.
Chi tende un laccio vi resterà preso.

Cf. *He who digs a PIT for others falls in himself.*

o Ecclesiasticus 27, 26 / Siràcide 27, 26; Psalms 9, 15; 34, 6-7; 56, 8-9; 140, 9 / Salmi 9, 16; 34, 7; 56, 7; 140, 9

1987 SNOW for a se'nnight is a mother to the earth, for ever after a stepmother.
La neve per otto dì è alla terra come mamma, da indi in là come matrigna.

1988 What SOBERNESS conceals, drunkenness reveals.
Vino e sdegno fan palese ogni disegno.
Bocca ubriaca scopre il fondo del cuore.

Sim. *He speaks in his drink what he thought in his drouth.*

1989 Keep SOMETHING for a rainy day.
I quattrini bianchi van serbati pei giorni neri.

Var. *Lay up against a rainy day.*
Sim. *Keep something for him that rides on the white horse / Spare when you're young and spend when you're old.*
Cf. *For AGE and want save while you may: no morning sun lasts a whole day / Make ample PROVISION for old age.*

1990 SOMETHING is better than nothing.
È meglio qualcosa che nulla.
Meglio poco che niente.

Var. *Better something than nothing.*
Sim. *Better some of a pudding than none of a pie.*
Cf. *Half a LOAF is better than no bread.*

1991 Every man is the SON of his own works.
Ciascun è figlio delle sue opere.

1992 Marry your SON when you will, your daughter when you can.
Accasa il figlio quando vuoi e la figlia quando puoi.

1993 Great men's SONS seldom do well.
I gran personaggi o non hanno figliuoli o non son saggi.

1994 SOON enough, if well enough.
Chi fa bene, fa presto.
Assai presto si fa quel che si fa bene.

Sim. *Well done, soon done.*

1995 SOON learnt, soon forgotten.
Presto imparato, presto dimenticato.

1996 SOON ripe, soon rotten.
Quel che presto matura, poco dura.

1997 Of thy SORROW be not too sad, of thy joy be not too glad.
Gioia e sciagura sempre non dura.
Il male non dura e il bene non regna.

1998 SORROW for a husband is like a pain in the elbow, sharp and short.
Il dolore dell'occhio, del ginocchio, del gomito e della moglie è grande, ma dura poco.

1999 SORROW is always dry.
Il dolore è sempre asciutto.

2000 SORROW treads upon the heels of mirth.
Dopo il dolce ne vien l'amaro.

    Cf. *After LAUGHTER, tears / LAUGH before breakfast, you'll cry before supper / SADNESS and gladness succeed each other / He that SINGS on Friday will weep on Sunday.*

2001 When SORROW is asleep, wake it not.
Le disgrazie quando dormono non bisogna svegliarle.

Sim. *Wake not a sleeping lion.*
Cf. *Let sleeping DOGS lie.*

2002 SORROWS remembered sweeten present joy.
Il ricordarsi del male raddoppia il bene.

Sim. *The remembrance of past sorrow is joyful.*
Cf. *That which was BITTER to endure may be sweet to remember.*

2003 There is no SOUND more pleasing than one's own praises.
Ognuno ama sentirsi lodare.

2004 Of SOUP and love, the first is the best.
Alle zuppe e agli amori, i primi sono i migliori.

    Cf. *No LOVE like the first love / Old LOVE will not be forgotten.*

2005 As you SOW, so you reap.
Come seminerai, così raccoglierai.
Si raccoglie quel che si semina.
Ognuno raccoglie quel che ha seminato.

    o Galatians 6, 7 / Galati 6, 7

2006 He that does not SOW does not mow.
Chi non semina non raccoglie.

2007 SOW thin and mow thin.
Chi mal semina, mal raccoglie.

2008 SOW with the hand and not with the whole sack.
Bisogna seminar con la mano e non col sacco.

2009 You must SOW ere you reap.
Chi vuol raccogliere, semini.

2010 **Forbear not SOWING because of birds.**
Non cessar per gli uccelli di seminar piselli.
Non devi evitare di seminare per paura delle cornacchie.
Non bisogna ristare per le passere di seminar panico.

2011 **He that SOWS in the highway tires his oxen and loses his corn.**
Chi semina sulla strada, stanca i buoi e perde la semenza.

2012 **One SOWS and another reaps.**
Uno semina e un altro raccoglie.

Cf. *One beats the BUSH and another catches the birds / Little DOGS start the hare, the great get her.*

o John 4, 37 / Giovanni 4, 37

2013 **Better SPARE at brim than at bottom.**
È meglio risparmiare all'orlo che al fondo.

2014 **It is too late to SPARE when the bottom is bare.**
Tardi si risparmia quando non se n'ha più.

2015 **SPARE at the spigot, and let it out at the bung-hole.**
Bisogna guardare il lume nello stoppino e non nell'olio.

Sim. *Penny wise and pound foolish.*

2016 **SPARING is a great revenue.**
L'economia è una gran raccolta.

2017 **SPARING is the first gaining.**
Il risparmio è il primo guadagno.

Cf. *A PENNY saved is a penny gained.*

2018 **Of a small SPARK a great fire.**
Piccola favilla accende gran fuoco.
Di picciol favilla nasce gran fuoco.
Poca favilla gran fiamma seconda.

Var. *A little spark kindles a great fire / A small spark makes a great fire.*
Cf. *A little FIRE burns up a great deal of corn.*

o Ecclesiasticus 11, 32 / Siràcide 11, 34; James 3, 5 / Giacomo 3, 5

2019 **He cannot SPEAK well that cannot hold his tongue.**
Chi non sa tacer, non sa parlare.

o Ecclesiasticus 32, 8 / Siràcide 32, 8

2020 **SPEAK fitly, or be silent wisely.**
O taci, o di' cosa migliore del silenzio.

Cf. *SILENCE is often the best answer / No WISDOM to silence.*

2021 **To SPEAK without thinking is to shoot without looking.**
Parlar senza pensare è come tirare senza mirare.

Cf. *First THINK, and then speak.*

2022 **He that SPEAKS sows and he that holds his peace gathers.**
Chi parla, semina; chi tace raccoglie.

Var. *He that speaks sows; he that hears reaps / Who speaks sows; who keeps silence, reaps.*

2023 **He that SPEAKS the thing he should not hears the thing he would not.**
Chi dice quel che vuole, ode quel che non vorrebbe.

Var. *He who says what he likes shall hear what he does not like.*

2024 **He that has a good SPEAR, let him try it.**
Chi ha buona lancia, la provi al muro.

2025 **More have repented SPEECH than silence.**
Mai nocque il tacere, ma l'aver parlato.

Cf. *SILENCE does seldom harm / Be STILL, and have thy will.*

2026 **SPEECH is silver, but silence is golden.**
La parola è d'argento, il silenzio è d'oro.

Var. *Silence is golden.*

2027 **To a good SPENDER, God is the treasurer.**
A buon spenditore Iddio è tesoriere.
All'uomo elimosiniero Iddio è tesoriero.

2028 **In SPENDING lies the advantage.**
Nello spendere consiste l'utile.
Denaro sepolto non fa guadagno.

2029 **Get thy SPINDLE and thy distaff ready and God will send thee flax.**
A tela ordita Dio manda il filo.

Cf. *GOD helps those who help themselves.*

2030 **By one and one the SPINDLES are made.**
A uno a uno si fanno le fusa.

Cf. *FEATHER by feather, the goose is plucked.*

2031 **The SPIRIT is willing, but the flesh is weak.**
Lo spirito è forte, ma la carne è debole.

o Matthew 26, 41 / Matteo 26, 41; Mark 14, 38 / Marco 14, 38; John 6, 63 / Giovanni 6, 63

2032 Who SPITS against the wind, it falls in his face.
Chi sputa in su, lo sputo gli torna sul viso.
Var. *Who spits against the heaven, it falls in his face.*
Sim. *Evil that comes out of thy mouth flieth into thy bosom.*
Cf. *An ARROW shot upright falls on the shooter's head / Piss not against the WIND.*

2033 "If" and "An" SPOILS many a good charter.
Col ma e col se non si fa niente di ben.

2034 That is well SPOKEN that is well taken.
Le parole non sono mal dette se non sono mal prese.

2035 He should have a long SPOON that sups with the devil.
Chi vuol mangiar col diavolo bisogna aver cucchiaio lungo.

2036 Throw out a SPRAT to catch a mackerel.
Bisogna rischiare la scardova per aver il salmone.
Var. *Throw out a sprat to catch a salmon (herring, whale) / Bait a sprat to catch a herring.*

2037 That which doth blossom in the SPRING will bring forth fruit in the autumn.
Primavera per l'occhio e l'autunno per la bocca.

2038 It is too late to shut the STABLE-DOOR after the horse has bolted.
Dopo che i cavalli sono presi, serrar la stalla.
Non chiudere la stalla quando i buoi sono scappati.
Chiudere la stalla quando sono fuggiti i buoi.

Var. *It is too late to shut the stable-door when the steed is stolen / There is no use in closing the barn door after the horse is stolen.*
Cf. *When a thing is done, ADVICE comes too late / When the HOUSE is burned down, you bring water / It is easy to be WISE after the event.*

2039 If the STAFF be crooked, the shadow cannot be straight.
Bacchetta torta non fa ombra dritta.

2040 It is an ill STAKE that cannot stand one year in the ground.
Cattivo è quel palo che non può star un anno in terra.

2041 The higher STANDING, the lower fall.
Chi monta più in alto che non deve, cade più in basso che non crede.
Chi più alto sale, fa maggior caduta.

Sim. *The bigger they are, the harder they fall.*
Cf. *Hasty CLIMBERS have sudden falls / The higher the MOUNTAIN, the greater descent.*

2042 **If you STEAL for others, you shall be hanged yourself.**
Chi ruba per altri è impiccato per sé.

2043 **It is the first STEP that is difficult.**
Il passo più difficile è quello dell'uscio.

    Var. *The hardest step is over the threshhold / The first step is the only difficulty.*
    Cf. *Every BEGINNING is hard / The greatest STEP is that out of doors.*

2044 **STEP after step the ladder is ascended.**
A scaglion a scaglion si sale la scala.

2045 **The greatest STEP is that out of doors.**
Il più duro passo è quello della soglia.

    Cf. *Every BEGINNING is hard / It is the first STEP that is difficult.*

2046 **Take heed of a STEPMOTHER: the very name of her suffices.**
Chi ha matrigna, di dietro si signa.

2047 **Dress up a STICK and it does not appear to be a stick.**
Vesti un bastone e ti parrà un signore.
Vesti uno zuccone e pare un barone.
Vesti una colonna, la pare una bella donna.

    Sim. *Apparel makes the man.*
    Cf. *The COAT makes the man / Fine FEATHERS make fine birds.*

2048 **It is easy to find a STICK to beat a dog.**
Tosto si trova il bastone per dare al cane.

    Sim. *A staff is quickly found to beat a dog.*
    Cf. *He that would hang his DOG gives out first that he is mad.*

2049 **Be STILL, and have thy will.**
Chi sa tacer all'occasione guadagna più che col parlare.

    Cf. *SILENCE does seldom harm / More have repented SPEECH than silence.*

2050 **The STING is in the tail.**
Nella coda sta il veleno.

    Sim. *Bitter end.*

2051 **A STITCH in time saves nine.**
Un punto in tempo ne salva cento.

    Var. *A stitch in time saves nine, and sometimes ninety-nine.*
    Sim. *He that repairs not a part, builds all.*
    Cf. *Who REPAIRS not his gutter, repairs his whole house / The TAILOR that makes not a knot loses a stitch.*

2052 **A little STONE in the way overturns a great wain.**
Piccola pietra gran carro riversa.

2053 **A rolling STONE gathers no moss.**
Sasso che rotola non fa muschio.
Pietra mossa non fa muschio.

Var. *Rolling stones gather no moss.*

2054 **A STONE in the well is not lost.**
La pietra è nel pozzo.

2055 **Between two STOOLS one falls to the ground.**
Chi in due scanni vuol sedere, darà in terra del messere.

2056 **He must STOOP who has a low door.**
Dove l'uscio è basso, bisogna inchinarsi.

Sim. *Stoop low and it will save you many a bump through life.*

2057 **STORE is no sore.**
Abbondanza di bene non nuoce.
Meglio troppo che troppo poco.

Sim. *Plenty is no plague.*

2058 **After a STORM comes a calm.**
Dopo la tempesta viene il sereno.

Sim. *After black clouds, clear weather.*

2059 **To stumble at a STRAW and leap over a block.**
Inciampar contro una paglia e balzar sopra un tronco.

2060 **Who has skirts of STRAW needs fear the fire.**
Chi ha coda di paglia, non s'avvicini al fuoco.

Cf. *He that has a HEAD of wax must not walk in the sun.*

2061 **Cross the STREAM where it is ebbest.**
Chi non vede il fondo non guadi il torrente.

Sim. *No safe wading in an unknown water.*

2062 **It is ill striving against the STREAM.**
È un cattivo andare contro la corrente.

Var. *In vain it is to strive against the stream / Strive not against the stream.*

2063 **A man's STUDIES pass into his character.**
Chi di scienza è amatore, a lungo andare avrà onore.

2064 **He that STUMBLES and falls not mends his pace.**
Chi inciampa e non cade, avanza cammino.

2065 **He that STUMBLES twice over one stone deserves to break his shins.**
Chi inciampa due volte nella medesima pietra, non merita compassione.

2066 **The STYLE is the man.**
Lo stile è l'uomo.

2067 **SUBTLETY is better than force.**
La destrezza val più che viva forza.

2068 **SUCCESS has many fathers, while failure is an orphan.**
La vittoria trova cento padri, e nessuno vuole riconoscere l'insuccesso.

2069 **A SUIT at law and a urinal bring a man to hospital.**
Processo, taverna e orinale mandan l'uomo all'ospedale.

2070 **Although the SUN shine, leave not thy cloak at home.**
Né d'estate né d'inverno non andar senza mantello.

2071 **If it rains when the SUN is shining, the devil is beating his wife.**
Quando è sole e piove, il diavolo mena moglie.

2072 **Men use to worship the rising SUN.**
Il sole che nasce ha più adoratori di quel che tramonta.

2073 **Never let the SUN go down on your anger.**
Non lasciar tramontare il sole sulla tua ira.

Var. *Let not the sun go down upon your wrath.*

o Ephesians 4, 26 / Efesini 4, 26

2074 **The March SUN raises, but dissolves not.**
Il sole di marzo muove e non risolve.

2075 **The SUN loses nothing by shining into a puddle.**
Anche il sole passa sopra il fango, e non s'imbratta.

2076 **The SUN shines on all the world.**
Per tutto si leva il sole.
Il sole splende per tutti.

Var. *The sun shines on the just and the unjust / The sun shines upon all alike.*

o Matthew 5, 45 / Matteo 5, 45

2077 **There is nothing new under the SUN.**
Niente di nuovo sotto il sole.
Non vi è nulla di nuovo sotto il sole.

Var. *Nothing new under the sun.*

o Ecclesiastes 1, 9 / Qoèlet 1, 9

2078 **Where the SUN enters, the doctor does not.**
Dove entra il sole non entra il medico.

2079 **He that is SURETY for a stranger shall smart for it.**
Chi garantisce per un estraneo si troverà male.

o Proverbs 11, 15 / Proverbi 11, 15

2080 **A pitiful SURGEON spoils a sore.**
Medico pietoso fa la piaga verminosa.

2081 **One SWALLOW does not make a summer.**
Una rondine non fa primavera.

Cf. *One FLOWER makes no garland.*

2082 **The SWAN sings when death comes.**
Il cigno canta morendo.

2083 **He that will SWEAR will lie.**
Chi giura è bugiardo.

2084 **A ground SWEAT cures all disorders.**
Chi muore esce d'affanni.

2085 **Everyone should SWEEP before his own door.**
Se ognuno spazzasse da casa sua, tutta la città sarebbe netta.
Chi ha mangiato i bacelli, spazzi i gusci.

Var. *If every man would sweep his own doorstep the city would soon be clean / If you want the town clean, sweep before your own door.*

2086 **No SWEET without some sweat.**
Chi non suda, non ha roba.

Cf. *A HORSE that will not carry a saddle must have no oats / No PAIN, no gain / He that will not WORK shall not eat.*

2087 **Good SWIMMERS at length are drowned.**
I più destri nuotatori sogliono morire annegati.
I buoni nuotatori alfin si affogano.

2088 **All they that take the SWORD shall perish with the sword.**
Tutti coloro che avran presa la spada, periranno per la spada.
Tutti quelli che mettono mano alla spada periranno di spada.

Cf. *He who lives by the SWORD dies by the sword.*

o Matthew 26, 52 / Matteo 26, 52; Revelation 13, 10 / Apocalisse 13, 10

2089 **He who lives by the SWORD dies by the sword.**
Chi di spada ferisce, di spada perisce.
Chi di coltello ferisce, di coltello perisce.

Sim. *He that strikes with the sword shall be stricken with the scabbard.*
Cf. *All they that take the SWORD shall perish with the sword.*

2090 It is ill putting a SWORD in a madman's hand.
Non mettere il rasoio in mano ad un pazzo.
Non mettere il rasoio in mano ad un fanciullo.

Var. *Do not put a sword into your enemy's hands / It is ill putting a sword in a child's hand.*

2091 One SWORD keeps another in the sheath.
Una spada tien l'altra nel fodero.
Un coltello fa tener l'altro nella guaina.

2092 They shall beat their SWORDS into ploughshares.
Ed essi delle loro spade fabbricheranno zappe.

o Isaiah 2, 4 / Isaia 2, 4

T

2093 At a round TABLE there's no dispute of place.
A tavola rotonda non si contende del luoco.

2094 The TABLE robs more than a thief.
La tavola ruba più che non fa un ladro.

2095 The TAIL does often catch the fox.
La troppa coda ammazza la volpe.
La volpe ha paura della sua coda.

2096 The TAILOR that makes not a knot loses a stitch.
Chi non fa nodo perde il punto.

    Sim. *He that repairs not a part builds all.*
    Cf. *Who REPAIRS not his gutter repairs his whole house / A STITCH in time saves nine.*

2097 A hundred TAILORS, a hundred millers, and a hundred weavers are three hundred thieves.
Trenta mugnai, trenta beccai, trenta sartori, trenta fattori, fan centoventi ladri.

2098 One 'TAKE IT' is worth more than two 'I'll give you'.
È meglio un "ti do" che cento "ti prometto".
È meglio un tieni, tieni, che cento piglia, piglia.

    Var. *Better is one 'take it' than two 'you shall have' / One "take it" is more worth than two "thou shalt have it".*
    Cf. *Better to HAVE than wish / One TODAY is worth two tomorrows.*

2099 Always TAKING OUT of the meal-tub, and never putting in, soon comes to the bottom.
Non mettere e cavare, si seccherebbe il mare.
Chi cava e non mette, le possessioni si disfanno.

2100 The greatest TALKERS are the least doers.
Chi parla molto agisce poco.

    Sim. *Much bruit and little fruit.*
    Cf. *Great BOAST and little roast / Great BRAGGERS, little doers / Much CRY and little wool / A long TONGUE is a sign of a short hand.*

2101 **TALKING pays no toll.**
Parole non pagan dazio.

2102 **He who TALKS much errs much.**
Chi molto parla, spesso falla.

Var. *He who talks much says many foolish things.*

2103 **Every man to his TASTE.**
Ognuno ha i suoi gusti.

Sim. *Everyone as they like best.*
Cf. *There is no ACCOUNTING for tastes / TASTES differ.*

2104 **To him that has lost his TASTE, sweet is sour.**
A gusto guasto non è buono alcun pasto.
Al gusto infermo ogni buon cibo annoia.

2105 **TASTES differ.**
Tutti i gusti sono gusti.
Ognuno ha i suoi gusti.

Sim. *Everyone as they like best.*
Cf. *There is no ACCOUNTING for tastes / Every man to his TASTE.*

2106 **TEACHING others teaches yourself.**
Insegnando s'impara.
Chi altri insegna, se stesso ammaestra.

Var. *One learns in teaching.*

2107 **Nothing dries sooner than TEARS.**
Niente s'asciuga così presto come le lacrime.

2108 **Good that the TEETH guard the tongue.**
Quando senti gli altrui mancamenti, chiudi la lingua tra i denti.

2109 **He who has TEETH has no bread, and he who has bread has no teeth.**
Chi ha denti non ha pane, e chi ha pane non ha denti.
Quando c'è il pane mancano i denti.
Dio manda i biscotti a quelli che non hanno denti.

Var. *They have most bread who have least teeth.*
Sim. *The Gods send nuts to those who have no teeth.*

2110 **If you cannot bite, never show your TEETH.**
Se non puoi mordere, non mostrar mai i denti.
Chi non può mordere, non mostri i denti.

Var. *Never show your teeth unless you can bite.*

2111 **A THIEF passes for a gentleman when stealing has made him rich.**
Il birbante quando si arricchisce diventa galantuomo.

2112 **He is a THIEF indeed that robs a thief.**
In casa di ladri non ci si ruba.

2113 **Once a THIEF, always a thief.**
Chi ruba una volta è sempre ladro.

Cf. *Once a KNAVE, and ever a knave.*

2114 **Save a THIEF from the gallows and he will help to hang you.**
Dispicca l'impiccato, impiccherà poi te.

Var. *Save a thief from the gallows and he will hate you.*
Sim. *Save a stranger from the sea, and he'll turn your enemy.*

2115 **The THIEF does fear each bush an officer.**
Al ladro fa paura anche un sorcio.

Sim. *A guilty conscience feels continual fear.*

2116 **When it thunders the THIEF becomes honest.**
Quando v'è tuono, il ladro divien buono.
Quando non si può più, si torna al buon Gesù.

2117 **Little THIEVES are hanged, but great ones escape.**
S'impiccano i ladrucci, e non i ladroni.
A rubar poco si va in galera, a rubar tanto si fa carriera.

Var. *Petty thieves are hanged, the great ones go free.*
Cf. *LAWS catch flies but let hornets go free.*

2118 **The great THIEVES hang the little ones.**
I ladri grandi fanno impiccare i piccoli.
Ladro piccolo non rubare, che il ladro grande ti fa impiccare.

Sim. *The great put the little on the hook.*
Cf. *Big FISH eat little fish.*

2119 **When THIEVES fall out, honest men come by their own.**
Quando i ladri contrastano, gli uomini da bene riscuoteranno lor beni.

2120 **One THING leads to another.**
Da cosa nasce cosa.
Da cosa nasce cosa, e il tempo la governa.

2121 **That THING which is rare is dear.**
Cosa rara, cosa cara.

2122 **The THING that's done has an end.**
Cosa fatta, capo ha.

Var. *The thing that's done is not to do.*
Cf. *What's DONE cannot be undone.*

2123 All THINGS thrive at thrice.
Tutte le cose belle sono tre.
Ogni trino è perfetto.

Var. *All good things go by threes.*

2124 Lay THINGS by, they may come to use.
Metti la roba in un cantone, che poi viene l'occasione.
Metti la roba in un cantone, ché viene tempo ch'ella ha stagione.

2125 The best THINGS come in small packages.
Le spezie migliori stanno nei sacchetti piccoli.

Var. *Good things are wrapped up in small parcels.*

2126 The best THINGS may be abused.
Ogni buona cosa si può abusare.

2127 First THINK, and then speak.
Prima il pensare e poi il parlare.
Pensa tre volte prima di parlare.
Pensa oggi e parla domani.

Var. *Always think before you speak / Think first and speak afterwards.*
Cf. *Think on the END before you begin / To SPEAK without thinking is to shoot without looking.*

2128 THINK much, speak little, and write less.
Pensa molto, parla poco e scrivi meno.

2129 THINKING is very far from knowing.
Credere non vuol dire sapere.

2130 He THINKS not well that thinks not again.
Mal pensa chi non contropensa.

2131 Men cut large THONGS of other men's leather.
Del cuoio d'altri si fanno le corregge larghe.

Sim. *Men are very generous with what costs them nothing / To cut large shives of another's loaf.*
Cf. *All MEN are free of other men's goods.*

2132 It early pricks that will be a THORN.
La spina cresce pungendo.

Cf. *The THORN comes forth with the point forwards.*

2133 The THORN comes forth with the point forwards.
Al nascer la spina porta la punta in cima.

Cf. *It early pricks that will be a THORN.*

2134 He that goes barefoot must not plant THORNS.
Chi semina spine non vada scalzo.

Var. *He who scatters thorns should not go barefooted / He who goes barefooted shouldn't plant briars.*

2135 THOUGHT is free.
I pensieri non pagano gabelle.
I pensieri sono esenti dal tributo, ma non dall'inferno.

Var. *Thoughts be free from toll.*

2136 Second THOUGHTS are best.
I secondi pensieri sono i migliori.

2137 The THREAD breaks where it is weakest.
Il filo si rompe dove è più debole.

Sim. *The chain is no stronger than its weakest link.*

2138 He THREATENS who is afraid.
Tal minaccia che vive con paura.
Chi più teme, minaccia.

Var. *A man may threaten, and yet be afraid.*

2139 After THUNDER comes rain.
Tanto tuonò che piovve.

2140 TIE it well, and let it go.
Legala bene, e poi lasciala andare.

2141 Knotty TIMBER must have sharp wedges.
A legno duro, accetta tagliente.
A duro ceppo, dura accetta.

Sim. *A crabbed knot must have a crabbed wedge.*

2142 Be ruled by TIME, the wisest counsellor of all.
Il tempo dà consiglio.

2143 He that has TIME and looks for time, loses time.
Chi ha tempo, non aspetti tempo.
Chi tempo ha e tempo aspetta, tempo perde.

2144 He that has TIME has life.
Chi ha tempo, ha vita.

2145 Take TIME by the forelock.
L'occasione ha i capelli dinanzi.

2146 There is a TIME for everything.
Ogni cosa a suo tempo.
Ogni cosa ha il suo tempo.

Sim. *Everything has its time.*

o Ecclesiastes 3, 1 / Qoèlet 3, 1

2147 There is a TIME to be born, and a time to die.
Vi è tempo di nascere e tempo di morire.

o Ecclesiastes 3, 2 / Qoèlet 3, 2

2148 There is a TIME to love, and a time to hate.
C'è un tempo per amare e un tempo per odiare.

o Ecclesiastes 3, 8 / Qoèlet 3, 8

2149 There is a TIME to speak, and a time to be silent.
C'è un tempo per parlare e uno per tacere.

o Ecclesiastes 3, 7 / Qoèlet 3, 7

2150 There is a TIME to weep, and a time to laugh.
Vi è tempo di piangere e tempo di ridere.

o Ecclesiastes 3, 4 / Qoèlet 3, 4

2151 TIME and straw make medlars ripe.
Col tempo e con la paglia si maturano le nespole.

Cf. *With TIME and art the leaf of the mulberry-tree becomes satin.*

2152 TIME and tide wait for no man.
Il tempo scorre incessantemente come l'acqua.
Il tempo passa e porta via ogni cosa.

Var. *Time shall teach thee all things.*

2153 TIME cures all things.
Il tempo guarisce tutti i mali.
Il tempo sana ogni cosa.

Cf. *TIME is a great healer.*

2154 TIME devours all things.
Il tempo consuma ogni cosa.

2155 TIME discloses all things.
Il tempo scopre tutto.

Sim. *Time will tell.*

o Matthew 10, 26 / Matteo 10, 26; Mark 4, 22 / Marco 4, 22

2156 **TIME flies.**
Il tempo fugge.
Il tempo vola.

Var. *Time flees away without delay / Time has wings.*

2157 **TIME is a file that wears and makes no noise.**
Il tempo è una lima sorda.

2158 **TIME is a great healer.**
Il tempo è un gran medico.

Cf. *TIME cures all things.*

2159 **TIME is money.**
Il tempo è denaro.

Sim. *Time is capital: invest it wisely.*

2160 **TIME is the rider that breaks youth.**
Il tempo è'l cozzone che doma la gioventù.

2161 **TIME lost cannot be won again.**
Tempo perduto mai più si riacquista.

Cf. *An OCCASION lost cannot be redeemed.*

2162 **TIME tames the strongest grief.**
Il tempo mitiga ogni gran piaga.
Il tempo doma ogni cosa.

Var. *Time and thinking tames the strongest grief.*

2163 **TIME tries truth.**
Il tempo scopre la verità.

Sim. *Time is the father of truth.*
Cf. *TRUTH is time's daughter.*

2164 **With TIME and art the leaf of the mulberry-tree becomes satin.**
Col tempo una foglia di gelso divien seta.

Cf. *TIME and straw make medlars ripe.*

2165 **Other TIMES, other manners.**
Altri tempi, altri costumi.

2166 **TIMES change and we with them.**
Mutansi i tempi e noi con essi.

2167 **Here TODAY and gone tomorrow.**
Oggi in figura, domani in sepoltura.

Sim. *Today gold, tomorrow dust / Today a man, tomorrow none.*

2168 I TODAY, you tomorrow.
Oggi a me, domani a te.

    o Ecclesiasticus 38, 22 / Siràcide 38, 24

2169 If TODAY will not, tomorrow may.
Quel che non avvien oggi, può avvenir domani.

2170 One TODAY is worth two tomorrows.
È meglio un presente che due futuri.

    Cf. *Better to HAVE than wish / One "TAKE IT" is more worth than two "Thou shalt have it".*

2171 Stuff TODAY and starve tomorrow.
Oggi fave, domani fame.

2172 TODAY a man, tomorrow a mouse.
Oggi mercante, domani viandante.
Oggi è Caifasso chi ieri fu Giovanni.

2173 TODAY is the scholar of yesterday.
Del primo giorno, scolaro è il secondo.
Un giorno è maestro dell'altro.

2174 Never put off till TOMORROW what you can do today.
Non rimandare a domani, quello che puoi fare oggi.
Quel che puoi fare oggi, non rimandare a domani.

    Sim. *Work today, for you know not how much you may be hindered tomorrow.*

2175 Ye know not what shall be on the TOMORROW.
Non sapete ciò che sarà domani.

    o James 4, 14 / Giacomo 4, 14

2176 A honey TONGUE, a heart of gall.
Volto di miele, cuor di fiele.
Parole di miele spesso sono piene di fiele.

2177 A long TONGUE is a sign of a short hand.
Lunga lingua, corta mano.

    Sim. *Much bruit and little fruit.*
    Cf. *Great BOAST and little roast / Great BRAGGERS, little doers / Much CRY and little wool / The greatest TALKERS are the least doers.*

2178 He who uses his TONGUE will reach his destination.
Chi lingua ha, a Roma va.
Domandando si va per tutto.

    Sim. *Make use of your tongue and you will find out.*

2179 **The lame TONGUE gets nothing.**
Chi non chiede, non ottiene.

Sim. *He that cannot ask, cannot live / Dumb men get no land.*
Cf. *He that speaks not, GOD hears not.*

2180 **The TONGUE ever turns to the aching tooth.**
La lingua batte dove il dente duole.

2181 **The TONGUE is sharper than the sword.**
Ferisce più la lingua che la spada.
Ne ammazza più la lingua che la spada.
Cattive lingue tagliano più che spade.

Sim. *Words cut more than swords.*

o Ecclesiasticus 28, 18 / Siracide 28, 19

2182 **The TONGUE is the rudder of our ship.**
La lingua timon del corpo.

2183 **The TONGUE talks at the head's cost.**
Non dica cosa la lingua che la paghi colla testa.

Sim. *A fool's tongue is long enough to cut his own throat.*

o Proverbs 13, 3; 21, 23 / Proverbi 13, 3; 21, 23

2184 **TONGUE breaks bone and herself has none.**
La lingua non ha osso, ma rompe il dosso.

Var. *The tongue is not steel, yet it cuts.*

o Proverbs 25, 15 / Proverbi 25, 15; Ecclesiasticus 28, 18 / Siràcide 28, 18

2185 **TOO MUCH breaks the bag.**
Il troppo bene sfonda la cassetta.

Cf. *COVETOUSNESS breaks the bag / You can have TOO MUCH of a good thing.*

2186 **TOO MUCH money makes one mad.**
Il molto fa l'uomo stolto.

2187 **TOO MUCH spoils, too little does not satisfy.**
Il troppo guasta, e il poco non basta.

2188 **You can have TOO MUCH of a good thing.**
Il troppo è troppo.
Il troppo storpia.
Il troppo stroppia.

Sim. *Enough is enough / More than enough is too much.*
Cf. *ABUNDANCE of things engenders disdainfulness / COVETOUSNESS breaks the bag / TOO MUCH breaks the bag.*

2189 **Quickly TOO'D and quickly go, quickly will thy mother have moe.**
Chi presto indenta, presto sparenta.
Chi presto inossa, presto in fossa.

2190 **As the TOUCHSTONE tries gold, so gold tries men.**
Al paragone si conosce l'oro.

2191 **A TRADE is better than service.**
Chi ha l'arte, ha ufficio e beneficio.

Sim. *Trade is the mother of money.*

2192 **He that learns a TRADE has a purchase made.**
Impara l'arte e mettila da parte.

2193 **Two of a TRADE seldom agree.**
Il tuo nemico è quello dell'arte tua.
Quello è tuo nemico che è di tuo ufficio.

Sim. *One potter envies another / The herringman hates the fisherman.*

2194 **Who has a TRADE, has a share everywhere.**
Chi ha un mestiere in man, dappertutto trova pan.

Cf. *He who has an ART has everywhere a part.*

2195 **A man of many TRADES begs his bread on Sunday.**
Quattordici mestieri, quindici infortuni.

Sim. *Jack of all trades, and master of none.*

2196 **TRANSLATORS, traitors.**
Traduttori, traditori.
Traduttore, traditore.

2197 **A TRAVELLER may lie with authority.**
Ha bel mentir chi vien da lontano.

Var. *Old men (soldiers) and travellers may lie by authority.*
Cf. *Long WAYS, long lies.*

2198 **He that TRAVELS far knows much.**
Chi viaggia s'istruisce.
Viaggiando s'impara.

o Ecclesiasticus 34, 10 / Siràcide 34, 10

2199 **TREACHERY will come home to the traitor.**
L'inganno va a casa dell'ingannatore.

Sim. *Subtility set a tap and caught itself.*

2200 The TREASON is loved, but the traitor is hated.
Tradimento amato, traditor odiato.
Tradimento piace assai, traditor non piacque mai.

Sim. *A king loves the treason but hates the traitor.*

2201 Where your TREASURE is, there will your heart be also.
Dove è il tuo tesoro, ivi è il tuo cuore.

o Matthew 6, 21 / Matteo 6, 21

2202 Lay not up for yourselves TREASURES upon earth.
Non accumulatevi tesori sulla terra.

o Matthew 6, 19 / Matteo 6, 19

2203 A good TREE cannot bring forth evil fruit.
L'albero buono non può far frutti cattivi.

Sim. *Good fruit of a good tree.*

o Matthew 7, 18 / Matteo 7, 18

2204 A TREE is known by its fruit.
Dal frutto si conosce l'albero.
La pianta si conosce dal frutto.

o Matthew 7, 19; 12, 33 / Matteo 7, 19; 12, 33

2205 A TREE often transplanted bears not much fruit.
Albero spesso trapiantato, mai di frutti è caricato.

Cf. *Remove an old TREE and it will wither to death.*

2206 He that leans on a good TREE, a good shadow covers him.
Chi a buon albero s'appoggia, buona ombra lo ricopre.

Cf. *Honour the TREE that gives you shelter.*

2207 He that loves the TREE loves the branch.
Chi ama la pianta ama il ramo.
Chi ama l'arbore, ama il ramo.

2208 Honour the TREE that gives you shelter.
Bisogna rispettare l'albero per la sua ombra.

Cf. *He that leans on a good TREE, a good shadow covers him.*

2209 In the place where the TREE falleth, there it shall be.
Quando l'albero cade, ove egli cade quivi resta.

Var. *As a tree falls, so shall it lie.*

o Ecclesiastes 11, 3 / Qoèlet 11, 3

2210 **It is only at the TREE loaded with fruit that people throw stones.**
I migliori alberi sono i più battuti.

2211 **Like TREE, like fruit.**
Quale la pianta, tali i frutti.

2212 **Remove an old TREE and it will wither to death.**
Albero vecchio trapiantato mai di frutti è caricato.

    Var. *You cannot shift an old tree without it dying.*
    Cf. *A TREE often transplanted bears not much fruit.*

2213 **When the TREE is fallen every one runs to it with his axe.**
Quando l'albero è in terra, ognuno corre a farvi legna.
Dall'albero caduto tutti si fanno legna.
Sopra l'albero caduto ognuno corre a far legna.

    Var. *When the tree is fallen, everyone goes to it with his hatchet / When an oak is fallen, every man becomes a wood-cutter.*

2214 **Great TREES are good for nothing but shade.**
Gli alberi grandi fanno più ombra che frutto.

2215 **A little and good fills the TRENCHER.**
Poco e buono empie il tagliere.

2216 **There are TRICKS in every trade.**
Ogni bottega la sua malizia.

2217 **Do not TRIUMPH before victory.**
Non convien cantar trionfo prima della vittoria.

2218 **He that seeks TROUBLE, never misses.**
Chi cerca rogna, rogna trova.
Chi cerca briga, l'accatta.

    Cf. *HARM watch, harm catch.*

2219 **What everybody says must be TRUE.**
Bisogna che sia vero quel che tutti dicono.

    Var. *It is true that all men say.*
    Cf. *When all men say you are an ASS, it is time to bray.*

2220 **In TRUST is treason.**
Chi si fida è l'ingannato.
Chi spesso fida, spesso grida.
Chi a tutti facil crede, ingannato si vede.

    Sim. *Quick believers need broad shoulders / Trust is the mother of deceit / He who trusteth not is not deceived.*
    Cf. *DISTRUST is the mother of safety.*

2221 Put not your TRUST in princes.
Non vi confidate in principi.

o Psalms 146, 3 / Salmi 146, 3

2222 TRUST is dead, ill payment killed it.
Credenza è morta, il mal pagar l'uccise.

2223 Follow not TRUTH too near the heels, lest it dash out thy teeth.
Chi segue la verità troppo presso potrà aver i denti spezzati.

Sim. *Truth has a scratched face.*

2224 Hide not the TRUTH from your confessor, your doctor or your lawyer.
Al confessore, medico e avvocato, non tenere il ver celato.

Var. *Always tell your doctor and your lawyer the truth / Conceal not the truth from thy physician and lawyer / Hide nothing from thy minister, physician and lawyer.*

2225 Nothing hurts like the TRUTH.
Non c'è niente che offenda come la verità.

2226 The TRUTH is always green.
La verità è verde.

2227 There is TRUTH in wine.
La verità è nel vino.

Var. *In wine there is truth.*

2228 TRUTH and oil are ever above.
L'olio e la verità tornano alla sommità.
La verità viene sempre a galla.

Var. *Truth and oil always come to the top.*
Sim. *Truth will out.*
Cf. *TRUTH is mighty and will prevail.*

2229 TRUTH begets hatred.
La verità genera odio.
La verità è madre dell'odio.
Del vero s'adira l'uomo.

Sim. *Truth finds foes, where it makes none.*

2230 TRUTH has a good face, but bad clothes.
La verità ha una buona faccia, ma cattivi abiti.

2231 TRUTH has no answer.
Il vero non ha risposta.

2232 **TRUTH is mighty and will prevail.**
La verità ha una gran forza.

Sim. *Truth will out.*
Cf. *TRUTH and oil are ever above.*

2233 **TRUTH is time's daughter.**
La verità è figliuola del tempo.

Sim. *Time is the father of truth / Truth is God's daughter.*
Cf. *TIME tries truth.*

2234 **TRUTH lies at the bottom of a well.**
La verità sta in fondo a un pozzo.

2235 **TRUTH may be blamed, but cannot be shamed.**
La verità può languire, ma non perire.

2236 **TRUTH needs no colours.**
La verità è senza varietà.

2237 **All TRUTHS are not to be told.**
Ogni vero non è ben detto.
Ogni verità non è da dire.

2238 **The more you stir a TURD, the worse it stinks.**
La merda, più la giri, più puzza.
Lo sterco più si rimescola e più pute.

2239 **Best to bend while it is a TWIG.**
Piega l'albero quando è giovane.
L'albero si raddrizza quando è piccolo.
Finché la pianta è tenera bisogna drizzarla.

Var. *Bend the tree while it is young.*

2240 **One cannot be in TWO places at once.**
Non si può essere in due luoghi allo stesso tempo.

U

2241 Better UNBORN than untaught.
È meglio non nato che non insegnato.

2242 Who UNDERSTANDS ill answers ill.
Chi male intende, peggio risponde.

2243 The UNEXPECTED always happens.
Vien più presto quel che non si spera.

2244 UNION is strength.
L'unione fa la forza.

> Var. *In union there is strength.*
> Cf. *UNITED we stand, divided we fall.*

2245 UNITED we stand, divided we fall.
L'ordine è pane, il disordine è fame.

> Cf. *UNION is strength.*

V

2246 **VAINGLORY blossoms but never bears.**
Gloria mondana, gloria vana, fiorisce e non grana.

2247 **VANITY of vanities, all is vanity.**
Vanità delle vanità, tutto è vanità.

    o Ecclesiastes 1, 2 / Qoèlet 1, 2

2248 **VARIETY is charming.**
La varietà diletta.

2249 **VARIETY is the spice of life.**
La vita è bella perché è varia.

2250 **A VAUNTER and a liar are near akin.**
Credi al vantatore, come al mentitore.

2251 **Raw pulleyn, VEAL and fish make the churchyards fat.**
Vitella, pollastro e pesce crudo ingrassan il cimitero.

2252 **The noblest VENGEANCE is to forgive.**
La miglior vendetta è il perdono.
Il perdono è la più bella vendetta.

  Sim. *Pardons and pleasantness are great revenges of slanders.*

2253 **A little VENOM bittereth much sweet.**
Poco fiele fa amaro molto miele.

  Sim. *One drop of poison infects the whole tun of wine.*

2254 **There is no VENOM to that of the tongue.**
Non c'è veleno pari ad una cattiva lingua.

2255 **Nothing VENTURE, nothing gain.**
Chi non risica, non rosica.
Chi non s'avventura, non ha ventura.

  Var. *Nothing venture, nothing have.*
  Sim. *He that counts all costs will never put plough in the earth.*

2256 **Empty VESSELS make the greatest sound.**
Sono le botti vuote quelle che cantano.

  Var. *Empty vessels make the most sound.*

2257 VICE is often clothed in virtue's habit.
Con l'ombra della virtù si dipinge il vizio.

2258 What maintains one VICE would bring up two children.
Costa più un viziolo che un figliuolo.

2259 Where VICE is vengeance follows.
Nessun vizio senza supplizio.

2260 He gets a double VICTORY who conquers himself.
Doppia vittoria acquista chi se stesso vince.

2261 It is a great VICTORY that comes without blood.
Gran vittoria è quella che si vince senza sangue.

2262 Make the VINE poor and it will make you rich.
Fammi povera, ti farò ricco.

2263 Take a VINE of a good soil, and the daughter of a good mother.
Di buona terra to' la vigna, di buona madre to' la figlia.

2264 The VINE brings forth three grapes: the first of pleasure, the second of drunkenness, the third of sorrow.
Nell'uva sono tre vinaccioli: uno di sanità, uno di letizia, e uno di ubriachezza.

2265 The VINE embraces the elm.
Ogni vite vuole il suo palo.

2266 Take heed of the VINEGAR of sweet wine.
Guardati da aceto di vin dolce.

2267 Nothing that is VIOLENT is permanent.
Violenza non dura a lungo.
Cosa violente non è permanente.

2268 No VIPER so little, but has its venom.
Ogni serpe ha il suo veleno.

2269 He that sows VIRTUE reaps fame.
Chi semina virtù, fama raccoglie.

2270 Make a VIRTUE of necessity.
Fare di necessità virtù.
Il savio fa della necessità virtù.

Cf. *To make the best of a bad JOB.*

2271 There is no VIRTUE that poverty destroys not.
Non c'è virtù che povertà non guasti.

2272 VIRTUE is a jewel of great price.
Più val che l'oro, della virtù il tesoro.

2273 VIRTUE is found in the middle.
La virtù sta nel mezzo.

2274 VIRTUE is its own reward.
La virtù è premio a se stessa.

2275 VIRTUE is the only true nobility.
Dalla virtù la nobiltà procede.
Chi di virtù non ha lo scudo, mancatagli la roba, resta nudo.

Var. *Virtue is the best title of nobility.*

2276 He cannot be VIRTUOUS that is not rigorous.
Non è virtuoso chi non sa esser rigoroso.

2277 The VOICE of the people, the voice of God.
Voce di popolo, voce di Dio.

o Daniel 10, 6 / Daniele 10, 6; Revelation 19, 6 / Apocalisse 19, 6

2278 He that goes and comes makes a good VOYAGE.
Chi va e torna, fa buon viaggio.

W

2279 **All things come to those who WAIT.**
Il tempo viene per chi sa aspettare.
Chi aspettar può, ha ciò che vuole.

    Var. *Everything comes to him who waits.*

2280 **To WAIT for one who never comes by, to be in bed and sleepless lie, to serve and not to satisfy, are reasons three to make one die.**
Aspettare e non venire; stare a letto e non dormire; ben servir e non gradire, son tre cose per morire.

2281 **WAIT and see.**
Chi vivrà, vedrà.

2282 **A WALL between preserves love.**
Per amistà conservare, muri bisogna piantare.

    Cf. *A HEDGE between keeps friendship green / Love your NEIGHBOUR, yet pull not down the hedge.*

2283 **A white WALL is a fool's paper.**
Muro bianco, carta di pazzi.
Muraglia bianca, carta di matto.

    Var. *White walls are fools' writing paper.*

2284 **WALLS have ears.**
I muri hanno orecchi.

    Cf. *FIELDS have eyes, and woods have ears.*

2285 **WALNUTS and pears you plant for your heirs.**
Chi pianta noce non mangia noci.
Chi pianta datteri non ne mangia.

2286 **A just WAR is better than an unjust peace.**
Anzi una guerra giusta che pace finta.

2287 **He that makes a good WAR makes a good peace.**
Chi fa buona guerra, ha buona pace.
Chi ben guerreggia, ben patteggia.

2288 In WAR, hunting, and love men for one pleasure a thousand griefs prove.
In guerra, nella caccia e negli amori, per un piacer mille dolori.
Di cani, uccelli, armi e amori, per un piacer mille dolori.
    Sim. *Hunting, hawking, and paramours, for one joy a hundred displeasures.*
    Cf. *Short PLEASURE, long pain.*

2289 In WAR it is not permitted twice to err.
Durante la battaglia, più di una volta non si sbaglia.
Gli errori nelle guerre divengono pianti.

2290 WAR makes thieves, and peace hangs them.
La guerra fa i ladri, e la pace li impicca.
    Var. *War makes the thief, and peace brings him to the galows.*

2291 WAR with all the world, and peace with England.
Guerra con tutto il mondo e pace con l'Inghilterra.

2292 When WAR begins then hell opens.
Quando comincia la guerra, si apre l'inferno.
Guerra cominciata, inferno scatenato.

2293 Good WARE makes quick markets.
La buona mercanzia trova subito spaccio.
La buona mercanzia si loda da se stessa.

2294 Ill WARE is never cheap.
Non s'ha mai buon mercato di cattiva mercanzia.

2295 Pleasing WARE is half sold.
Cosa cara tenuta, è mezza venduta.

2296 Proffered WARE stinks.
Mercanzia che si proferisce cala il doppio del prezzo.

2297 Of all WARS peace is the end.
La guerra cerca la pace.

2298 Good WATCH prevents misfortune.
La buona cura scaccia la mala ventura.

2299 Dirty WATER will quench fire.
Anche l'acqua sporca spegne il fuoco.
Ogni acqua spegne il fuoco.
    o Ecclesiasticus 3, 30 / Siràcide 3, 29

2300 In the deepest WATER is the best fishing.
Nel mar grosso si pigliano i pesci grossi.

2301 Let none say, I will not drink WATER.
Non serve dire: Di tal acqua non beverò.

Var. *Do not say, I'll never drink of this water.*
Sim. *Never say never.*

2302 Much WATER goes by the mill that the miller knows not of.
Assai acqua passa per il mulino che il molinaro non se n'accorge.

2303 Much WATER has run under the bridge since then.
È passata molt'acqua sotto il ponte.

2304 Running WATER carries no poison.
Acqua che corre non porta veleno.

2305 Under WATER, famine; under snow, bread.
Sott'acqua fame e sotto neve pane.

2306 WATER afar off quenches not fire.
Acqua lontana non spegne fuoco vicino.

2307 WATER, fire, and soldiers, quickly make room.
Acqua, vento, soldato e fuoco, da per tutto si fanno far luoco.
Acqua e fuoco presto si fan loco.

2308 We never know the worth of WATER till the well is dry.
Pozzo secco, acqua stimata.

Var. *You never miss the water till the well runs dry.*
Cf. *The COW knows not what her tail is worth till she has lost it* / *A GOOD thing lost is a good thing valued.*

2309 Still WATERS run deep.
Acqua cheta rovina i ponti.
Acque chete fanno le cose, e stansi chete.

Cf. *Take heed of still WATERS, the quick pass away.*

2310 Stolen WATERS are sweet.
Pan rubato ha buon sapore.

Var. *Stolen pleasures are sweet.*
Cf. *Forbidden FRUIT is sweet.*

o Proverbs 9, 17 / Proverbi 9, 17

2311 Take heed of still WATERS, the quick pass away.
Dall'acqua cheta mi guardi Dio, che dalla corrente mi guarderò io.

Cf. *Still WATERS run deep.*

2312 The longest WAY round is the shortest way home.
La più lunga strada è la più prossima a casa.

2313 **The nearest WAY is commonly the foulest.**
La scorciatoia non è mai la più comoda.

2314 **Who leaves the old WAY for the new will find himself deceived.**
Chi lascia la via vecchia per la nuova, ingannato spesso si ritrova.

Sim. *He that leaves the highway to cut short, commonly goes about.*

2315 **Long WAYS, long lies.**
Lunga via, lunga bugia.

Cf. *A TRAVELLER may lie with authority.*

2316 **There are three WAYS: the church, the sea, the court.**
Tre cose fan l'uomo guadagnare: scienza, corte e mare.
Scienza, casa, mare, molto fan l'uomo avanzare.

2317 **The WEAKEST go to the wall.**
Gli stracci vanno all'aria.

2318 **Little WEALTH, little care.**
Poca roba, poco pensiero.

2319 **Men get WEALTH and women keep it.**
Gli uomini fanno la roba, e le donne la conservano.

2320 **The greatest WEALTH is contentment with a little.**
Contentezza passa ricchezza.

Sim. *He hath enough who is contented with little / Content is more than a kingdom.*
Cf. *He is RICH enough that wants nothing.*

2321 **WEALTH got by labour is sweet in the enjoyment.**
Pane di sudore ha gran sapore.

2322 **WEAPONS breed peace.**
L'armi portan pace.

2323 **No WEATHER is ill if the wind be still.**
Se non fosse vento o femmina matta, non vi saria mal tempo né mala giornata.

2324 **Better WED over the mixen than over the moor.**
Moglie e buoi dei paesi tuoi.
Moglie e ronzino, pigliali dal vicino.

2325 **Ill WEEDS grow apace.**
L'erba cattiva cresce in fretta.

Sim. *Ill weeds wax well.*

2326 WEEDS never die.
La mala erba non muore mai.
L'erba cattiva non muore mai.
La mal erba non si spegne mai.

Sim. *The frost hurts not the weeds.*

2327 We WEEPING come into the world, and weeping hence we go.
Tutti si nasce piangendo e nessuno muore ridendo.

Sim. *We are born crying, live complaining, and die disappointed.*

2328 WEIGH justly and sell dearly.
Pesa giusto, e vendi caro.

2329 WEIGHT and measure take away strife.
Misura e pesa, non avrai contesa.

2330 They are WELCOME that bring.
Chi porta è sempre il benvenuto.
Ben venga chi ben porta.

Cf. *If thou wilt COME with me, bring with thee.*

2331 All's WELL that ends well.
Tutto è bene quel che finisce bene.

2332 He that would be WELL needs not go from his own house.
Chi sta bene, non si muova.
Chi vuol star bene, non bisogna spartirsi di casa sua.

Sim. *When you are well hold yourself so.*

2333 Never be weary of WELL doing.
Non stanchiamoci di fare il bene.

　　o Galatians 6, 9 / Galati 6, 9

2334 The worst WHEEL of a cart creaks most.
La peggiore ruota è quella che cigola.
La più cattiva ruota del carro sempre più cigola.

Var. *The worst wheel of a cart makes the most noise.*

2335 He who greases his WHEELS helps his oxen.
Ungi la ruota, se vuoi che il carro cammini.
Perché vada il carro, bisogna unger le ruote.
A voler che il carro non cigoli, bisogna ungere bene le ruote.

2336 A man cannot WHISTLE and drink at the same time.
Non si può ad un tempo bere e fischiare.

Var. *One cannot drink and whistle at once.*
Sim. *A man cannot spin and reel at the same time / No man can sup and blow together.*
Cf. *A man cannot have his MOUTH full of flour and also blow the fire.*

2337 **Every WHITE hath its black, and every sweet its sour.**
Non c'è miele senza fiele.
Non c'è dolce senza amaro.

Cf. *No JOY without annoy.*

2338 **It is an ill thing to be WICKED, but worse to be known so.**
È mala cosa esser cattivo, ma è peggio esser conosciuto.

2339 **A fair WIFE and a frontier castle breed quarrels.**
Chi ha bella donna e castello in frontiera, non ha mai pace in lettiera.

2340 **A good WIFE makes a good husband.**
La buona moglie fa il buon marito.

Sim. *Behind every great man there is a great woman / Behind every successful man there is a woman.*

2341 **Commend not your WIFE, wine, nor horse.**
La persona non s'ha da vantar di tre cose, buon vino, bella moglie e borsa piena.

2342 **He that has a WIFE has strife.**
Chi ha moglie, ha doglie.

2343 **He that has no WIFE beats her oft.**
Tal castiga la moglie che non l'ha, ché quando l'ha, castigar non la sa.
Chi non ha moglie ben la batte, chi non ha figliuoli ben li pasce.

2344 **He that loses his WIFE and sixpence has lost a tester.**
Chi perde la moglie e un quattrino ha gran perdita del quattrino.

2345 **The cunning WIFE makes her husband her apron.**
Donne danno, fanno gli uomini e gli disfanno.

2346 **The first WIFE is matrimony, the second company, the third heresy.**
La prima è moglie, la seconda compagnia, la terza eresia.

2347 **The WIFE is the key of the house.**
La moglie è la chiave di casa.

2348 **There is one good WIFE in the country, and every man thinks he has her.**
Se v'è in paese una buona moglie, ciascuno crede che sia la sua.

2349 **Who has a fair WIFE needs more than two eyes.**
Chi è bella ti fa far sentinella.

2350 A good WIFE's a goodly prize, saith Solomon the wise.
Donna buona vale una corona.

o Proverbs 12, 4; 18, 22; 31, 10 / Proverbi 12, 4; 18, 22; 31, 10

2351 A WILFUL man will have his way.
La volontà fa tutto.

Cf. *Where there's a WILL, there's a way.*

2352 He that WILL not when he may, when he will he shall have nay.
Chi non vuol quando può, non può quando vuole.
Chi non fa quando può, non fa quando vuole.

2353 Take the WILL for the deed.
Buona volontà supplisce a facoltà.

2354 Where there's a WILL, there's a way.
Volere è potere.
A chi vuole, non mancano modi.

Sim. *Nothing is impossible to a willing heart (mind).*
Cf. *A WILFUL man will have his way.*

2355 Where your WILL is ready, your feet are light.
Dove la voglia è pronta, le gambe sono leggere.

2356 WILL buys and money pays.
Volontà fa mercato, ma danari pagano.

2357 You WIN some, you lose some.
Oggi si perde e doman si guadagna.

2358 A little WIND kindles, much puts out the fire.
Piccolo vento accende il fuoco, e il grande l'estingue.

2359 As the WIND blows, you must set your sail.
Bisogna voltar la vela secondo il vento.
Bisogna navigare secondo il vento.

2360 Come with the WIND, go with the water.
Ciò che vien per acqua, per acqua tornerà.

Sim. *Light come, light go / Lightly gained, quickly lost.*
Cf. *EASY come, easy go.*

2361 Every WIND is ill to a broken ship.
A nave rotta ogni vento è contrario.

2362 Piss not against the WIND.
Chi piscia contro il vento, si bagna la camicia.

Var. *Puff not against the wind.*
Cf. *An ARROW shot upright falls on the shooter's head / Who SPITS against the wind, it falls in his face.*

2363 **The WIND in one's face makes one wise.**
Vento al visaggio rende l'uomo saggio.
Vento o disagio rende l'uomo saggio.

2364 **They that sow the WIND shall reap the whirlwind.**
Chi semina vento raccoglie tempesta.

Var. *If you sow the wind, you reap the whirlwind / Sow the wind and reap the whirlwind.*

o Hosea 8, 7 / Osea 8, 7

2365 **Good WINE engenders good blood.**
Buon vino fa buon sangue.

2366 **Good WINE needs no bush.**
Il buon vino non ha bisogno di frasca.
Il buon vino non vuol frasca.

2367 **He that drinks not WINE after salad is in danger of being sick.**
Chi vin non beve dopo l'insalata, aspetti d'esser ammalato.

2368 **Of WINE the middle, of oil the top, and of honey the bottom, is the best.**
Olio dapprima, vino del mezzo, e miele di fondo.

2369 **The best WINE is that a body drinks of another man's cost.**
Il miglior vino è quello che si beve in casa d'altri.

2370 **When the WINE is in, the wit is out.**
Vino dentro, senno fuori.
Dov'entra il bere se n'esce il sapere.

2371 **WINE and youth increase love.**
Vino e gioventù, doppio incendio alla lussuria.

2372 **WINE by the savour, bread by the colour.**
Il vino al sapore, il pane al colore.

2373 **WINE in the bottle does not quench thirst.**
Il vin nel fiasco non cava la sete di corpo.

2374 **WINE is a turncoat.**
Amicizia stretta dal vino non dura da sera al mattino.

Var. *Wine is a turncoat, first a friend, then an enemy.*

2375 **WINE is old men's milk.**
Il vino è il latte dei vecchi.

2376 **WINE is the glass of the mind.**
L'uomo si conosce al bicchiere.

2377 **WINE makes glad the heart of man.**
Il vino allieta la vita.

> o Psalms 104, 15 / Salmi 103, 16; Zechariah 10, 7 / Zaccaria 10, 7; Ecclesiastes 10, 19 / Qoèlet 10, 19

2378 **He covers me with his WINGS, and bites me with his bill.**
Dio ti guardi da quella gatta che davanti ti lecca e di dietro ti graffia.
Chi ti vuol male ti liscia il pelo.
Tal ti ride in bocca che dietro te l'accocca.

2379 **Too light WINNING makes the prize light.**
Dove non è pericolo, non è gloria.

2380 **It is a hard WINTER when one wolf eats another.**
Quando il lupo mangia il compagno, creder si deve sterile la campagna.

2381 **No WISDOM to silence.**
Assai sa, chi tacer sa.
Chi parla rado, è tenuto a grado.

> Cf. *SILENCE is often the best answer / SPEAK fitly, or be silent wisely / A WISE head makes a close mouth.*

2382 **The poor man's WISDOM is as useless as a palace in a wilderness.**
A veste logorata poca fede vien prestata.

2383 **WISDOM has one foot on land, and another on sea.**
Il sapere ha un piede in terra e l'altro in mare.

2384 **WISDOM is better than strength.**
Buona la forza, meglio l'ingegno.
Meglio val sapienza che forza.

> o Ecclesiastes 9, 16 / Qoèlet 9, 16; Proverbs 24, 5 / Proverbi 24, 5

2385 **Without WISDOM wealth is worthless.**
Ricchezze senza lettere sono un corpo senz'anima.

2386 **A WISE head makes a close mouth.**
Una testa savia ha la bocca chiusa.

> Cf. *SILENCE is often the best answer / SPEAK fitly, or be silent wisely / No WISDOM to silence.*

2387 **A WISE man is never less alone than when he is alone.**
Il savio non è mai solo.

2388 **A WISE man needs not blush for changing his purpose.**
Il savio non si vergogna di mutar proposito.

2389 He commands enough that obeys a WISE man.
Assai comanda chi ubbidisce al saggio.

2390 He is not WISE who cannot play the fool.
Non è sempre savio chi non sa esser qualche volta pazzo.

2391 He is WISE that is rich.
Chi è ricco è savio.

2392 He seems WISE with whom all things thrive.
A chi la va bene par savio.
A chi la riesce bene, è tenuto per savio.

2393 He that is a WISE man by day is no fool by night.
Chi è tenuto savio di giorno non sarà mai pazzo di notte.

2394 If the WISE erred not, it would go hard with fools.
Se i savi non errassero, i matti s'impiccherebbero.

2395 It is easy to be WISE after the event.
Del senno di poi son piene le fosse.
Dopo il fatto ognuno è savio.

  Cf. *When a thing is done, ADVICE comes too late / When the HOUSE is burned down, you bring water / It is too late to shut the STABLE-DOOR after the horse has bolted.*

2396 No man is WISE at all times.
Niuno è savio d'ogni tempo.

  Sim. *Every man is a fool sometimes and none at all times.*
  Cf. *Every one has a FOOL in his sleeve / Every man is MAD on some point.*

2397 Send a WISE man on an errand, and say nothing to him.
Commetti al savio, e lascia fare a lui.
Accenna al savio, e lascia fare a lui.

2398 The WISE man must carry the fool upon his shoulders.
Bisogna che il savio porti il pazzo in ispalla.

2399 WISE men change their minds, fools never do.
Il savio non si vergogna di mutar proposito.

  Var. *A wise man changes his mind; a fool never.*

2400 WISE men have their mouth in their heart, fools their heart in their mouth.
I saggi hanno la bocca nel cuore, e i matti il cuore in bocca.

2401 WISE men learn by other men's harms; fools, by their own.
Impara a vivere lo sciocco a sue spese, il savio a quelle altrui.
Savio è colui che impara a spese altrui.

Sim. *It is good to beware by other men's harms / It is good to learn at other men's cost / He is happy whom other men's perils make wary / Learn wisdom by the follies of others.*

2402 If WISHES were horses, beggars would ride.
Se i desideri bastassero, i poveri andrebbero in carrozza.

Var. *If wishes would bide, beggars would ride.*

2403 WISHES never can fill a sack.
I desideri non empiono il sacco.

2404 A little WIT will serve a fortunate man.
Poco senno basta a cui fortuna suona.

2405 There is a WITNESS everywhere.
Dappertutto c'è un testimonio.

2406 WIVES and wind are necessary evils.
Il matrimonio è un male necessario.

Sim. *Women are necessary evils.*

2407 A WOLF in sheep's clothing.
Lupo in pelle d'agnello.

2408 It never troubles a WOLF how many the sheep be.
Anche delle pecore contate ne mangia il lupo.
Il lupo non guarda che le pecore sieno conte.

2409 Talk of the WOLF, and his tail appears.
Chi ha il lupo in bocca, l'ha sulla groppa.

Cf. *Talk of the DEVIL, and he is bound to appear.*

2410 The WOLF may lose his teeth, but never his nature.
Il lupo cambia il dente, ma non la mente.
Il lupo perde il pelo, ma non il vizio.

Cf. *The FOX may grow grey, but never good.*

2411 The WOLF must die in his own skin.
Nella pelle dov'è il lupo gli convien morire.

2412 To set the WOLF to keep the sheep.
Dare le pecore in guardia al lupo.

Var. *You give the wolf the wether to keep.*
Sim. *He sets the fox to keep his geese.*

o Matthew 10, 16 / Matteo 10, 16

2413 Who has a WOLF for his mate needs a dog for his man.
Chi ha il lupo per compare, porti il can sotto il mantello.

2414 **Who keeps company with the WOLF will learn to howl.**
Chi va col lupo impara ad ululare.
Chi pratica col lupo impara a urlare.

Var. *One must howl with the wolves.*

2415 **A fair WOMAN and a slashed gown find always some nail in the way.**
Bella donna e veste tagliuzzata sempre s'imbatte in qualche uncino.

2416 **A fair WOMAN without virtue is like palled wine.**
Bellezza senza bontà è come vino svanito.

2417 **A WOMAN, a dog, and a walnut tree, the more you beat them the better they be.**
Donne, asini e noci, voglion le mani atroci.

Var. *A spaniel, a woman, and a walnut-tree, the more they're beaten the better they be.*

2418 **A WOMAN and a cherry are painted for their own harm.**
Le donne e le ciliege son colorite per lor proprio danno.

2419 **A WOMAN and a glass are ever in danger.**
La donna e il vetro sempre in pericolo.

2420 **A WOMAN conceals what she knows not.**
Le donne tacciono quello che non sanno.

Var. *Women conceal all they know not.*

2421 **A WOMAN either loves or hates in extremes.**
La donna o ama o odia.

2422 **A WOMAN is flax, man is fire, the devil comes and blows the bellows.**
La donna è stoppa, l'uomo è fuoco, vien il diavol che ci soffia.

Var. *Man is straw, woman fire, and the devil blows / Man is fire, and woman tow; the devil comes and sets them ablaze.*

Cf. *FIRE cannot be hidden in flax / Keep FLAX from fire and youth from gaming.*

2423 **A WOMAN kissed is half won.**
Donna baciata, mezza guadagnata.

2424 **A WOMAN that loves to be at the window is like a bunch of grapes on the highway.**
Donna di finestra, uva di strada.

2425 **Tell a WOMAN she is fair and she will soon turn fool.**
Di' una volta a una donna che è bella, e il diavolo glielo ripeterà dieci volte.

2426 What a WOMAN wills, God wills.
Ciò che donna vuole, Dio lo vuole.

2427 Who has a WOMAN has an eel by the tail.
Chi piglia l'anguilla per la coda e la donna per la parola, può dire di non tener nulla.
Chi piglia l'anguilla per la coda, può dire di non tener nulla.

Sim. *As much hold of his word as a wet eel by the tail / He holds a wet eel by the tail.*

2428 Never choose your WOMEN or your linen by candlelight.
Né donna né tela a lume di candela.
Né donna né tela, non guardare al lume di candela.

Var. *Choose neither a woman nor linen by candlelight / Don't pick women or horses by candlelight.*

2429 The more WOMEN look in their glass, the less they look to their house.
Donna specchiante, poco filante.

2430 Three WOMEN and a goose make a market.
Tre donne e un'oca fan un mercato.
Tre donne e un papero fanno un mercato.
Due donne e un'oca fanno un mercato.
Tre donne fanno un mercato, e quattro fanno una fiera.

Sim. *Many women, many words; many geese, many turds.*
Cf. *Where there are WOMEN and geese, there wants no noise.*

2431 Where there are WOMEN and geese, there wants no noise.
Dove son femmine e oche, non vi son parole poche.

Sim. *Many women, many words; many geese, many turds.*
Cf. *Three WOMEN and a goose make a market.*

2432 WOMEN and hens are lost by gadding.
Le donne e le galline per troppo andare si perdono.

2433 WOMEN are saints in church, angels in the street, devils in the kitchen, and apes in bed.
Le donne son sante in chiesa, angeli in strada, diavole in casa, civette alla finestra e gazze alla porta.

2434 WOMEN are the devil's nets.
La donna, per piccola che sia, la vince il diavolo in furberia.
La donna ne sa una più del diavolo.
La donna ne sa un punto più del diavolo.

2435 WOMEN change as often as the wind.
Donna e luna, oggi serena e domani bruna.

Var. *Women are as wavering as the wind.*
Sim. *A woman is a weathercock / A woman's mind and winter wind change oft / Women, wind and fortune are ever changing.*

2436 WOMEN laugh when they can, and weep when they will.
La donna ride quando puole e piange quando vuole.
Femmina piange da un occhio e dall'altro ride.
Donna si lagna, donna si duole, donna s'ammala quando ella vuole.

2437 WOMEN, priests and poultry, have never enough.
Donne, preti e polli non son mai satolli.
Preti, frati, monache e polli non si trovano mai satolli.

Var. *Children, chickens and women never have enough.*

2438 WONDER is the daughter of ignorance.
La meraviglia, dell'ignoranza è figlia.

2439 A little WOOD will heat a little oven.
A piccol forno poca legna basta.

2440 Green WOOD makes a hot fire.
Le legne verdi colle secche fan buon fuoco.

2441 He cannot see the WOOD for the trees.
Non può veder il bosco per gli alberi.
Non si può vedere il bosco per gli alberi.

Var. *You cannot see the wood for the trees.*
Sim. *You cannot see the city for the houses.*

2442 Lay on more WOOD; ashes give money.
Metti pur su legna, che in ogni modo la cenere val denari.

2443 Better give the WOOL than the sheep.
È meglio perdere la lana che la pecora.

2444 Many go out for WOOL, and come home shorn.
Andar per lana e tornarsene tosi.
Fare come i pifferi di montagna, che andarono per suonare e furono suonati.

2445 A WORD and a stone let go cannot be called back.
Parola detta e sasso tirato non torna indietro.
Parola detta e sasso tirato non fu più suo.
Sasso tratto e parola detta non tornano indietro.
Parola di bocca e pietra gettata, chi la riaspetta perde la giornata.

Sim. *A word spoken is past recalling / Words have wings and cannot be recalled.*

2446 An honest man's WORD is as good as his bond.
Tra galantuomini una parola è uno strumento.

2447 From WORD to deed is a great space.
Dal detto al fatto, c'è un gran tratto.
Fra dire e fare si consumano di molte scarpe.
Fra il dire e il fare, c'è di mezzo il mare.

Cf. *SAYING and doing are two things / SAYING is one thing, and doing another.*

2448 Half a WORD is enough for a wise man.
A buon intenditor mezza parola basta.

Sim. *A word to a wise man is enough.*
Cf. *Few WORDS to the wise suffice.*

o Mark 4, 9 / Marco 4, 9

2449 Many a true WORD is spoken in jest.
Burlando si dice il vero.
Non v'è peggio burla che la vera.

Var. *There's many a true word said in jest.*

2450 One ill WORD asks another.
Una parola cattiva ne domanda un'altra.

2451 One WORD spoken in sport requires another.
Una parola tira l'altra.

Sim. *One word leads to another.*

2452 Fair WORDS and foul deeds.
Belle parole e cattivi fatti.

2453 Fair WORDS break no bones.
Le buone parole non rompono i denti.

Cf. *Fair WORDS hurt not the mouth.*

2454 Fair WORDS fill not the belly.
Il ventre non si sazia di parole.
Le parole non empiono il corpo.

Cf. *Good WORDS fill not a sack.*

2455 Fair WORDS hurt not the mouth.
Un bel parlare non scortica la lingua.
Non scortica la lingua il parlar dolce.

Cf. *Fair WORDS break no bones.*

2456 Few WORDS to the wise suffice.
A buon intenditor, poche parole.

Sim. *A word to a wise man is enough.*
Cf. *Half a WORD is enough for a wise man.*

2457 Fine WORDS dress ill deeds.
Le buone parole acconciano i mali fatti.

2458 For mad WORDS deaf ears.
A parole lorde, orecchie sorde.

Var. *For foolish talk deaf ears.*

2459 Good WORDS and ill deeds deceive wise and fools.
Belle parole e cattivi fatti, ingannano savi e matti.

2460 Good WORDS anoint us, and ill do unjoint us.
Le buone parole ungono, e le cattive pungono.

2461 Good WORDS cool more than cold water.
Una buona parola smorza più che una caldaia d'acqua.
Più spegne una buona parola che un secchio d'acqua.

Cf. *A soft ANSWER turneth away wrath.*

2462 Good WORDS fill not a sack.
Le parole non empiono il sacco.

Sim. *Many words will not fill a bushel.*
Cf. *Fair WORDS fill not the belly.*

2463 Good WORDS without deeds are rushes and reeds.
Detto senza fatto, ad ognun par misfatto.

2464 He who gives fair WORDS feeds you with an empty spoon.
Chi ti dà ciancie, imbocca colla cucchiara vuota.

2465 In many WORDS the truth goes by.
Il troppo parlare la verità fa errare.

Sim. *In many words a lie or two may escape / Truth needs not many words.*

2466 Keep off and give fair WORDS.
Dà pur belle parole, ma tien salda la borsa.

2467 Kind WORDS go a long way.
Le buone parole trovano buon luogo.

Cf. *A man's HAT in his hand, never did him any harm / LIP-HONOUR costs little, yet may bring in much.*

2468 WORDS and feathers the wind carries away.
Parole e piume, se le porta il vento.
Sim. *Words are but wind.*
Cf. *WORDS fly, writings remain.*

o Ecclesiasticus 28, 18 / Siràcide 28, 19

2469 WORDS fly, writings remain.
Le parole volano, gli scritti rimangono.
Le parole volano, quel ch'è scritto rimane.
Sim. *Words are but wind.*
Cf. *WORDS and feathers the wind carries away.*

2470 After the WORK is done, repose is sweet.
Dopo il lavoro è dolce il riposo.

2471 All WORK is noble.
Il lavoro nobilita l'uomo.

2472 As the WORK, so the pay.
Quale il lavoro, tale la mercede.
Tale il lavoro, tale il salario.

o I Corinthians 3, 8 / I Corinzi 3, 8; II Corinthians 5, 10 / II Corinzi 5, 10; Revelation 22, 12 / Apocalisse 22, 12; Psalms 62, 12 / Salmi 61, 11; Proverbs 24, 12,29 / Proverbi 24, 12,29; Jeremiah 25, 14 / Geremia 25, 14; Matthew 16, 27 / Matteo 16, 27; II Timothy 4, 14 / II Timoteo 4, 14

2473 He that will not WORK shall not eat.
Chi non lavora, non mangia.
Var. *If you won't work, you shan't eat.*
Sim. *No mill, no meal.*
Cf. *A HORSE that will not carry the saddle must have no oats / No PAIN, no gain / No SWEET without some sweat.*

o II Thessalonians / II Tessalonicesi 3, 10

2474 The WORK shows the workman.
L'opera loda il maestro.
Cf. *The WORKMAN is known by his work.*

2475 To WORK is to pray.
Chi lavora, prega.
Il lavorare è un mezzo orare.
Sim. *Toil is prayer / They that work not, cannot pray.*

2476 **A bad WORKMAN quarrels with his tools.**
Cattivo lavoratore a ogni ferro pon cagione.
Al cattivo zappatore, ogni zappa da dolore.

2477 **The WORKMAN is known by his work.**
All'opera si conosce il maestro.

Cf. *The WORK shows the workman.*

2478 **If the WORLD will be gulled, let it be gulled.**
Il mondo vuol essere ingannato.

2479 **In the WORLD, who knows not to swim goes to the bottom.**
Il mondo è come il mare, e vi s'affoga chi non sa nuotare.
Mondo rotondo, chi non sa nuotar vassene a fondo.

Cf. *The WORLD is a ladder for some to go up and some down.*

2480 **The gown is his that wears it, and the WORLD his that enjoys it.**
Il mondo è di chi se lo piglia.

2481 **The WORLD is a ladder for some to go up and some down.**
Il mondo è fatto a scale, chi le scende e chi le sale.

Sim. *Thus fareth the world, that one goeth up and another goeth down.*
Cf. *In the WORLD, who knows not to swim goes to the bottom.*

2482 **The WORLD is a small place.**
Il mondo è piccolo.

Var. *It's a small world / The world is but a little place, after all.*

2483 **The WORLD is a wide parish.**
C'è per tutti posto sotto il sole.

Var. *The world is a wide place.*

2484 **The WORLD is full of fools.**
Il mondo è una gabbia di matti.
Al mondo ci sono più pazzi che briciole di pane.
È infinito il numero degli stolti.

Sim. *Knaves and fools divide the world.*

2485 **This WORLD is a stage and every man plays his part.**
Teatro è il mondo e l'uomo è marionetta.

Var. *All the world's a stage, and all the men and women merely players.*

2486 To travel through the WORLD it is necessary to have the mouth of a hog, the legs of a stag, the eyes of a falcon, the ears of an ass, the shoulders of a camel, and the face of an ape, and overplus, a satchel full of money and patience.
Per camminar salvo per il mondo convien avere bocca di porco, gambe di cervo, occhio di falcone, orecchie d'asino, spalle di cammello, viso di scimmia, e per giunta, una bisaccia piena di quattrini e pazienza.

2487 We must take the WORLD as we find it.
Bisogna prendere il mondo come viene.

Var. *The world is as you take it.*

2488 When I die, the WORLD dies with me.
Morto io, morto il mondo.
Morto io, morto ognun, ed il porco.

Cf. *After us the DELUGE.*

2489 Even a WORM will turn.
Anche il verme ha la sua collera.

Var. *Tread on a worm and it will turn.*
Cf. *The FLY has her spleen and the ant her gall.*

2490 A green WOUND is soon healed.
Ogni mal fresco si sana presto.

2491 WRITING destroys the memory.
Chi scrive non ha memoria.

2492 It is better to suffer WRONG than to do wrong.
È meglio ricevere un torto che farlo.

2493 No WRONG without a remedy.
Ogni male ha il suo rimedio.

2494 Two WRONGS don't make a right.
Due torti non fanno una ragione.
Due neri non fanno un bianco.

Y

2495 **A plum YEAR, a dumb year.**
Anno susinaio, poche fastella.

2496 **A snow YEAR, a rich year.**
Anno nevoso, anno fruttuoso.
Anno di neve, anno di bene.

2497 **Say no ill of the YEAR till it be past.**
Non dir mal dell'anno finchè passato non sia.

Cf. *Praise a fair DAY at night.*

2498 **It will be all the same a hundred YEARS hence.**
In cento anni e cento mesi, l'acqua torna ai suoi paesi.
Di qui a cento anni tanto varrà il lino quanto la stoppa.

Var. *It will be all one a thousand years hence.*

2499 **Once in ten YEARS, one man has need of another.**
Ogni dieci anni un uomo ha bisogno dell'altro.

2500 **YEARS know more than books.**
Gli anni sanno più dei libri.
Molto più fanno gli anni che i libri.

2501 **If the YOUNG man would and the old man could, there would be nothing undone.**
Se il giovane sapesse e il vecchio potesse, non v'è cosa che non si facesse.

2502 **Of YOUNG men die many, of old men scape not any.**
Dei giovani ne muor qualcuno, dei vecchi non ne campa nessuno.

2503 **YOUNG men may die, but old must die.**
Si muore giovani per disgrazia e vecchi per dovere.

2504 **YOUNG men's knocks old men feel.**
Bravure da giovani, doglie da vecchi.

2505 **What's YOURS is mine, and what's mine is my own.**
Quello che è tuo è mio, e quel che è mio è mio.

2506 **An idle YOUTH, a needy age.**
Giovane ozioso, vecchio bisognoso.

Var. *A young courtier, an old beggar.*
Sim. *If you lay upon roses when young, you'll lie upon thorns when old.*

o Ecclesiasticus 25, 3 / Siràcide 25, 5

2507 Growing YOUTH has a wolf in his belly.
Ragazzo crescente ha la lupa nel ventre.
Cf. *Small BIRDS must have meat.*

2508 Reckless YOUTH makes rueful age.
Gioventù disordinata fa vecchiezza tribolata.
In gioventù sfrenato, in vecchiezza abbandonato.
Chi ride in gioventù, piange in vecchiaia.

2509 What YOUTH is used to, age remembers.
Chi da giovane ha un vizio, in vecchiaia fa sempre quell'uffizio.

Sim. *Whoso learneth young forgets not when he is old.*
Cf. *What we first LEARN, we best know.*

o Proverbs 22, 6 / Proverbi 22, 6

2510 Who that in YOUTH no virtue uses, in age all honour him refuses.
Chi non segue la virtù in giovinezza, sfuggir il vizio non potrà poi in vecchiezza.

2511 YOUTH and white paper take any impression.
I ragazzi son come la cera, quel che vi s'imprime, resta.

2512 YOUTH will have its course.
Gioventù vuol fare il suo corso.

2513 It is easy to cry YULE at other men's cost.
Si balla bene sulla sala degli altri.

INDEX

abide, to 1074, 1136, 1877
above 180, 261, 2228
abroad 225, 1853
absence 1914
absent 738, 1325, 1462
abuse, to 2126
accommodate, to 1672
accord 586
according 336, 1290
accusation 359
accuse, to 674
ache, to 347, 1050
Adam 521
advantage 2028
adversity 759
afar 966, 1406, 2306
affirmative 1590
afraid 680, 2138
after 289, 462, 471, 487, 524, 627, 712, 768, 908, 938, 1032, 1138, 1198, 1272, 1423, 1475, 1544, 1573, 1734, 1735, 1786, 1896, 1987, 2038, 2044, 2058, 2139, 2367, 2395, 2470
afterwards 1735
again 82, 269, 608, 645, 1471, 2130, 2161
against 746, 866, 1086, 1468, 1559, 2032, 2062, 2362
age 193, 1631, 1809, 2506, 2508, 2509, 2510
agree, to 109, 293, 1234, 1713, 2193
air 739
alarm, to 1910
alehouse 1197
alike 439, 1505
all 9, 12, 81, 121, 140, 150, 152, 179, 254, 270, 291, 318, 335, 392, 397, 439, 463, 465, 469, 485, 489, 507, 515, 543, 608, 629, 659, 742, 744, 824, 835, 903, 919, 926, 927, 959, 984, 997, 1024, 1057, 1064, 1101, 1168, 1177, 1193, 1225, 1254, 1301, 1340, 1383, 1395, 1425, 1473, 1482, 1483, 1484, 1485, 1492, 1515, 1531, 1544, 1639, 1646, 1651, 1655, 1659, 1670, 1672, 1703, 1746, 1768, 1771, 1813, 1858, 1860, 1885, 1889, 1929, 1946, 1968, 2076, 2084, 2088, 2123, 2142, 2153, 2154, 2155, 2237, 2247, 2279, 2291, 2297, 2331, 2392, 2396, 2471, 2498, 2510
alms 865, 1092
alone 229, 343, 354, 665, 2387
also 887, 1562, 2201
altar 362, 1802
altogether 1138
always 2, 32, 88, 280, 313, 432, 498, 656, 756, 776, 880, 991, 1028, 1074, 1170, 1172, 1354, 1355, 1999, 2099, 2113, 2226, 2243, 2415
among 828
amongst 1803
ample 1809
angel 1420, 2433
anger 2073
angry 1166
annoy 1211
anoint, to 1626, 2460
another 78, 96, 222, 233, 248, 269, 377, 494, 530, 567, 594, 670, 691, 751, 802, 809, 816, 830, 845, 904, 1011, 1014, 1051, 1134, 1169, 1241, 1242, 1309, 1329, 1358, 1392, 1572, 1635, 1678, 1725, 1743, 1867, 1894, 1935, 1979, 1982, 1986, 2012, 2091, 2120, 2369, 2380, 2383, 2450, 2451, 2499
answer (n.) 1816, 1817, 1818, 1954, 2231, 2242
answer, to 820
ant 793
anvil 1008
anybody 569

INDEX

anyone 538
anything 1533
ape, apes 43, 1788, 2433, 2486
appear, to 496, 1609, 2047, 2409
appetite 1477
April 1444
apron 2345
arms 1233, 1351
art 60, 150, 1110, 1164, 1581, 1768, 2164
ascended 2044
ashamed 620, 1116, 1767
ashes 574, 2442
ask, to 375, 488, 645, 820, 865, 1144, 1365, 1565, 1816, 1875, 1925, 1940, 2450
asleep 971, 2001
ass 221, 421, 1100, 1135, 1912, 1950, 2486
assaulted 1414
asunder 947
asylum 1193
attend, to 548
authority 2197
autumn 2037
autumnal 23
avail, to 458
avarice 1771
avaunt 894
axe 2213

Bacchus 295
back 149, 516, 593, 941, 1912, 2445
bad 132, 152, 205, 302, 331, 354, 566, 568, 709, 757, 826, 1113, 1208, 1281, 1339, 1524, 1551, 1602, 1662, 1776, 1830, 1859, 1877, 1887, 2230, 2476
bag 396, 439, 632, 2185
bait 777
bald 1045
bare 1947, 2014
barefoot 2134
bark, to 559, 562, 1015
barking 556, 1541
barn 51, 1444

barrel 1242
basket 629
bathwater 89
battle 18, 1310, 1820
bauble 806
beam 691
beans 1165
bear, to 244, 246, 404, 413, 664, 668, 1099, 1131, 1200, 1794, 2205, 2246
beard 105, 219, 1031
beast 53, 743, 1420
beat, to 75, 248, 560, 563, 605, 1127, 2048, 2092, 2343, 2417
beating 2071
beauty 732
become, to 982, 2116, 2164
bed 476, 597, 1313, 1575, 2280, 2433
bee 789
before 102, 128, 249, 278, 303, 411, 563, 637, 781, 876, 975, 1198, 1217, 1270, 1348, 1350, 1455, 1482, 1651, 1785, 1786, 1876, 1881, 1918, 2085, 2217
beforehand 1676
beg, to 488, 865, 2195
beggar 828, 1784, 1976, 2402
begging 1544
begin, to 206, 299, 436, 478, 637, 650, 708, 1589, 2292
beginning 234, 621, 633, 1378, 1664
behind 156, 503, 1350, 1555, 1651, 1973
beholden 1323
being 1367, 1767, 1898, 2367
believe, to 140, 146, 543, 690, 801, 1296, 1535, 1907
bell 379
bellows 2422
belly 516, 683, 1405, 1716, 2454, 2507
bellyful 153
below 1087
bend, to 2239
best 86, 155, 251, 332, 433, 492, 675, 773, 774, 775, 797, 806, 836, 886, 972, 1091, 1095, 1163, 1204, 1208, 1271, 1273, 1285, 1427, 1429, 1469,

INDEX

1506, 1682, 1711, 1714, 1839, 1944, 1954, 2004, 2125, 2126, 2136, 2239, 2300, 2368, 2369
better 22, 66, 73, 100, 118, 124, 125, 131, 145, 154, 185, 186, 225, 226, 228, 312, 354, 368, 408, 432, 490, 518, 550, 561, 624, 625, 633, 641, 655, 669, 695, 721, 739, 762, 829, 870, 877, 917, 955, 966, 970, 973, 1043, 1047, 1048, 1049, 1060, 1061, 1075, 1202, 1239, 1266, 1288, 1344, 1454, 1459, 1460, 1574, 1592, 1596, 1617, 1674, 1721, 1776, 1783, 1808, 1832, 1892, 1939, 1948, 1982, 1990, 2013, 2067, 2191, 2241, 2286, 2324, 2384, 2417, 2443, 2492
between 240, 1008, 1010, 1015, 1077, 1397, 1828, 2055, 2282
bewail, to 419
beware, to 204, 863, 928, 1422, 1597, 1801
beyond 12
big 683, 767, 935
bill 2378
bind, to 1876
bird 248, 262, 417, 739, 741, 1599, 2010
bit 1002, 1930
bitch 952
bite, to 385, 452, 556, 558, 559, 572, 786, 1206, 1557, 2110, 2378
bitten 1910
bitter 116, 123, 171, 178, 179, 1719, 2253
black 104, 499, 894, 1083, 1937, 2337
blame 1200
blamed 2235
bleating 1930
bless, to 878, 1694
blessed 1719
blessing 307, 1332, 1470
blind 177, 188, 387, 840, 841, 984, 1040, 1170, 1373, 1402
blind, to 17, 913
bliss 384
block 323, 2059

blood 2261, 2365
blossom, to 1006, 2037, 2246
blow, to 40, 609, 1168, 1540, 1562, 2359, 2422
blush, to 1660, 2388
body 1057, 1504, 1949, 2369
bog 890
boil, to 1758, 1761
boiling 1760
bold 341
bolted 2038
bond 2446
bone 293, 560, 568, 578, 585, 586, 1260, 1476, 2184, 2453
book 2500
booty 511
born 289, 702, 763, 811, 828, 1021, 1252, 1436, 1463, 1742, 2147
borne 244
borrow, to 209, 607
bosom 1120, 1985
both 55, 85, 185, 188, 686, 1014
bottle 2373
bottom 775, 2013, 2014, 2099, 2234, 2368, 2479
bound 496, 1190
boy 216
brain 143, 1003, 1055, 1888
brambles 597
bran 515, 986
branch 2207
brave 839
bray, to 80, 81
bread 47, 441, 579, 599, 997, 1115, 1344, 1479, 2109, 2195, 2305, 2372
break, to 33, 90, 154, 215, 396, 1465, 2065, 2137, 2160, 2184, 2185, 2453
breaker 1276
breakfast 1113, 1270
breaking 1638
breast 414, 1361
bred 201
breed, to 321, 416, 610, 707, 2322, 2339
bridge 642, 2303
bridle 1804, 1828

INDEX

bright 269
brim 2013
bring, to 54, 177, 275, 327, 335, 346, 355, 441, 663, 668, 948, 952, 1157, 1328, 1444, 1466, 1603, 1740, 1854, 1956, 2037, 2069, 2203, 2258, 2264, 2330
brittle 438
broken 371, 888, 1617, 1728, 1873, 2361
broth 370, 1761
brother 1974, 1976
brought 855, 1556
brows 894
build, to 1700, 1811
building 1197
built 1151, 1865
bunch 2424
bung-hole 2015
burden 19, 68, 941, 1108, 1691
burn, to 755, 1153, 1942
burned 1037, 1157
burnt 306, 760
burst, to 145
bury, to 451, 454
bush 159, 2115, 2366
bushel 876
business 250, 1363
butter 1479
buttocks 1135
buy, to 182, 407, 476, 699, 1410, 1445, 1472, 1521, 2356

cabbage 569, 1702
cable 1557
cackle, to 628, 1084
Caesar 260
calendar 467
calf 244
call, to 141, 1023, 1637, 1724
called 1442, 2445
calling 666
calm 2058
camel 925, 2486
candle 794, 897
candlelight 2428

Candlemas 269
canter, to 345
capers 1516
capon 226
cap 824
captain 654
care 1854, 1964, 2318
caress 372
carried 303
carrion 419
carry, to 73, 111, 147, 698, 970, 1124, 1691, 2304, 2398, 2468
cart 2334
case 670
cask 1725
cast, to 519, 1467, 1600, 1957
castle 241, 652, 2339
cat 305, 1237, 1559
catch, to 104, 169, 172, 175, 248, 282, 287, 401, 575, 611, 771, 787, 861, 1027, 1032, 1033, 1279, 1508, 1560, 1971, 2036, 2095
caught 102, 170, 777, 1297, 1558
cause 1218
cause, to 1610
cease, to 294
certain 472
chaff 175
change, to 56, 792, 1109, 1293, 1730, 1919, 2166, 2399, 2435
changing 2388
chapel 951
character 2063
charming 2248
charter 2033
chasten, to 301
chastise, to 302, 1277
chastity 109
cheap 155, 968, 1969, 2294
cheaper 460
cheat, to 512
cheese 224, 255
cherry 530, 2418
chest 870
chicken 313, 425, 862

239

INDEX

chiding 1158,
child 1864, 1928
children 9, 242, 715, 719, 1632, 2258
chips 324, 1761
choice 245
choked 980
choose, to 667, 1152, 2428
chooser 129
chosen 1442
Christians 1207
Christmas-pie 504
church 141, 362, 951, 1197, 1885, 2316, 2433,
churchyard 1707, 2251
churls 1731
circus 223
city 1487, 1729, 1844
clad 43
clap, to 264
claws 1324
clean, to 239
cleanse, to 1001
clear 359, 1709
clerk 504, 1792
client 1283
cling, to 1098
cloak 2070
cloister 1538
close, to 594, 1560, 2386
closed 202, 508
cloth 336
clothed 2257
clothes 938, 2230
clothing 2407
clout 1467
clouting 1877
clown 754
cloy, to 1102
clutch, to 604
coarse 500
cobweb 885
cock 1155, 1913
cock-stride 440
coffers 694

cold 51, 284, 295, 938, 1017, 1074, 1160, 1840, 2461
colour 180, 187, 331, 2236, 2372
colt 1226
comb 1058, 1136
come, to 15, 18, 46, 76, 269, 287, 324, 325, 328, 425, 442, 449, 473, 475, 529, 546, 584, 617, 665, 666, 764, 766, 904, 908, 971, 1062, 1085, 1106, 1178, 1186, 1264, 1268, 1323, 1509, 1511, 1553, 1563, 1607, 1612, 1734, 1736, 1760, 1772, 1812, 1848, 1878, 1922, 2058, 2082, 2099, 2119, 2124, 2125, 2133, 2139, 2199, 2261, 2278, 2279, 2280, 2327, 2360, 2422, 2444
comfit 100
comfort 818
command (n.) 429
command, to 349, 1619, 1923, 2389
commend, to 1764, 2341
commit, to 722, 1200
common 463, 705, 1137
commonly 1534, 2313
companion 110, 1159
company 1859, 2346, 2414
compelled 1369
complain, to 1899
conceal, to 1988, 2420
concealing 60
conceive, to 1214
confess, to 489
confessed 720
confessor 1459, 1933, 2224
conquer, to 1068, 2260
conqueror 1400
conscience 905
consent 1955
consider, to 1243
consist, to 60
constant 602, 999
consult, to 13
consume, to 267
contain, to 279
contempt 707

INDEX

contend, to 1086
content 160, 1579
contented 1503
contentment 2320
continual 1503
control, to 728
convent 1539
convince, to 1643
cooked 258
cookery 1162
cook (n.) 940
cook, to 1027
cool 1444, 1561, 2461
corn 755, 939, 1696, 1873, 2011
corner 1152
correct, to 728
corrupt, to 351
cost (n.) 2183, 2369, 2513
cost, to 222, 1328
cottage 1382
cough 1362
counsel 34, 799, 803, 923, 1408, 1438, 1606
counsellor 2142
count, to 852, 1534
country 1421, 1800, 2348
couple 1170
course 1394, 2512
court 1382, 2316
cover (n.) 1759
cover, to 1050, 1370, 1746, 2206, 2378
covered 553, 756, 1712
coverlet 1106, 1290
covetousness 1968
cow 254, 264, 1424, 1563
coward 1583
crack, to 1222
cradle 700, 831, 851
craft 391
crafty 406
crashing 570
creaking 277
creak, to 2334
credit 1833
crime 698

cripple 1297
crooked 2039
cross 503, 1794, 2061
cross-bow 26
crown (n.) 1939
crown, to 635
crow (n.) 420
crow, to 342, 1155
cruel 1201
curst 399, 557
cry, to 1270, 2513
cudgel, to 1827
cunning 2345
cup 601
cure (n.) 418, 1783
cure, to 24, 1318, 2084, 2153
cured 527, 811
cushion 1174
custom 383
cut, to 213, 336, 577, 1012, 1417, 1472, 2131

dam 1226
dance, to 846, 1111
danger 433, 735, 914, 963, 1936, 2367, 2419
dangerous 486, 914
dark 291
dash, to 2223
daughter 714, 1546, 1547, 1548, 1551, 1992, 2233, 2263, 2438
daughter-in-law 1550
day 20, 48, 269, 440, 525, 616, 751, 768, 891, 1050, 1093, 1102, 1399, 1544, 1609, 1865, 1989, 2393
dead 56, 104, 122, 419, 437, 454, 495, 521, 558, 561, 920, 975, 1031, 1229, 1338, 1462, 1777, 2222
deadly 526
deaf 464, 1170, 2458
deal 755
dear 6, 130, 222, 372, 407, 968, 1096, 1733, 2121
dearly 2328
death 233, 234, 258, 373, 470, 473, 1006,

INDEX

1314, 1315, 1377, 1633, 1684, 1835, 1867, 1974, 2082, 2212
debt 118, 469, 1674, 1762, 1795, 1967
debtor 408
deceit 479
deceitful 732
deceive, to 479, 1117, 1452, 2459
deceived 1452, 2314
deceptive 44
deed 1198, 2353, 2447, 2452, 2457, 2459, 2463
deemer 554
deep 1940, 2300, 2309
defence 86
defend, to 929
defiled 1727
defy, to 1709
degree 799
delight 1823, 1972
delve, to 8
denial 464
deny, to 919
deprive, to 599
depth 996
descent 1554
desert 1824, 1825
deserve, to 2065
design 1942
desire, to 139, 1751
desperate 528
despise, to 799, 1309, 1789
destination 2178
destiny 1022
destroy, to 849, 2271, 2491
destruction 1079
devil 126, 268, 308, 414, 490, 507, 509, 651, 718, 939, 940, 945, 951, 1005, 1174, 1754, 1794, 1884, 2035, 2071, 2422, 2433, 2434
devilish 1961
devour, to 1101, 1909, 2154
die, to 199, 206, 207, 208, 384, 390, 393, 657, 822, 956, 1023, 1118, 1340, 1343, 1577, 2089, 2147, 2280, 2326, 2411, 2488, 2502, 2503

differ, to 2105
difficult 2043
dig, to 1726
dine, to 1850
dirt 1700
dirty 1322, 2299
disarmed 1680
discerned 1449
disclose, to 2155
discover, to 752, 1274
discretion 1625
disdainfulness 3
disease 1834
disgrace 1778
dish 1840
disorder 2084
dispose, to 1434
disposition 1922
dispute 1610, 2093
dissolve, to 2074
distaff 831, 2029
ditch 188, 495
divided 1232, 2245
divine 66, 661, 985
do, to 28, 31, 230, 348, 453, 497, 538, 539, 541, 588, 595, 721, 753, 950, 1190, 1192, 1234, 1331, 1533, 1537, 1559, 1793, 1866, 1993, 2174, 2217, 2399, 2460, 2492
doctor 48, 368, 462, 930, 2078, 2224
dog 231, 286, 293, 372, 385, 564, 577, 1002, 1047, 1206, 1541, 2048, 2413, 2417
doing 1356, 1893, 1894, 2333
done 15, 137, 322, 542, 547, 549, 1036, 1189, 1609, 1880, 2122, 2470
door 298, 409, 498, 508, 848, 1223, 1531, 1772, 2045, 2056
double (adj.) 2260
double, to 662, 735
doubtful 1705
doubt, to 1250
dove 610, 1911
dower 111
down 16, 580, 596, 663, 704, 1157, 1595, 2073, 2481

INDEX

downwards 776
Dr. Diet 1711
Dr. Merryman 1711
Dr. Quiet 1711
dragon 1909
draw, to 112, 297, 530, 614, 1138, 1139, 1499, 1522, 1578
dread, to 306
dream (n.) 1114, 1312
dream, to 1715
dress, to 2047, 2457
dressed 765
drink (n.) 153
drink, to 236, 333, 618, 627, 1129, 1142, 1635, 2301, 2336, 2367, 2369
drive, to 83, 494, 1161, 1396, 1572, 1743, 1964, 1983
drowned 286, 1021, 2087
drunkenness 1988, 2264
dry (adj.) 225, 226, 373, 614, 743, 1444, 1999, 2308
dry, to 2107
due 491, 1104, 1978
dumb 2495
dunghill 341
Dutchman 1197
duty 1618
dwell, to 409, 1598
dying 1253

each 161, 449, 1790, 1879, 2115
eagle 272
ear 70, 151, 749, 1569, 2284, 2258, 2486
early 119, 169, 320, 955
earnest 1689
earn, to 779
earth 553, 744, 904, 1481, 1712, 1746, 1853, 1987, 2202
earthly 66
ease 526
easier 265, 493, 871, 1764, 1811
easily 583, 854
Easter 326, 327, 1207, 1291
easy 617, 1066, 2048, 2395, 2513
eat, to 79, 80, 176, 263, 288, 292, 304, 333, 343, 419, 564, 569, 619, 767, 779, 823, 867, 876, 980, 1026, 1199, 1222, 1476, 1479, 1872, 2380, 2473
eaten 227, 719, 1840, 1932
eating 46, 1140
edge 719
effect 294, 1719
egg 164, 415, 1083, 1638
eight 1150
elbow 692, 1998
elephant 792
eloquence 1363
else 569, 915
embrace, to 994, 1357, 2265
embroidered, to 421
embroidery 1075
emperor 1755
empty 1489, 1874, 2256, 2464
end (n.) 131, 136, 450, 465, 639, 898, 1308, 1664, 1832, 2122, 2297
end, to 1491, 2331
ending 132, 133, 1378
endure, to 68, 178, 630, 1252, 1659, 1764
endured 424, 972
enemy 61, 157, 750, 882, 914, 929, 1160, 1920
engage, to 1460
engender, to 3, 2365
England 708, 2291
Englishman 1197
enjoy, to 974, 2480
enjoyment 2321
enough 333, 709, 716, 847, 1248, 1510, 1733, 1846, 1859, 1903, 1994, 2389, 2437, 2448
enrich, to 1750
enriched 1699, 1784
enter, to 141, 265, 1661, 2078
equal 468, 744, 1383, 1458, 1482
equality 889
escape, to 376, 1138, 2117
estate 906
esteem, to 1421

243

INDEX

Eve 8
evening 663, 1545
ever 74, 407, 1238, 1253, 1489, 1500, 1792, 1987, 2228, 2419
every 57, 65, 134, 190, 246, 251, 279, 334, 385, 386, 389, 413, 443, 672, 721, 777, 798, 806, 807, 844, 911, 964, 986, 995, 1069, 1089, 1093, 1129, 1227, 1258, 1275, 1333, 1409, 1421, 1423, 1424, 1425, 1426, 1427, 1428, 1429, 1430, 1431, 1480, 1492, 1499, 1667, 1668, 1690, 1691, 1759, 1817, 1897, 1937, 1956, 1991, 2103, 2213, 2216, 2337, 2348, 2361, 2485
everybody 726, 872, 1536, 2219
everyone 722, 1290, 1732, 1944, 2085
everything 135, 634, 801, 1320, 1371, 1601, 1835, 1902, 2146
everywhere 64, 2194, 2405
evil 351, 397, 415, 448, 966, 972, 1119, 1259, 1395, 1441, 2203, 2406
exceeding 1502
except 852, 960, 1246
excessive 1212
excuse 1182, 1567
excused 522
expect, to 434, 664, 812
expected 909, 1733
expel, to 1392
expensive 1146
extract, to 789
extreme 1220, 2421
eye 185, 224, 256, 265, 304, 387, 416, 420, 511, 609, 679, 749, 833, 913, 1072, 1317, 1367, 1564, 1569, 1706, 1833, 2349, 2486

face 77, 111, 1014, 1213, 1778, 2032, 2230, 2363, 2486
fade, to 113
failure 2068
fain 1598
faintly 488, 1070
fair 116, 269, 270, 447, 461, 696, 701, 748, 851, 851, 896, 1070, 1128, 1147, 1213, 1388, 1647, 1713, 1870, 1882, 2339, 2349, 2415, 2416, 2425, 2452, 2453, 2454, 2455, 2464, 2466
fairest 417, 1647, 1870
fair-weather 883
faith 1219, 1365, 1398, 1534
faithful 868
falcon 2486
fall (n.) 330, 1785, 2041
fall, to 49, 59, 82, 90, 188, 280, 568, 682, 1232, 1263, 1687, 1726, 1929, 1961, 1971, 1981, 1986, 2032, 2055, 2064, 2119, 2209, 2245
fallen 2213
falling 1403, 1824
false 359, 1801
fame 2269
familiar 646
familiarity 1551
famine 2305
far 49, 162, 958, 1257, 1452, 1592, 1598, 2129, 2198
fare, to 93
farthing 1666
fashion 1423
fast, to 146, 230, 623
fat 22, 143, 226, 688, 1090, 1235, 1347, 1666, 1707, 1744, 2255
father 308, 309, 316, 501, 716, 1928, 2068
fatten, to 832, 1707, 1744
fault 553, 662, 678, 881, 1162, 1200, 1426, 1437, 1712
faulty 724
favour, to 838, 839
fear (n.) 226, 432, 470, 963, 1374, 1393, 1854, 1900,
fear, to 40, 284, 359, 544, 737, 1119, 1289, 1325, 1611, 1856, 1941, 2060, 2115
feast 823, 1503
feather 39, 173, 740, 980, 2468
fed 763, 1011
feed, to 235, 262, 271, 773
feel, to 1098, 1415, 2504

INDEX

felled 1615
fellowship 1364, 1770
female 481
fence 991
fever 659
few 350, 647, 721, 1221, 1442, 2456
fifty 1020
fight, to 144, 751
fighting 1657
file 2157
fill (n.) 41
fill, to 51, 609, 987, 1334, 1444, 2215, 2403, 2454, 2462
filth 1747
find, to 108, 497, 721, 868, 969, 1162, 1305, 1350, 1386, 1465, 1567, 1908, 2048, 2314, 2415, 2487
fine 262, 741, 1601, 2457
finger 369, 504, 907, 1098, 1626
finish, to 350
fire 305, 306, 311, 784, 893, 961, 1346, 1562, 1597, 1941, 1980, 1981, 1982, 2018, 2060, 2299, 2306, 2307, 2358, 2422, 2440
firmness 1365
first 6, 14, 195, 234, 377, 436, 650, 729, 763, 764, 765, 766, 799, 849, 763, 764, 765, 766, 799, 849, 949, 1191, 1197, 1265, 1285, 1389, 1618, 1714, 1896, 1928, 1957, 2004, 2017, 2043, 2127
fish 288, 437, 767, 905, 1538, 1600, 1892, 2251
fishing 782
fist 808
fit (adj.) 349
fit, to 1946
fitly 2020
five 853
flatterer 796
flax 758, 2029, 2422
flay, to 1938
flea 580
fleece, to 1938
flesh 200, 201, 769, 772, 773, 2031

flight 269
flock (n.) 824, 1934, 1937
flock, to 173
flour 1562
flower 54, 113, 123, 1665, 1667
fly (n.) 611, 1101, 1279, 1560, 1760
fly, to 1400, 1735, 1772, 2156, 2469
flying 642, 711
folk 1849
follow, to 374, 430, 736, 791, 1786, 1935, 2223, 2259
folly 110, 817, 1246, 1274
fonder 1
fool 94, 125, 285, 314, 317, 379, 606, 641, 723, 805, 825, 838, 1090, 1150, 1215, 1729, 1827, 1928, 1933, 2283, 2390, 2393, 2394, 2398, 2399, 2400, 2401, 2425, 2459, 2484
foolish 735
foot 288, 529, 1092, 1561, 1946, 2355, 2383
forbear, to 101, 2010
forbidden 892
force 1755, 2067
forearmed 834
forecast (n.) 1644
forecast, to 1703
forelock 1621, 2145
foreseen, 475
forever 875
forget, to 640, 1407, 1792
forgetful 1046
forgive, to 661, 2252
forgiven 1960
forgotten 227, 435, 1391, 1857, 1886, 1995
form 86, 1028
formidable 58
fort 1197
forth 54, 177, 952, 1556, 2037, 2133, 2203, 2264
fortunate 1705, 2404
fortune 57, 640, 746, 1068, 1644
forty 1020
forwards 2133

245

INDEX

foul, to 163, 252, 696, 700, 851, 1001
found 205, 871, 1555, 2273
fountain 1545
four 693, 1123, 1551
fox 864, 988, 1326, 2095
free 297, 1279, 1483, 2135
French 1198
Frenchman 1197
friar 540
Friday 1963
friend 176, 641, 644, 647, 750, 774, 869, 872, 875, 887, 929, 1042, 1202, 1240, 1314, 1449, 1497, 1506, 1520, 1748, 1803, 1805, 1831, 1849, 1852, 1917
friendship 759, 1077
fright, to 172
frontier 2339
fruit 116
fruitful 1853
full 142, 144, 146, 152, 391, 597, 902, 1011, 1079, 1374, 1562, 1716, 1876, 2484, 2486
fulsome 1347, 1736
funeral 1449
furred 858
furrier 855
furrow 1648
fury 1671

gadding 2432
gain (n.) 1358, 1654
gain, to 847, 898, 1284, 1493, 1494, 1693, 2255
gaining 2017
gall 789, 793, 2176
gallon 787
gallows 355, 1848, 2114
game 632
gaming 784
gander 979
garden 1024, 1667
gardener 569
garland 790
garment 1862

gate 844, 960
gather, to 272, 1016, 1637, 1747, 2022, 2053
gay 454
generally 531
generation 904
gentle 1066
gentleman 8
gentleness 1171
Germans 1198
get, to 130, 194, 580, 582, 760, 771, 878, 1091, 1725, 1859, 2179, 2260
girdle 857, 1097, 1225
give, to 67, 199, 298, 375, 378, 491, 514, 670, 754, 803, 818, 837, 909, 915, 918, 945, 975, 1016, 1056, 1092, 1242, 1438, 1470, 1501, 1549, 1625, 1681, 1723, 1915, 1939, 2098, 2208, 2442, 2443, 2464, 2466
giving 880
glad 1479, 1997, 2377
gladness 1879
glass 706, 842, 1051, 2376, 2411, 2429
glitter, to 959
glory 1665
gloves 282, 1009
gluttony 142
gnaw, to 578
go, to 42, 76, 84, 118, 120, 121, 197, 212, 230, 265, 277, 308, 529, 590, 617, 632, 957, 958, 960, 1022, 1075, 1076, 1129, 1257, 1279, 1280, 1282, 1289, 1387, 1452, 1509, 1530, 1544, 1553, 1575, 1635, 1728, 1780, 1785, 1786, 1804, 1885, 1931, 2073, 2134, 2140, 2189, 2278, 2302, 2317, 2327, 2332, 2360, 2394, 2444, 2445, 2465, 2467, 2479, 2481
God 298, 329, 435, 599, 865, 878, 1425, 1433, 1434, 1470, 1502, 1526, 1588, 1681, 1686, 1754, 1841, 1857, 1900, 2027, 2029, 2277, 2426
gold 79, 439, 514, 747, 759, 886, 962, 1073, 1149, 1223, 1256, 1300, 1418, 2026, 2190

INDEX

golden 642, 1223, 2026
gone 269, 616, 983, 2167
good 12, 13, 29, 33, 34, 47, 65, 92, 97, 104, 133, 145, 157, 193, 205, 210, 230, 238, 268, 302, 344, 351, 356, 357, 360, 451, 456, 480, 523, 568, 662, 664, 748, 757, 780, 831, 859, 873, 874, 880, 946, 965, 969, 970, 1067, 1068, 1080, 1113, 1119, 1130, 1132, 1144, 1187, 1188, 1192, 1199, 1205, 1206, 1214, 1259, 1278, 1281, 1298, 1330, 1339, 1356, 1367, 1399, 1424, 1441, 1446, 1524, 1534, 1537, 1549, 1551, 1552, 1574, 1575, 1591, 1603, 1605, 1622, 1624, 1627, 1643, 1661, 1662, 1678, 1679, 1739, 1765, 1776, 1887, 1902, 1912, 1917, 1938, 2024, 2027, 2033, 2087, 2108, 2188, 2203, 2206, 2214, 2215, 2230, 2263, 2278, 2287, 2293, 2298, 2340, 2348, 2350, 2365, 2366, 2446, 2459, 2460, 2461, 2462, 2463,
goodly 2350
goods 1483
goose, geese 740, 824, 863, 866, 981, 1715, 2430
gosling 979
got 130, 516, 916, 2321
govern, to 716, 1230, 1827
gown 1283
grace 1246
grain 990
granary 990
grandmother 513
grapes 719, 2264, 2424
grass 1133, 1984
gratis 96
grave 1125, 1201
grease, to 2335
great 6, 93, 98, 196, 198, 218, 242, 304, 317, 429, 466, 582, 597, 724, 728, 755, 805, 755, 805, 908, 935, 998, 1108, 1187, 1332, 1413, 1443, 1505, 1554, 1582, 1608, 1616, 1789, 1796, 1822, 1921, 1940, 1993, 2016, 2018, 2052, 2117, 2118, 2158, 2214, 2261, 2272, 2447
greedy 1140
green 327, 1077, 2226, 2440, 2490
greener 991
greet, to 884
grey 275, 291, 663, 859, 1006, 1055
grief 444, 798, 1107, 1212, 1668, 2162, 2288
grieve, to 689
grind, to 766, 879, 1498, 1501, 1502
gripping 1036
ground 1596, 2040, 2055, 2084
grow, to 1, 295, 302, 821, 859, 989, 992, 1277, 1616, 1667, 1736, 1968, 2325
growing 2507
guard (n.) 730
guard, to 2108
guests 768
guide, to 1246
gulled 2478
gutter 1836

habit 2257
hair 275, 1005
half 103, 137, 138, 185, 406, 483, 521, 527, 720, 1063, 1306, 1344, 1411, 1414, 1419, 1576, 1848, 1916, 1939, 1960, 2295, 2423, 2448
halt, to 409, 411
halter 1138, 1140
halting 584
hammer 39, 41, 570
hand 28, 35, 159, 252, 497, 548, 686, 694, 739, 754, 831, 966, 1038, 1132, 1731, 2008, 2090, 2177
handle, to 1098
handsome 1019, 1020
hang, to 566, 1225, 2114, 2118, 2290
hanged 483, 1495, 1576, 1629, 1868, 2042, 2117,
happen, to 1148, 2243
happiness 363, 1521
happy 308, 1024, 1170, 1510
harbour, to 198

INDEX

hard 47, 134, 411, 868, 1025, 1165, 1603, 2380, 2394
hardest 668
hare 401, 575, 582, 583, 587
harm 953, 1033, 1038, 1953, 2401, 2418
harmless 1011, 1404
harp 74
haste 34, 1456
hasty 177, 330
hatch, to 1508
hate, to 148, 738, 1183, 1704, 2148, 2421
hated 2200
hateful 1765
hatred 458, 1551, 2229
haunt, to 785
have, to 33, 39, 65, 71, 102, 116, 135, 174, 185, 199, 228, 263, 269, 304, 307, 322, 330, 332, 356, 377, 408, 450, 528, 543, 545, 547, 551, 567, 630, 640, 687, 719, 749, 852, 951, 963, 973, 1124, 1144, 1175, 1233, 1298, 1307, 1478, 1479, 1510, 1519, 1551, 1556, 1562, 1565, 1566, 1631, 1656, 1661, 1663, 1674, 1681, 1698, 1719, 1739, 1849, 1851, 1855, 1912, 1917, 2025, 2035, 2049, 2141, 2188, 2189, 2284, 2351, 2352, 2400, 2437, 2486, 2512
hay 439, 1444, 1466
head 59, 85, 104, 347, 663, 743, 776, 975, 1120, 1173, 1440, 1489, 2183, 2386
headache 418
headed 1495
heal, to 930, 931, 1708
healed 1416, 2490
healer 2158
healthful 1438
healthy 119, 120
heap 1853
hear, to 74, 138, 161, 311, 459, 464, 543, 613, 695, 944, 1330, 1535, 1682, 1749, 2023

heart 1, 4, 414, 689, 690, 696, 1017, 1112, 1213, 2176, 2201, 2377, 2400
heaven 221, 265, 933, 960, 1082, 1450, 1781
heavy 19
heavy-heeled 1546
hedge 1595
heed 753, 1541, 1651, 2046, 2266, 2311
heel 1046, 2000, 2223
heir 810, 977, 2285
hell 230, 649, 1075, 2292
help (n.) 548, 955, 1588
help, to 285, 380, 663, 704, 932, 953, 987, 1187, 1333, 1536, 1568, 2114, 2335
hen 625, 630, 1155, 2432
heretic 982
hero 1435
herring 1745
hide (n.) 1359,
hide, to 758, 1362, 1960, 2224
high 42, 468, 656, 682, 1151, 1554, 1588, 2041
highway 989, 2011, 2424
hinder, to 34
hindmost 506, 575
hindrance 98
hire 1255
hired 1121
hit, to 183
hoist, to 1882
hold, to 33, 41, 268, 631, 799, 1248, 1717, 1873, 2019, 2022
hole 1558
holy 1001, 1536, 1792
home 76, 225, 299, 425, 565, 584, 652, 699, 860, 1861, 2070, 2199, 2312, 2444
honest 1485, 2116, 2119, 2446
honey 122, 123, 787, 789, 791, 1519, 2176, 2368
honour, to 461
hoop 1242
hope (n.) 296, 1316
hope, to 1856

INDEX

hornet 1279
horns 399, 1649
horse 73, 76, 238, 278, 343, 344, 649, 688, 785, 910, 992, 1199, 1269, 1571, 1651, 2038, 2341, 2402
horseback 126, 529
horse-manger 708
hospital 2069
host 372
hot 743, 1195, 1757, 2440
hounds 1167
house 293, 593, 798, 802, 827, 922, 1221, 1227, 1236, 1412, 1455, 1462, 1597, 1627, 1718, 1824, 1836, 1868, 1982, 1983, 2332, 2347, 2429
housewife 831
howl, to 560, 2414
hue 181
human 660, 661, 1961
humility 1788
hump 1159
hundred 99, 256, 614, 647, 716, 717, 804, 815, 1640, 1762, 1843, 1978, 2097, 2498
hunger 1118
hungry 262, 786
hunt, to 1029
hunting 2288
hurt, to 38, 1169, 1226, 2225
husband 108, 1998, 2340, 2345
husbandman 748
hussies 292

ice 1465
idle 497, 507
idleness 1379
ignorance 61, 2438
ill 93, 163, 186, 197, 322, 369, 376, 455, 477, 483, 552, 554, 588, 659, 662, 670, 736, 746, 781, 976, 977, 1068, 1184, 1185, 1268, 1308, 1413, 1445, 1576, 1593, 1604, 1794, 1970, 2040, 2062, 2090, 2222, 2242, 2294, 2323, 2325, 2338, 2361, 2450, 2457, 2459, 2460, 2497

impoverishing 243
impression 2511
improve, to 62
impudence 1181
incarnate 651
inch 1486
inconvenience 1766
increase, to 1245, 2371
index 697
infirmities 1370
ingratitude 1810
inherit, to 1481
inheritance 115, 731, 1926
injure, to 50
injuring 1662
injustice 1220
inn 1152
intention 1080
invention 1585
invitation 372, 1146
invite, to 1952, 1979
Ireland 650
iron 39, 1009, 1194, 1224, 1872
Italianate 651

jade 1129
January 990
jealous 1367
jealousy 1376
jest (n.) 877, 1203, 1689, 2449
jest, to 77, 681
jewel 2272
joined 947
joy 1997, 2002
judge, to 45, 187, 1214
judgement 22
jump, to 893
just 2286,
justice 1220, 1410
justify, to 636
justly 2328

keep, to 48, 231, 353, 357, 377, 437, 467, 567, 734, 743, 784, 868, 934, 1077, 1087, 1564, 1698, 1859, 1901, 1962, 1989, 2091, 2319, 2412, 2414, 2466

INDEX

kettle 894
key 52, 1176, 1661, 2347
kid 430
kill, to 24, 162, 924, 1024, 1212, 2222
kin 1240
kind 2467
kindred 828
kindle, to 2358
kindly 1745
king 283, 387, 632, 731, 980, 1229, 1261, 1280, 1755
kingdom 265, 303, 364, 1234, 1385
kinsfolk 1449
kinsman 1592, 1917
kiss, to 1012, 1424, 2423
kitchen 2433
knave 1238
knife 253, 1417
knock (n.) 2504
knock, to 844, 848, 975, 1603
knot 2096
knotty 2141
know, to 28, 70, 166, 167, 208, 251, 309, 319, 353, 381, 402, 490, 502, 527, 533, 543, 607, 710, 802, 805, 858, 921, 972, 1000, 1172, 1248, 1285, 1324, 1427, 1677, 1852, 1900, 1904, 1914, 1919, 1921, 1942, 1944, 1945, 2175, 2198, 2204, 2302, 2308, 2338, 2420, 2477, 2479, 2500
knowing 2129
knowledge 676

labour 85, 2321
lack 1288
ladder 2044, 2481
lady 1070
laid 264, 381, 1697
lake 1129
lamb 943, 1206
lame 1812, 2179
lament, to 458
land 1397, 1622, 1898, 1901, 2383
lanthorn 1608
large 1236, 2131

largely 1299
lark 1971
last 6, 340, 601, 794, 901, 942, 1172, 1271, 1714, 1728, 1870
last, to 20, 891, 899
lasting 1191
late 16, 320
lather, to 103
Latin 805
latter 439
laugh, to 900, 1210, 1271, 1284, 1354, 1411, 2150, 2436
law 427, 605, 1182, 1258, 1276, 1282, 1353, 1441, 1482, 1580, 1584, 2069
lawfully 1278
lawless 1375
lawyer 504, 995, 2224
lay, to 493, 628, 1083, 1084, 1822, 2124, 2202, 2442
lazy 210, 1347
lead, to 83, 188, 454, 981, 1665, 1860, 2120
leaf 116, 2164
lean (adj.) 22, 143, 710, 785
lean, to 2206
leap, to 224, 430, 1348, 1832, 2059
learn, to 32, 94, 409, 588, 589, 1180, 1336, 1630, 1780, 1819, 2192, 2401, 2414
least 80, 844, 1030, 1099, 1175, 1249, 2100
leather 2131
leave (n.) 1656
leave, to 1204, 1723, 1973, 2070, 2314
lecture 833
left 28, 567, 653
leg 147, 280, 1123, 1307, 2486
leisure 1175, 1456
lend, to 645, 1122, 1520, 1939
lender 211
length 855, 856, 1290, 2087
lengthened 440
Lent 1516
less 105, 538, 994, 996, 997, 1534, 2428, 2387, 2429

INDEX

lesser 667
lest 682, 2223
let, to 28, 209, 236, 340, 400, 405, 454, 476, 569, 581, 613, 685, 713, 947, 1120, 1129, 1252, 1279, 1289, 1294, 1337, 1476, 1675, 1691, 1780, 1804, 1957, 2015, 2024, 2073, 2140, 2301, 2445, 2478
letter 694, 1072, 1294,
leveller 466
liar 705, 2250
liberal 395
liberty 100, 912, 1453, 1906
lick, to 369, 574, 1096, 1650, 1915
lie (n.) 501, 598, 2315
lie, to 117, 219, 339, 495, 580, 581, 606, 833, 1067, 1656, 1828, 2028, 2083, 2197, 2234, 2280
life 63, 451, 454, 461, 1024, 1295, 2144, 2249
lifeless 727
light-heeled 1546
light, to 267
like (adv.) 32, 87, 113, 193, 425, 530, 569, 570, 713, 714, 743, 906, 1206, 1228, 1389, 1461, 1514, 1536, 1538, 1548, 1713, 1784, 1791, 1818, 1853, 1883, 1998, 2211, 2225, 2416, 2424
like, to 16, 599, 806, 1280, 1318, 1319, 1364, 1429
lime 170
line 445, 567
lined 1283
linen 2428
lining 334
lion 58, 69, 561, 563, 565, 1031, 1047, 1048
lip 1010, 1037
litter 1714
little 160, 198, 218, 220, 264, 317, 333, 422, 582, 622, 631, 648, 710, 755, 767, 880, 950, 993, 1003, 1054, 1065, 1236, 1251, 1328, 1347, 1384, 1412, 1565, 1579, 1616, 1674, 1751, 1757, 1832, 1903, 1915, 2052, 2117, 2118, 2128, 2187, 2215, 2253, 2268, 2318, 2320, 2358, 2404, 2439
live, to 25, 30, 229, 281, 333, 390, 471, 518, 520, 533, 619, 736, 743, 751, 822, 922, 1111, 1118, 1253, 1341, 1382, 1782, 2089
living 454, 561, 1839
lizard 1048, 1910
loaded 79, 2210,
loadstone 1380
lock 990, 1224
lodge, to 1268
lone 1936
long 23, 63, 148, 214, 277, 328, 794, 819, 899, 921, 942, 1003, 1229, 1233, 1253, 1331, 1341, 1342, 1384, 1561, 1610, 1733, 1737, 1831, 1845, 1867, 2035, 2177, 2315, 2467
longed 616
longest 450, 2312
look, to 283, 682, 734, 910, 1143, 1367, 1415, 1657, 2143, 2429
looking 184, 2021
looking-glass 184
loophole 1275
loose 1650
Lord 1752
lordship 1364
lose, to 85, 145, 392, 680, 825, 847, 877, 1202, 1231, 1301, 1493, 1494, 1520, 1611, 1861, 1930, 1939, 2011, 2075, 2096, 2143, 2344, 2357, 2410,
loss 407
lost, to 145, 402, 480, 485, 532, 871, 965, 1571, 1620, 2054, 2104, 2161, 2344, 2432
lot 366
lottery 1447
loud 7, 1155, 1347
love (n.) 226, 273, 274
love, to 16, 161, 168, 310, 319, 372, 571, 579, 685, 881, 952, 956, 1039, 1040, 1058, 1210, 1366, 1368, 1380, 1384, 1389, 1396, 1403, 1424, 1595, 1655, 1772, 1861, 1896, 2004, 2148, 2200, 2207, 2282, 2288, 2371, 2421, 2424

lover 108, 1210
low 468, 1078, 1151, 2041, 2056
luck 523, 1239
lucky 273, 274
lunatic 1193
lurk, to 503
lye 85

mackerel 2036
mad 317, 849, 1286, 1663, 2186, 2458
made 228, 412, 747, 842, 901, 1450, 1742, 2030, 2111, 2192
madman 2090
madness 36
magnifying 706
Mahomed 1553
maid 285, 1437, 1514
maintain, to 2258
maize 1715
make, to 1, 11, 27, 99, 106, 117, 119, 122, 131, 133, 176, 190, 193, 238, 310, 317, 338, 344, 362, 403, 468, 478, 492, 504, 525, 537, 601, 603, 615, 622, 642, 645, 688, 741, 744, 790, 808, 810, 813, 814, 815, 841, 849, 876, 896, 900, 935, 996, 1018, 1025, 1034, 1035, 1044, 1046, 1090, 1101, 1142, 1165, 1170, 1203, 1208, 1213, 1236, 1237, 1286, 1304, 1346, 1367, 1383, 1405, 1443, 1448, 1465, 1487, 1513, 1528, 1529, 1530, 1546, 1547, 1583, 1586, 1587, 1590, 1633, 1638, 1642, 1648, 1685, 1706, 1718, 1741, 1761, 1774, 1776, 1793, 1805, 1809, 1815, 1831, 1853, 1862, 1896, 1905, 1928, 1932, 1933, 1950, 1958, 1986, 2081, 2096, 2151, 2157, 2186, 2251, 2256, 2262, 2270, 2278, 2280, 2287, 2290, 2293, 2307, 2340, 2345, 2363, 2377, 2379, 2386, 2430, 2440, 2494, 2508
male 481
mallet 975
Mammon 954
man, men 11, 13, 24, 25, 29, 33, 53, 57, 81, 88, 98, 105, 167, 183, 184, 185, 187, 202, 204, 206, 208, 217, 229, 233, 237, 246, 251, 252, 265, 312, 315, 338, 348, 353, 355, 357, 366, 387, 393, 394, 406, 413, 451, 452, 457, 473, 477, 507, 510, 517, 544, 553, 567, 604, 622, 643, 645, 662, 710, 744, 747, 773, 802, 803, 804, 820, 823, 836, 844, 867, 868, 900, 905, 911, 916, 934, 947, 1023, 1038, 1078, 1115, 1150, 1160, 1166, 1192, 1225, 1227, 1278, 1286, 1329, 1358, 1408, 1409, 1419, 1424, 1432, 1433, 1448, 1451, 1461, 1464, 1483, 1485, 1492, 1515, 1529, 1534, 1562, 1573, 1589, 1607, 1627, 1628, 1632, 1633, 1635, 1640, 1649, 1699, 1748, 1749, 1750, 1753, 1775, 1776, 1777, 1827, 1850, 1851, 1868, 1921, 1962, 1966, 1975, 1976, 1982, 1983, 1991, 1993, 2063, 2066, 2069, 2072, 2103, 2119, 2131, 2152, 2172, 2190, 2195, 2288, 2319, 2336, 2348, 2351, 2369, 2375, 2377, 2382, 2387, 2388, 2389, 2393, 2396, 2397, 2398, 2399, 2400, 2401, 2404, 2413, 2422, 2446, 2448, 2485, 2499, 2501, 2502, 2503, 2504, 2513
mankind 659
manners 351, 1109, 2165
mar, to 769, 939, 1448, 1729, 1934
marble 1439
March 2074
mare 1135, 1530, 1947
mark 183, 656
marked 928
market 826, 870, 1359, 2293, 2430
marriage 193, 1207
married 702
marry, to 242, 1485, 1633, 1992
Martinmas 1089
master 65, 71, 686, 688, 813, 832, 946, 1309, 1524, 1678, 1689, 1905, 1914, 1918
mate 857, 2413
matrimony 2346

INDEX

May 52, 53, 54, 1200, 1444, 1457
may 31, 33, 116, 128, 178, 183, 205, 244, 283, 307, 332, 541, 546, 575, 583, 586, 592, 600, 751, 803, 804, 859, 884, 888, 1010, 1011, 1031, 1078, 1122, 1123, 1141, 1269, 1323, 1328, 1339, 1417, 1446, 1544, 1557, 1559, 1583, 1625, 1719, 1730, 1832, 1834, 1850, 1851, 1861, 1887, 1949, 2124, 2126, 2169, 2197, 2235, 2352, 2410, 2503
meal 66, 220, 515, 574, 709
meal-tub 2099
mean, to 512, 710, 1797, 1955
means (n.) 636
measure (n.) 618, 2329
measure, to 1471, 1474, 1486, 1626
meat 145, 152, 153, 174, 225, 620, 936, 940, 1260, 1753
medicine 1273
medlar 2151
meet, to 237, 677, 884, 967, 1471
memory 408, 1298, 2513
mend, to 302, 769, 1267, 1492, 2064
mention, to 1868
Mercury 190
merry 352, 814, 1711
mickle 1054
middle 2273, 2368
might 882, 973
mightier 1692
mighty 1738, 2232
mile 524
milk 423, 1563, 2375
mill 788, 879, 1499, 2302
miller 2097, 2302
mind 697, 771, 833, 868, 934, 1059, 1730, 1951, 2376, 2399
mine 1144, 2505
mirror 684
mirth 1645, 2000
mischief 1508
misfortune 2298
miss, to 140, 1446, 2218
mistake 1180

mixen 2324
mock, to 410
money 553, 645, 800, 870, 1063, 1269, 1291, 1371, 1395, 1399, 1522, 1528, 1672, 1952, 2159, 2186, 2356, 2442, 2486
monk 403, 509, 856, 1651
moon 1540
moor 1207, 2324
more 538, 600, 686, 693, 717, 779, 787, 802, 891, 924, 1007, 1239, 1300, 1349, 1490, 1543, 1566, 1578, 1739, 1896, 1941, 1947, 1967, 2003, 2025, 2095, 2098, 2238, 2349, 2417, 2429, 2442, 2461, 2500
morning 20, 386, 663, 1149, 1823, 1972
morrow 1591
morsel 318, 1010, 1841
mortal 23, 1484
moss 2053
most 80, 247, 878, 1139, 1191, 1249, 1343, 2334
mote 691
moth 332
mother 307, 310, 316, 436, 523, 534, 676, 714, 845, 1177, 1181, 1585, 1606, 1768, 1769, 1987, 2189, 2263
mountain 703, 884, 905, 1545, 1553
mouse, mice 282, 287, 289, 290, 293, 1323, 1325, 1556, 2172
mouth 4, 179, 253, 568, 910, 936, 1024, 1097, 1100, 1149, 1263, 1519, 1653, 1775, 2386, 2400, 2555, 2486
move, to 703
mow, to 2006, 2007
much 10, 195, 215, 220, 307, 367, 422, 532, 579, 627, 631, 909, 1050, 1065, 1102, 1117, 1199, 1274, 1286, 1328, 1342, 1371, 1444, 1633, 1674, 1750, 1751, 1797, 1807, 1875, 1903, 2102, 2128, 2198, 2205, 2253, 2302, 2303, 2358
muck 1853
mud 326
mulberry-tree 2164

mule 1135
multitude 300
music 1111
must 1222, 1231, 1243, 1291, 1338, 1340, 1410, 1430, 1519, 1553, 1570, 1624, 1629, 1661, 1663, 1682, 1683, 1787, 1814, 1832, 1871, 1895, 1913, 1918, 1919, 1924, 1938, 2009, 2056, 2134, 2141, 2219, 2359, 2398, 2411, 2487, 2503,
mustard 1475
mute 998

nail 2415
name 566, 2046
nation 1806
nature 62, 426, 1614, 1755, 2410
naught 6, 1317
near 200, 329, 337, 775, 874, 1152, 1235, 1428, 1592, 1943, 2223, 2250, 2313
necessary 2406, 2486
necessity 2270
need (n.) 869
need, to 72, 231, 256, 367, 725, 737, 853, 857, 1053, 1126, 1408, 1518, 1611, 1624, 1679, 1710, 1925, 2060, 2236, 2332, 2349, 2366, 2388, 2413, 2499
needle 265, 1589, 1690
needy 2506
neighbour 50, 698, 1281, 1413, 1552
neither 144, 375, 526, 569, 694, 772, 828, 1032, 1074, 1240, 1368, 1495, 1540, 1917
nephew 945
nest 160, 163, 165, 168
net 781, 857, 2434
never 27, 32, 45, 49, 82, 127, 131, 142, 162, 286, 293, 296, 347, 404, 455, 480, 556, 558, 586, 620, 628, 653, 657, 692, 805, 811, 850, 859, 880, 884, 888, 891, 899, 936, 976, 978, 985, 999, 1020, 1021, 1038, 1070, 1079, 1121, 1128, 1129, 1130, 1205, 1266, 1267, 1282, 1330, 1331, 1356, 1376, 1394, 1407, 1511, 1537, 1539, 1623, 1628, 1630, 1641, 1676, 1694, 1698, 1699, 1703, 1758, 1837, 1868, 1891, 2073, 2099, 2110, 2174, 2218, 2246, 2280, 2294, 2308, 2326, 2333, 2387, 2399, 2403, 2408, 2410, 2428, 2437
new 239, 576, 1353, 1396, 1477, 1886, 1958, 2077, 2314
news 1605
next 409, 522
nighest 1588
night 121, 442, 447, 525, 1050, 1399, 1823, 1972, 2393
nine 281, 2051
nobility 2275
noble 1922, 2252, 2471
nobody 259, 872
nod, to 1094
noise 570, 2157, 2431
none 189, 378, 459, 902, 963, 1082, 1463, 1465, 1639, 1916, 1947, 2184, 2301
nose 90
notary 240
note 166, 167
nothing 10, 92, 138, 140, 311, 367, 381, 393, 456, 472, 567, 588, 646, 653, 818, 837, 953, 973, 1036, 1154, 1217, 1231, 1248, 1250, 1401, 1513, 1611, 1612, 1701, 1725, 1797, 1807, 1819, 1846, 1847, 1881, 1990, 2075, 2077, 2107, 2179, 2214, 2225, 2255, 2267, 2397, 2501
nought 1567, 1613, 1878
nourish, to 1110, 1985
number 357
nut 1222

oar 197
oats 477, 1129
observant 867
observed 1292
occasion 552
odious 358

offering 1883
officer 2115
often 110, 198, 257, 398, 568, 622, 628, 1091, 1334, 1413, 1604, 1728, 1954, 1967, 2095, 2205, 2257, 2435
oil 774, 2228, 2368
old 13, 21, 24, 95, 175, 312, 316, 323, 342, 473, 502, 562, 576, 654, 773, 774, 854, 886, 1390, 1391, 1396, 1401, 1415, 1506, 1586, 1634, 1648, 1809, 1875, 1884, 1886, 1931, 1958, 1968, 2212, 2314, 2375, 2501, 2502, 2503, 2504
once 207, 325, 428, 432, 517, 844, 1153, 1238, 1472, 1510, 2113, 2240, 2499
one 33, 78, 96, 176, 204, 233, 235, 245, 248, 256, 293, 301, 387, 389, 494, 498, 530, 583, 586, 594, 600, 607, 612, 614, 627, 629, 644, 647, 680, 695, 715, 716, 717, 721, 728, 742, 790, 799, 807, 812, 815, 816, 827, 830, 845, 904, 934, 979, 982, 987, 982, 993, 1013, 1014, 1060, 1073, 1090, 1132, 1134, 1186, 1190, 1218, 1225, 1234, 1241, 1242, 1263, 1304, 1321, 1322, 1356, 1358, 1392, 1412, 1460, 1492, 1558, 1572, 1615, 1639, 1640, 1667, 1704, 1706, 1725, 1730, 1743, 1762, 1793, 1803, 1894, 1903, 1916, 1918, 1934, 1935, 1946, 1978, 1979, 1985, 2003, 2012, 2030, 2040, 2055, 2065, 2081, 2091, 2098, 2117, 2118, 2120, 2170, 2186, 2213, 2240, 2258, 2280, 2288, 2348, 2363, 2380, 2383, 2450, 2451, 2499
one-fourth 1535
onion 271
only 138, 453, 1368, 2210, 2275
open (adj.) 592, 783, 1125, 1564, 1778
open, to 594, 848, 1223, 1224, 1531, 2292
opinion 1488
opportunity 1583
orator 1742
orphan 320, 2068

other 33, 141, 181, 230, 267, 349, 398, 547, 548, 612, 814, 867, 991, 1013, 1082, 1402, 1479, 1483, 1726, 1879, 2042, 2106, 2131, 2165, 2401, 2513
ought 30, 410, 546, 555
ounce 1509, 1762, 1773
out 4, 89, 123, 127, 185, 201, 270, 298, 304, 305, 381, 416, 420, 494, 612, 804, 878, 890, 1154, 1161, 1393, 1396, 1403, 1467, 1538, 1572, 1743, 1772, 1878, 1948, 1951, 1952, 1983, 2015, 2036, 2045, 2119, 2223, 2358, 2370, 2444
oven 2439
over 423, 430, 516, 601, 638, 689, 698, 1078, 1254, 2059, 2065, 2324
overcome, to 638, 1254, 1670
overplus 2486
over-ruler 745
overturn, to 2052
owe, to 1677, 1847
own 309, 318, 341, 369, 381, 400, 417, 431, 643, 644, 691, 698, 802, 806, 867, 1069, 1073, 1131, 1159, 1218, 1221, 1227, 1258, 1309, 1417, 1421, 1429, 1430, 1431, 1499, 1597, 1641, 1647, 1691, 1775, 1790, 1800, 1944, 1982, 1991, 2003, 2085, 2119, 2274, 2332, 2401, 2411 2418, 2505
owner 734, 1156
ox 624, 626, 627
oxen 112, 1578, 2011, 2335

pace 958, 2064
package 2125
paid 909
pain 1655, 1734, 1735, 1737, 1998
paint, to 499, 2418
pair 614, 1046
palace 2382
pale 1540
palled 2416
pan 1179
paper 2283, 2511
paradise 649

INDEX

pardon (n.) 725
pardon, to 1623
parents 317
parish 1792, 2483
part (n.) 64, 687, 1099, 2485
part, to 800, 1770
parties 1064
pass, to 432, 444, 1581, 1614, 2063, 2111, 2311
past 435, 1498, 1857, 2497
patching 1875
Pater Noster 512
paternoster 1696
patience 1321, 1582, 1684, 2486
Paul 1863
paved 1080
paw 305
pawn 632
pay (n.) 2472
pay, to 107, 232, 469, 478, 1291, 1724, 1762, 1810, 1814, 1863, 2101, 2356
payer 210
payment 1512, 2222
peace 624, 1248, 1332, 2022, 2286, 2287, 2290, 2291, 2297, 2322
peach 750
pear 1091, 2285
peel, to 750
pence 1723
penetrate, to 1781
penny 1693, 1697, 1723
people 1175, 1228, 1555, 1791, 2210, 2277
pepper 1702
perfect 889, 1393, 1774
performance 1796
performing 1798
peril 1551
perish, to 434, 1302, 2088
perjuries 1210
permanent 2267
permit, to 729, 2289
person 304
Peter 1863
philosopher 106

physic 526
physician 95, 526, 810, 931, 984, 995, 1582
pick, to 420, 1476
picking 313
pick-purse 97
pig 952
pike 1049
pillow 360
pilot 1658
pinch, to 1787, 1944, 1945
pine, to 900
pipe, to 846
pippins 404
pitied 655
pitiful 1547, 2080
pity 1752
place 2240
plant, to 404, 1024, 2134, 2285
play, to 74, 290, 760, 794, 864, 1723, 1731, 2390, 2485
players 1349
pleasant 1720
please, to 701, 950, 1204, 1221
pleasing 2003, 2295
pleasure 249, 446, 618, 1650, 2264, 2288
plenty 1466, 1685, 1702, 1803
ploughshares 2092
pluck, to 740, 1959
plum 2495
plum-tree 1240
pocket 901
poet 1656
point 1409, 2133
poison 2304
poke 1717
policy 1095
poor 27, 108, 315, 510, 822, 1115, 1738, 1741, 1754, 1829, 1850, 1922, 2262, 2382
possible 927
post 1294
pot 995, 1179, 1264, 1931
pottage 1329
poultry 861, 2437

INDEX

pound 1509, 1644, 1645, 1695, 1773
poverty 365, 1176, 1235, 2271
power 1247
praise (n.) 2003
praise, to 310, 374, 447, 816, 817, 1087, 1539, 1598, 1690, 1790, 1901
pray, to 511
preach, to 863, 866
precept 669, 1773
prepare, to 1683
present 16, 738, 1325, 2002
preserve, to 2282
pretty 1347
prevent, to 2298
prey, to 860
price 12, 1368, 2272
prick, to 72, 2132
pride 510, 1551, 1740
priest 1663, 1718, 2437
prince 2221
prison 100, 1388
prodigal 712
produce, to 202
profess, to 799
proffered 1717, 2296
prologue 1887
promise, to 818
proper 911
propose, to 1434
prosper, to 382, 976
prosperity 1551
proud 1131, 1347
prove, to 671, 1807, 1949, 2288
provender 1131
provoked 1671
public 1322, 1536
pudding 906
puddle 2075
pull, to 804, 1031, 1595, 1867
punish, to 949
punishment 723, 1844, 1927, 1956, 1966
purchase 2192
pure 1813
purgatory 649
purpose 2388

purse 853, 885, 1334, 1518, 1519, 1678
pursue, to 1826
put, to 278, 298, 421, 629, 947, 1015, 1120, 1154, 2090, 2099, 2174, 2221, 2358

quarrel (n.) 995, 2339
quarrel, to 2476
quarreling 584
quartan 24
quench, to 2299, 2306, 2373
question 820
quick 1215, 1338, 2293
quickly, to 371, 918, 967, 1214, 2189, 2307
quiet 322
quit, to 296

race-horses 899
ragged 339
rags 1075
rain (n.) 55, 269, 335, 663, 948, 1983, 2139
rain, to 53, 225, 1540, 2071
rainbow 1823
rainy 1989
raise, to 493, 2074
rare 2121
raven 171
raw 2251
razor 1097
reach, to 221, 988, 2178
ready 1263, 2029, 2355
roasted 1263
reap, to 2012, 2269
reason 17, 1381, 1821, 2280
receive, to 912, 917
reckless 2508
reckoning 1147
red 104, 663, 935, 1005, 1112, 1540, 1972
redeem, to 1620, 1952
redemption 1081
redressed 720
reeds 2463

257

INDEX

refuse, to 1537, 2510
reign, to 1230
relation 874
relics 1790
religion 681
remain, to 1961, 2469
remedy 433, 528, 1397, 1668, 2493
remember, to 178, 535, 868, 2002, 2509
remove, to 2212
render, to 260
renewing 1403
rent 1808
repair, to 1836
repay, to 1922
repeat, to 1088
repent, to 203, 484, 1456, 1457, 2025
repentance 1664, 1684
repose 2470
reputed 1845
require, to 748, 1817, 2451
respected 1838
rest, to 524, 743, 1682
restoring 920
return, to 453, 573, 1028
reveal, to 1906, 1988
revenge 458
reverse 1480
reward 1103, 1927, 2274
rich, 11, 265, 365, 537, 553, 822, 1020, 1753, 2111, 2262, 2391, 2496
riches 315, 394, 1351, 1574
rid 1859
ride, to 73, 126, 1135, 1141, 1143
rider 1571, 2160, 2402
riding 33
rifled 1573
right (adj.) 28, 544, 1496
right (n.) 1231, 2494
rigorous 2276
ring 514, 1105
ripe 1026, 1687, 1996, 2151
rise, to 118, 119, 120, 386, 765
rising 955, 2072
river 1413, 1552
road 1287

roasted 1263
roast 196, 225
rob, to 149, 362, 593, 2094, 2112
robbery 673
robe 1862
rock 1871
rod 779
roll, to 1345, 1525
rolling 2053
Romans 1866
Rome 762, 1860
room 2307
roost, to 425
root 397, 1395
rose 1313
rose-water 1192
rotten 50, 1996
royal 1287
rudder 2182
rueful 2508
rule, to 427, 536, 671, 672, 1385, 1871, 2142
ruled 431
run, to 289, 434, 585, 587, 601, 751, 862, 1032, 1125, 1126, 1394, 1858, 2213, 2303, 2304, 2309
runaway 1539
running 1125, 1126, 2304
rushes 2463
rust 1390

sack 939, 987, 2008, 2403, 2462
sad 1155, 1997
saddle (n.) 75, 700, 851, 1124, 1127
saddle, to 343, 1134
safe 1487
safely 957
safety 474, 534
said 171, 894, 988, 1881
sail (n.) 2359
sail, to 1703, 1898
saint 592, 718, 950, 2433
sake 865
salad 2367
salt 180, 375, 876

INDEX

saluted 1845
same 632, 789, 2336, 2498
satchel 2486
satin 2164
satisfy, to 2187, 2280
sauce 1163, 1478
save, to 20, 639, 1693, 1800, 2051, 2114
savour (n.) 2372
savour, to 180, 1745
say, to 81, 311, 456, 512, 539, 540, 550, 902, 1306, 1331, 1497, 1549, 1682, 1895, 2219, 2301, 2397, 2497
scabbed 1136, 1934
scabby 1058, 1547
scald, to 1329
scalded 284
scape, to 2502
scarlet 43
scholar 2173
schoolmasters 717
score 1973
scrape, to 1085
scratch, to 91
scratching 621
scrub, to 78
sea 32, 782, 905, 1192, 1703, 1780, 1858, 2316, 2383
season (n.) 825
season, to 1889
second 14, 426, 729, 762, 799, 2136
security 1551
sedan 1076
see, to 138, 186, 189, 286, 689, 690, 691, 693, 898, 990, 1159, 1329, 1406, 1542, 1577, 1635, 1637, 1682, 2281, 2441
seed 748
seek, to 753, 1753, 1890, 2218
seem, to 824, 2392
seldom 109, 382, 495, 967, 1953, 1993, 2193
self 551, 799
sell, to 102, 257, 407, 699, 912, 915, 1410, 1453, 2328
seller 256

send, to 513, 812, 936, 938, 939, 940
sentence 1215
sepulchre 783
sermon 148
serpent 1909
servant 211, 649, 757, 1524, 1905
serve, to 30, 394, 946, 954, 1464, 1701, 1924, 2280, 2404
served 764, 1676, 1919
service 2191
set, to 126, 401, 719, 2359, 2412
settle, to 1898
settling 1197
seven 1148, 1150
shabby 344
shade 2214
shadow 1004, 2039, 2206
shame 518, 905, 1357, 1767, 1786, 1958
shamed 2235
shape, to 941
share, to 1099
sharp 2513, 2141
sharper 2181
shave, to 94, 96, 103
shaven 1045
shaving 94, 107
sheath 2091
sheep 419, 474, 1912, 2407, 2408, 2412, 2443
shelter 2208
shepherd 1923, 1972
shine, to 247, 1044, 1542, 2070, 2076
ship 32, 1825, 2182, 2361
shipped 492
shipwreck 1899
shirt 337
shoe 742, 1571,
shoot, to 656, 658, 2021
shooter 59
shooting 162
shop 405, 1962
shore 286
shorn 943, 2444
short 36, 63, 214, 399, 525, 557, 797, 1140, 1291, 1307, 1737, 1781, 1831, 1998, 2177, 2312

INDEX

shoulders 698, 1135, 2398, 2486
show, to 42, 662, 1437, 2110
shower 54, 55, 269, 603
shunning 1981
shut, to 405, 1564, 2038
shuttle 1311
sick 509, 623, 920, 1112, 1438, 1710, 2367
sickness 21, 1062
side 991, 1361, 1651
sight 698, 1599
sign 640, 831, 1627, 1658, 2177
silence 2025, 2026, 2381
silent 605, 819, 964, 1422, 2020, 2149
silk 43
silly 1816
silver 334, 1224, 2026
simple 378
sin 300, 1277, 1959, 1961
since 2303
sinews 1527
sing, to 128, 161, 2082
singe, to 794
singly 1511
sinking 1825
sit, to 1000
six 744, 1150
skin 69, 102, 1326, 1359, 1943, 2411
skin-deep 114
skirt 2060
sky 1074, 1972
slap, to 77
slashed 2415
sleep, to 476, 570, 1440, 1544
sleeping 581, 861
sleepless 2280
sleeve 807, 866
slip, to 829, 1010
slow 985
slowly 1035, 1214, 1502
sluggards 1093
small 174, 196, 728, 1004, 1443, 1502, 1796, 1822, 2018, 2125, 2482
smart, to 2079
smell (n.) 1523

smell, to 279, 1761
smith 570, 1947
smoke 761, 1761, 1802
smooth 1394
snared 854
sneeze 878
snout 1912
snow 326, 752, 1540, 2305, 2496
sober 1237
soft 37, 360, 958
softly 957
soil 832, 2263
sold 826, 1368, 1733, 2295
soldered, to 888
soldiers 2307
solemn 1845
Solomon 2350
some 322, 362, 444, 971, 1409, 1891, 2086, 2357, 2415, 2481
something 92, 205, 682, 1188
sometimes 183, 268, 505, 1094
son 712, 713, 714, 716, 718, 945, 1090
soon 139, 158, 206, 227, 484, 777, 800, 1045, 1078, 1189, 1212, 1232, 1251, 1264, 1297, 1309, 1416, 1485, 1558, 1757, 1880, 1931, 1995, 1996, 2099, 2107, 2425, 2490
sore 786, 1317, 1890, 2057, 2080
sorrow 83, 446, 1245, 1645, 1762, 1921, 2264
sorry 1399
soul 198, 684, 1001, 1949
sound (adj.) 476, 748, 888, 1504
sound (n.) 2256
sour 719, 988, 1378, 1478, 2104, 2337
sow, to 2022, 2269, 2364
space 2447
Spaniard 1197
spare, to 292, 867, 1864
spatter, to 1779
speak, to 4, 7, 455, 457, 505, 722, 944, 964, 1065, 1071, 1249, 1296, 1445, 2127, 2128, 2149
spend, to 543, 895, 1207
spender 908

INDEX

spending 896
spent 516, 1185
spice 2249
spigot 2015
spin, to 321, 1256
spirit 1295
spit, to 179
spitting, to 362
spittle 830
spleen 793, 1339
spoil, to 370, 1864, 2080, 2187
spoken 2449, 2451
spoon 2464
spoonful 787
sport 2451
spot 1437
spots 1292, 1293
spread 1599, 1853
spring, to 1039
spur 238, 1126, 1361, 1828
squint-eyed 1706
squirted 304
staff 1141, 1451
stag 58, 2486
stage 2485
staggerer 1257
stake 1451
stand, to 35, 322, 730, 1874, 2040, 2245
standing 1747, 1969
starling 171
start, to 582
starve, to 398, 992, 2171
stay, to 942, 1011, 1294
steal, to 124, 626, 1092, 1303, 1721, 2111
stealing 866, 2111
steel 1239
stepdame 431
stepmother 845, 1987
steps 1978
stick, to 170, 340, 2047
still 41, 79, 577, 933, 1422, 1763, 1843, 2309, 2311, 2323
stink, to 768, 776, 1775, 1853, 2238, 2296

stitch 2096
stock 478
stolen 978, 2310
stomach 1102, 1440, 1753
stone 194, 304, 572, 602, 804, 922, 1025, 1051, 1260, 1387, 1439, 1897, 1957, 2065, 2210, 2445
stooping 1412
stopped 850
store 1750
storm 1550, 1658, 1756
straight 412, 1346, 1648, 2039
strain, to 925
stranger 2079
straw 390, 604, 830, 1209, 1418, 2151
street 2433
strength 2244, 2384
stretch, to 1290
stricken 1490
strife 1041, 2329, 2342
strike, to 41, 942, 1195
strive, to 170, 585
striving 2062
stroke 26, 828, 1615
strong 35, 756, 1020, 1377, 1820, 2162
study, to 142
stuff, to 2171
stumble, to 1123, 1130, 2059
sturgeon 1049
subtle 500
succeed, to 1879
succour 1042
such 136, 164, 165, 1315
suck, to 123, 316
sucking 1843
sudden 330, 1212
suet 906
suffer 264, 1342, 1899, 2492
suffice, to 1335, 2046, 2456
sufficient 448
suit 1207
summer 2081
sun 20, 386, 752, 1044, 1052, 1542
Sunday 443, 1963, 2195
sunshine 1891

sup, to 2035
supper 524, 1113, 1270, 1887
supperless 118, 121
support, to 715
sure 381, 1455, 1977
suspect, to 726
suspicion 261, 1763
swallow, to 578, 925
swans 903
sway, to 1705
sweat 2086
sweep, to 239
sweet, 178, 179, 200, 243, 525, 892, 1165, 1372, 1378, 1478, 1842, 2002, 2104, 2253, 2266, 2310, 2321, 2337, 2470
sweeten, to 2002
swell, to 1405
swept 1412
swift 1820
swim, to 32, 770, 775, 778, 1965, 2479
swine 1688, 1912
sword 924, 1122, 1385, 1692, 2088, 2089, 2181

table 457
tabor 1029
tail 42, 77, 400, 402, 510, 577, 579, 858, 1047, 1048, 1049, 1950, 2050, 2409, 2427
take, to 14, 104, 181, 294, 305, 331, 400, 407, 449, 477, 506, 514, 753, 754, 837, 915, 930, 949, 975, 1024, 1142, 1154, 1203, 1325, 1411, 1414, 1431, 1621, 1649, 1651, 1815, 1826, 1917, 1978, 2034, 2046, 2088, 2145, 2263, 2266, 2311, 2329, 2353, 2487, 2511
tale 1628, 1749
talk, to 328, 496, 1532, 2183, 2409
tall 1412, 1489
tame, to 2162
tarry, to 1455
taste 5
teach, to 150, 266, 576, 778, 813, 895, 1363, 2106

teacher 675, 1164
tear, to 416
tears 1272, 1738
tell, to 33, 192, 314, 543, 923, 1251, 1305, 1628, 1905, 2237, 2425
temper, to 943
tempest 1550
tempt, to 507
ten 695, 715, 1460, 1578, 2499
test 759
tester 2344
thank, to 184
thanks 931
thick 1736
thief 128, 615, 1642, 1830, 2094, 2097, 2113, 2290
thin 2007
thing 3, 15, 260, 350, 372, 502, 514, 549, 590, 633, 748, 927, 934, 965, 971, 979, 1134, 1254, 1429, 1473, 1593, 1670, 1672, 1721, 1771, 1798, 1813, 1889, 1893, 1894, 1902, 1983, 2023, 2153, 2154, 2155, 2188, 2279, 2338, 2392
think, to 417, 637, 722, 1030, 1071, 1134, 1184, 1263, 1402, 1505, 1647, 1967, 1970, 2130, 2348
third 585, 799, 977, 2264, 2346
thirst 995, 2373
thirsty 120
thirty 1020
thistles 79
thorn 1096, 1869
thousand 361, 1793, 2288
thread 56, 885, 1066
threatened 1490
three 241, 372, 748, 768, 891, 979, 1582, 1903, 1904, 1916, 1983, 2097, 2264, 2280, 2316, 2430
threefold 371
thrice 770, 1472, 2123
thrifty 712
thrive, to 977, 978, 1256, 1624, 2123, 2392
throat 783, 1962

INDEX

throw, to 73, 89, 572, 698, 804, 922, 1051, 1192, 1688, 2026, 2210
thrushes 1666
thunder (n.) 828
thunder, to 2116
tide 2152
tie, to 71, 557, 885, 1066
tiffs 1404
till 56, 375, 393, 402, 623, 1023, 1062, 1467, 1637, 1777, 2174, 2308, 2497
time 81, 1217, 1557, 1582, 1672, 1803, 1922, 1978, 2051, 2143, 2147, 2148, 2149, 2150, 2233, 2336, 2396
tinker 1179
tire, to 1121, 2011
today 625, 2174
together 55, 173, 272, 947, 1234
toil 83
toll 2101
tomorrow 625, 2167, 2168, 2169, 2170, 2171, 2172
tongue 504, 614, 829, 964, 1071, 1649, 2019, 2108, 2254
tools 2476
tooth, teeth 570, 679, 719, 1843, 2109, 2180, 2223, 2410
toothache 1568
top 2368
torment 1372
toss, to 121
touch, to 692, 1727, 1833
toy 1360
trade 1179, 1430, 2216
traitor 2196, 2199, 2200
transplanted 2205
travel, to 1269, 1900, 2486
traveller 663
tread, to 742, 1652, 2000
treason 2220
treasure 873
treasurer 2027
treat, to 882
tree 49, 1015, 1240, 2164, 2417, 2441
trencher 1915
trick 104, 576

trot, to 72, 1586
trouble 356, 1128, 1589, 2408
troubled 780
trough 1716
true 875, 1394, 1580, 1604, 2275, 2449
trumpeter 373
trust, to 574, 937, 1302
truth 314, 505, 532, 1296, 1302, 1305, 1551, 1793, 2163, 2465
try, to 607, 961, 1805, 2024, 2163, 2190
tumble, to 121
tune 1724
turn, to 508, 608, 662, 856, 1356, 1451, 1671, 2180, 2425, 2489
turncoat 2374
twelfth 440
twenty 301, 1020, 1803
twice 258, 918, 1145, 1632, 1899, 2065, 2289
two 33, 159, 195, 240, 293, 446, 451, 531, 585, 586, 667, 693, 827, 865, 1032, 1060, 1086, 1234, 1464, 1557, 1570, 1723, 1798, 1815, 1893, 1903, 1916, 2055, 2098, 2170, 2193, 2258, 2349, 2494

unbidden 1000
under 516, 1106, 1897, 2077, 2303, 2305
understand, to 1826
understanding 949
undone 158, 591, 2501
unjoint, to 2460
unjust 2286
unlawful 1617
unless 805, 1909
unlucky 273, 274
untaught 2241
unwilling 1167
upon 213, 390, 663, 989, 1534, 1752, 2000, 2202, 2398
upright 59, 1874
upset, to 1716
urinal 2069
use, to 423, 1278, 1470, 2072, 2124, 2178, 2510

INDEX

used 2509
useless 2382

vain 562, 732, 1599, 1600, 1655
valet 1435
valiant 1421, 1583
value 607
valued 965, 1062
vanities 2247
variant 843
varlet 43
velvet 1009,
vengeance 2259
vent, to 458
Venus 295
vice, vices 398, 1177, 1704, 1706
victory 2217
village 762
vinegar 787
vineyard 734
vintage 214
virtue 662, 1103, 1535, 1587, 1669, 2257, 2416, 2510
voice 1755, 1845
vomit 573

wag, to 579
wages 1925
waggon 352
wain 2052
wait, to 368, 1867, 2152
wake (n.) 1129
wake, to 570, 1114, 2001
walk, to 524, 1052, 1132, 1430
wall 1025, 1387, 1487, 1844, 2317
wallet 303, 852
walnut 2417
want, to 20, 88, 151, 257, 549, 552, 590, 621, 1128, 1517, 1543, 1571, 1628, 1683, 1720, 1771, 1846, 1848, 2431
wanting 1500
wanton 1237
war 624, 1262, 1400, 1527, 1681, 1683
ware 437, 438, 826
warehouse 1197

warm 333, 531, 1017, 1153, 1561
warning 1823, 1972
wash, to 85, 1013, 1014, 1322
wasp 789
waste 1034
waster 242
watch 1033, 1758
water 191, 284, 757, 769, 780, 817, 981, 1112, 1142, 1157, 1192, 1422, 1498, 1499, 1501, 1536, 1538, 1792, 1940, 1941, 2360, 2461
watering 821
wax 1052
way 127, 172, 352, 663, 1259, 1386, 2052, 2351, 2354, 2415, 2467
wayside 1151
weak 1680, 2031, 2137
wealth 1061, 1453, 2318, 2319, 2320, 2321, 2385
wealthy 119
wear, to 514, 602, 824, 1948, 2157, 2480
weariest 1652
weary 1046, 2333
weather 55, 748
weave, to 500
web 500
wedge 808, 2141
wed, to 451
week 1024
ween 1082
weep, to 312, 798, 996, 1963, 2150, 2436
weeping 1284, 2327
weigh, to 276, 1209, 1829
welcome 665, 999, 1497
well (adv.) 31, 103, 137, 144, 276, 321, 388, 509, 520, 545, 549, 550, 623, 846, 1040, 1234, 1341, 1382, 1405, 1406, 1407, 1454, 1494, 1625, 1676, 1782, 1839, 1859, 1919, 1925, 1970, 1993, 1994, 2019, 2034, 2130, 2140, 2331
well (n.) 804, 1728, 2054, 2234, 2308
wet 288, 771, 1444, 1466
wheat 228
wheel 277

INDEX

whelp 177, 1714
whet, to 1194, 1241
whirlwind 2364
white 327, 752, 824, 891, 935, 1083, 1128, 1540, 2283, 2511
whole 20, 410, 461, 1007, 1710, 1836, 1934, 2008
whore 83, 372, 828, 1129
wicked 203
wide 2483
wife 261, 293, 451, 836, 1024, 1122, 1128, 1129, 1170, 1171, 1173, 1419, 1500, 1586, 1947, 1983, 2071
wilderness 2382
wilfulness 1283
willingly 142
wind 943, 948, 1822, 1882, 2032, 2323, 2406, 2435, 2468
window 26, 298, 1772, 2424
wine 224, 279, 382, 886, 900, 1144, 1497, 2227, 2266, 2341, 2416
wing 38, 733, 794, 795, 862, 1602, 1855
winter 269
wipe, to 510
wisdom 339, 1171, 1534, 1806
wise 11, 119, 309, 641, 723, 799, 802, 803, 804, 819, 820, 823, 1020, 1056, 1198, 1331, 1485, 1636, 1827, 1911, 2142, 2350, 2363, 2448, 2456, 2459
wisely 1299, 2020
wish, to 13, 849, 1012, 1043
wisp 439
wither, to 1870, 2212
witness 240, 361, 1314
wiving 1022
wolf 474, 1161, 1432, 1932, 1933, 1936, 2380, 2507
woman, women 14, 270, 649, 900, 905, 1150, 1415, 1418, 1633, 2319
won 1070, 2116, 2423
wonderfully 365
wood 587, 905, 1289
wooden 379
woods 749, 1161
wool 84, 422

words 7, 167, 481, 482
work (n.) 497, 635, 686, 1018, 1436, 1673, 1991, 2477
work, to 1607
workman 2474
world 1252, 1269, 1436, 1507, 1526, 1635, 2076, 2291, 2327
worm 169
worry, to 583
worse 302, 470, 646, 1057, 1401, 1776, 1834, 2238, 2338
worst 836, 1091, 1137, 2334
worth 159, 402, 446, 883, 897, 962, 1073, 1300, 1418, 1640, 1644, 1645, 1677, 1773, 2098, 2170, 2308
worthless 2385
worthy 1255
wounds 18, 658
write, to 16, 1439, 2128
writings 2469
wrong 2, 531, 1355, 1641, 1646, 1856
wrongfully 1899
wroth 1264

year 52, 325, 521, 522, 1148, 1843, 1848, 1913, 2040, 2495, 2496
yelp, to 587
yesterday 2173
yield, to 254, 1596, 1906
young 24, 95, 316, 342, 345, 473, 773, 956, 1629, 1633, 1634, 1647, 1699, 1707, 1884, 1931, 1968
youth 105, 784, 2160, 2371

CPSIA information can be obtained at www.ICGtesting.com
Printed in the USA
LVOW041402141011

250554LV00001B/5/A